FLAWED VICTORY

NEW PERSPECTIVES IN AMERICAN HISTORY

UNDER THE EDITORSHIP OF

James P. Shenton

William L. Barney, THE ROAD TO SECESSION:
A New Perspective on the Old South

George Dargo, ROOTS OF THE REPUBLIC:
A New Perspective on Early American Constitutionalism

John M. Dobson, POLITICS IN THE GILDED AGE:
A New Perspective on Reform

Jack D. Foner, BLACKS AND THE MILITARY IN
AMERICAN HISTORY: *A New Perspective*

Gerald Sorin, ABOLITIONISM: *A New Perspective*

Flawed Victory

A New Perspective on the Civil War

William L. Barney

Foreword by James P. Shenton

PRAEGER PUBLISHERS
New York • Washington

To Kristina and Jeremy
for their patience and their love

———————————

Published in the United States of America in 1975
by Praeger Publishers, Inc.
111 Fourth Avenue, New York, N.Y. 10003

© 1975 by Praeger Publishers, Inc.

Library of Congress Cataloging in Publication Data
Barney, William.
  Flawed victory.
  (New perspectives in American history)
  Bibliography: p.
  1. United States—History—Civil War, 1861–1865.
I. Title.
E468.B32   973.7   74-14989
ISBN 0-275-52040-4
ISBN 0-275-85040-4 (pbk.)

Printed in the United States of America

Contents

Foreword

by James P. Shenton

No event in American history had more devastating results than the Civil War. For four years the nation was wracked by a seemingly endless blood letting. When the guns finally fell silent in the spring of 1865, more than 630,000 Americans had died. Americans had inflicted upon one another more casualties than had ever been sustained in a previous, or subsequent, foreign war. In the course of the struggle, a war of limited objectives had been translated into total war. The enemy was no longer armies alone but entire civilian populations. With a merciless logic, Lincoln and his government had accepted the proposition that nothing less than the gutting of the South would restore the Union. And with an uncompromising precision, the North insisted on nothing less than the unconditional surrender of the South. When final defeat engulfed the South, its economy was in shambles; vast stretches of its territory were ruined; and its social institutions rooted in slavery had been smashed. The Union had been restored but not as a community of equals. Rather, the subjugated southern third of the Union was obliged to face the fact of its conquest by the northern two-thirds of the Union. And, as one contemporary noted, the boundary between the two sections was drawn in blood.

Professor Barney has written a cogent, brilliant account of the agonizing struggle. His interpretation of the struggle perceives it as the collapse of, rather than proof of, the strength of the original union. The work of the founding fathers had been proven inadequate. Out of the struggle a new union had been forged. The institution of slavery had been smashed, and, momentarily, it seemed that the freedmen would be granted equality. But in the ensuing effort to create a more equal nation, the victory was flawed. Fulfillment of the sacrifices of the Civil War eluded Americans and bequeathed to subsequent generations the task of making equality for all, not a hollow promise, but a vibrant reality. More than a century after the guns stopped killing, the cost of the Civil War still remains unredeemed.

Preface and Acknowledgments

Despite continuing interest in the Civil War and despite the fact that America's identity as a nation is more intimately related to that war than to the revolution against the British, the war itself has, ironically, remained outside the mainstream of our interpretation of the American historical experience. The sheer scope of the war and the enormity of the social and political changes occasioned by the destruction of slavery seemed to require that the war be viewed apart from what preceded or followed it—as a great aberration rather than as a tragic conclusion and an uncertain beginning. At the same time, in recoiling from the immense slaughter of the war, we have made our collective atonement by sanctifying the results of the war as a shrine to our idealism in freeing the slaves and our selfless nationalism in preserving the Union. The result, especially in the popular imagination, has been the image of a holy war with a discrete historical existence.

In taking a fresh look at the Civil War, I hope not only to acquaint the reader with much of the latest research but also, more importantly, to develop an awareness of the war years as the watershed of American history. The first republic of the Founding Fathers collapsed in 1860, destroyed as much by the inertia of the Constitution as by the intransigence of Northerners and Southerners. To restructure the Union required a stretching of the Constitution to accommodate revolutionary techniques of economic organization and military mobilization, just as the effort to create a Southern Confederacy necessitated a centralization of controls that was at loggerheads with the defensive state-rights philosophy of the antebellum South. The political results, after a four-year war that had lasted longer and cost more than anyone had anticipated, were the establishment of the authority of nationalism and an effective end to the notion of a dual sovereignty divided between the federal government and the states. Abraham Lincoln's bold use of his authority as commander in chief marked a shift of power to the presidency that raised for the first time the specters of unrestrained executive leadership and uncompromising nationalism that would prove mixed blessings in the twentieth century.

The Northern victory was defined not so much by the creation of a new Union as by the evolution of a radically altered Union that was militarily patched together after the firing on Fort Sumter. In the central paradox of the war, the North had fought to strengthen a republicanism that was already flawed by the inherent limits of a Constitution that distrusted and precluded the use of centralized power for broadly based social goals. Having won a revolutionary war with a reactionary political philosophy, and having linked together emancipation and national unity only at the midpoint of the war, through a marriage of military convenience, the North lacked both the constitutional legitimacy and the moral urgency essential to controlling the postwar South and shaping a Reconstruction policy that would meet the needs of the freedmen. The persistence of a white-supremacist ideology throughout the nation and the reassertion of constitutional orthodoxy, breached during the war only because of military exigencies, were the surest evidence that the Union had been altered through not radically changed. It was still a white man's government that was incapable of embracing either racial equality or a national commitment to balance individual liberties with social justice.

Beginning with the military nature of the war and the special intensity of a civil war in a democratic culture, this volume in the New Perspectives in American History series will focus on the process by which the Civil War generation fought both for and against a quasi-revolutionary transformation of the Union. Precisely because the revolution was incomplete, the legacy of the Civil War is as timely and as tragic today as it was a century ago.

ACKNOWLEDGMENTS

I owe a debt of gratitude to Gladys S. Topkis and Vivien E. Fauerbach of Praeger Publishers for their editorial assistance and thoughtfulness, and to Professor James P. Shenton of Columbia University for granting me access to his research materials and for continuing to share with me his insights into American history. Ann Sampson, secretary of the History Department at Trenton State College, was more than generous in assisting me with the typing of the manuscript. To my wife, Elaine, and my children, Kristina and Jeremy, I owe the greatest debt for resigning themselves with understanding, if not always silence, to the family burdens imposed by my research.

WILLIAM L. BARNEY

Richboro, Pennsylvania
January, 1975

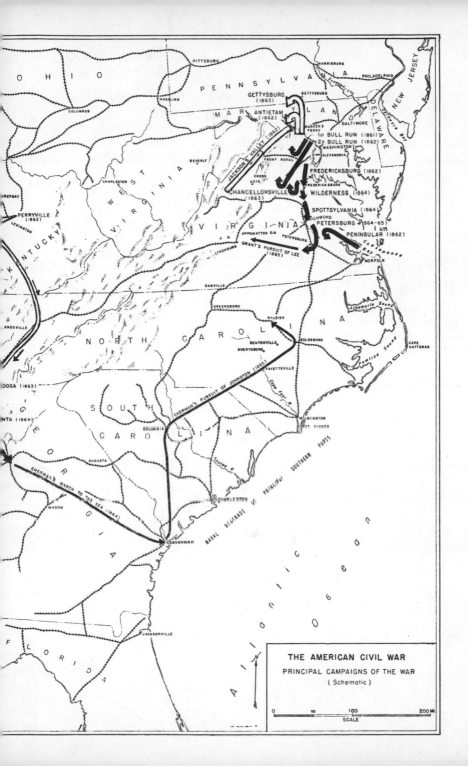

THE AMERICAN CIVIL WAR

PRINCIPAL CAMPAIGNS OF THE WAR

(Schematic)

1

The People's War

Ironies come cheaply in writing about the Civil War. The North, which went to war initially to preserve the Union as it was, with slavery intact, found that the war could be won only by restructuring the Union, with slavery destroyed. Southern whites, who went to war in large measure because they could not conceive of granting equality to their region's black population, found themselves at the end of the war in a position of inequality as regards the victorious North. As Lincoln noted in a speech in Baltimore in April, 1864, the nature and the impact of the war had been unforeseen. "When the war began, three years ago, neither party, nor any man, expected it would last till now. Each looked for the end, in some way, long ere today. Neither did any anticipate that domestic slavery would be much affected by the war. But here we are; the war has not ended, and slavery has been much affected."

The war was a grim educational experience that gradually eroded the illusions that had defined and sustained the initial responses of both the Union and the Confederacy to mobilization. Americans painfully learned that war is always a social process, and in so doing, they eventually had to face the central ambivalence of their conflict. On the one hand, the war was fought in pursuit of a political objective: restoration or division of the Union. On the other hand, the war, by its very nature, generated its own purposes and values. Lincoln finally led the North to victory only by adjusting his policies to this insight and by finding generals whose military strategy embodied a concept of total war.

Conquest Versus Maintenance

The most puzzling military aspect of the Civil War is not why the North finally won but, rather, how the South held out for so long. Given its immense economic disadvantages in war-making potential (the North in 1860 had over 90 per cent of the nation's industrial output), the ability of the Confederacy to survive a modern industrial war for four years is truly remarkable. Aside from the question of home-front mobilization, the prolonged defense of the Confederacy can be traced to the military and social realities of the war.

The North clearly had no choice but to adopt the offensive. Its objective of restoring the seceded states to the Union was, in effect, an imperial task of conquest, for it involved the reimposition of political authority over a vast territory controlled by a competing government. But the Confederacy, to achieve victory, had to hold what it already possessed; that is, it had only to maintain itself. Adding to the military problems of the North was the fact that the conflict evolved into a total war, in which victory or defeat was measured not so much by military statistics of battles won or lost as by the ability of one of the combatants to destroy the social fabric of its opponent. The South could be defeated only by bringing the war home to its individual citizens through a scorched-earth policy. Thus the Confederacy was able to sustain a war effort until it was literally overrun.

Lincoln and the Northern army and civilians were painfully slow to realize the fundamental military demands and complexities of an aggressive strategy of conquest. Their initial expectation, based primarily on the false assumption that the mass of Southerners was still Unionist at heart, was one of a quick and stunning victory. In his first mobilization order of April 15, 1861, Lincoln had called on the states and territories for only 75,000 three-month volunteers. As a private in the

6th Wisconsin Volunteers later recalled, "The sentiment then was quite universal that three months would close the war." Although Lincoln called for an additional 500,000 volunteers on May 3, the Virginia invasion launched in July, 1861, under the command of Irvin McDowell involved only 35,000 green, untrained troops. "Politics and popular emotion forced our first battle," noted a Maine volunteer, and the result was predictable. Owing as much to the inexperience of the soldiers and their officers as it did to the timely concentration via the Manassas Gap Railroad of two Confederate armies, the first battle of Bull Run ended in an ignominious federal rout. The disorganized and demoralized soldiers who streamed back into Washington in panicky flight did more than ruin the picnic festivities of the many congressmen who had followed along with their entourages to share in the anticipated victory. They revealed how totally unprepared the North was for a war of conquest.

Bull Run was a necessary and healthy antidote to the North's naïve optimism. It shocked the North into realization of the need for a huge, efficient, and well-trained army. George B. McClellan, soon to be one of the most maligned and perplexing of all Civil War generals, was given the task of organizing such an army. Fresh from a successful mountain campaign in West Virginia against no less an adversary than Robert E. Lee, McClellan went to Washington and willingly accepted the mantle of the Union's savior. Although many of his writings have an air of self-serving smugness, McClellan was exaggerating only slightly when he described the soldiers of McDowell's shattered army as "a collection of undisciplined, ill-officered and uninstructed men, who were, as a rule, demoralized and ready to run at the first shot," and "as insufficient in number as in quality." Working with these troops, as well as with the thousands of fresh recruits funneled into Washington by the governors, McClellan was in the paradoxical position by the spring of 1862 of having performed his administrative task too well. He had spent nine months creating what many felt was the finest army ever assembled on the North American continent, the Army of the Potomac. But precisely because hopes were so high and so much was expected of his army, anything less than the capture of Richmond would be regarded as failure.

When, in the spring of 1862, McClellan's army embarked on its Peninsular campaign (named after the peninsula to the southeast of Richmond, Virginia, between the York and James rivers), the North was again thinking in terms of a quick victory. Confidence ran high in the army. A private recollected, "It was a common expectation among us that we were about to end the rebellion." Under these conditions the resulting stalemate was regarded as a Confederate victory. Despite having inflicted proportionately much heavier casualties on Lee's troops —20,000 out of 80,000 engaged Confederates were killed, wounded, or missing in action—and despite having secured a defensive base on the James River just south of Richmond, McClellan's generalship was a bitter disappointment. Convinced that McClellan was too cautious, too likely to overestimate the enemy's forces and underestimate his own, Lincoln reorganized the Eastern armies with General John Pope in command and ordered McClellan to withdraw from the peninsula and join Pope's forces at Alexandria, Virginia.

After the second battle of Bull Run in late August, 1862, Lincoln would reappoint McClellan to the top Eastern command, just in time for McClellan to present him with Antietam, the Union victory that Lincoln used as justification for issuing the Preliminary Emancipation Proclamation. But the old confidence that a large and thoroughly organized army could end the war in a series of climactic victories could never be regained. Lincoln shuffled through commanders in the East in a desperate effort to find one who could inspire his trust, with results that were always disappointing and sometimes disastrous. Pope at Second Bull Run in August, 1862, Burnside at Fredericksburg in December, 1862, and Hooker at Chancellorsville in May, 1863, were all quickly and impressively outgeneraled by Lee. Still, despite his frustration, one suspects that Lincoln had half expected as much. Writing to the Republican general and politician Carl Schurz in November, 1862, Lincoln admitted, "I fear we shall at last find out that the difficulty is in our case, rather than in particular generals."

The "difficulty" rested in the exigencies of conducting a massive military offensive for which the Union was almost wholly unprepared. Nothing in the background of the Union generals had readied them for the modern total war they would have to wage. Tactics, logistics, intelligence, and medical services were all rooted in a strategic concept of limited war with fixed objectives to be secured by small armies suffering minimal casualties. The railroad, the telegraph, and the minié ball were to revolutionize the scope of war. Mass armies were now a logistical possibility, just as mass destruction was a military fact.

Although the forces of nationalism and revolutionary republicanism had spawned mass citizen armies in Europe in the Napoleonic era, no Civil War officer had had any experience with this new sociomilitary phenomenon. Many Civil War generals had read the writings of the Baron de Jomini, the most popular interpreter of Napoleonic warfare, and most were fascinated with the Napoleonic image of smashing, decisive battles, but for a practical guide the American officer corps naturally turned to its experience in the Mexican War. Despite the immense territorial gains wrested from Mexico in that war, the campaigns had been pre-Napoleonic in their stress on maneuver and avoidance of massive, bloody battles. Moreover, the armies had been small by Napoleonic standards. The main American army, Winfield Scott's invasion force, which had marched from Vera Cruz to Mexico City, had never exceeded 10,000 men. In contrast, Napoleon and his opposing generals had often commanded armies larger than 100,000. As training for the Civil War, the chief effect of the Mexican War was to confirm for American generals the military axiom that frontal infantry assaults in massed columns could consistently carry a defensive position. After all, the tactic had worked at Palo Alto and elsewhere: The Americans had attacked; the Mexicans had fired and then retreated.

In retrospect, it is hard to determine which was more responsible for the staggering casualties of the Civil War—the generals' infatuation with climactic battles or their inability to adjust to the suicidal obsolescence of traditional frontal assaults by infantry. While the generals overestimated the strategic importance of battles, so much that they often did not know what to do after a battle, whether a victory or defeat, they tragically underestimated the revolution in warfare wrought by the new rifled firearms.

Shock tactics could succeed before the Civil War because of

the inaccuracy of smoothbore muskets, the standard arm of the
infantry. Concerning these muskets, Ulysses S. Grant noted,
"At the distance of a few hundred yards a man might fire at
you all day without your finding out." Civil War armies,
however, were equipped with rifled muzzleloaders, usually the
.58-caliber Springfield or the .577-caliber Enfield rifle. What
made these rifles both practical and devastating was the introduction in the 1850's of the minié ball, an elongated bullet with
a hollow base that expanded upon firing. This expansion
permitted the bullet to fit snugly into the rifle's grooved barrel,
thereby greatly increasing its range and accuracy. Rifles now had
an effective range of 400 to 600 yards, and they could kill
at a distance of up to 1,000 yards. Such a withering fire could
be laid down that artillery gunners could no longer close in
for effective support of the advancing infantry. Artillery, rather
than aiding the offense in Napoleonic fashion, now functioned
best as another murderous defensive weapon.

The minié ball had shifted the advantages of warfare heavily,
usually decisively, over to the defense, which now had a normal
edge of 3 to 1 over its attackers. This ratio increased to 5 to 1
if the defense was entrenched behind breastworks or supported
by artillery. Although it was clear why only one out of eight
frontal assaults succeeded in the Civil War, the generals persisted
in their outmoded tactics, formations, and battle plans. The
results were murderous. Nine Confederate brigades attacked the
fortified Union position on Malvern Hill during the Peninsular
campaign.

> As each brigade emerged from the woods, from fifty to one hundred
> guns opened upon it, tearing great gaps in its ranks; but the
> heroes reeled on and were shot down by the reserves at the guns,
> which a few squads reached. Most of them had an open field half
> a mile wide to cross. . . . It was not war—it was murder.

This account of Malvern Hill by Confederate general D. H. Hill
could stand as well for numerous other engagements. "We were
lavish of blood in those days," remarked James Longstreet, one
of Lee's generals, "and it was thought to be a great thing to
charge a battery of artillery or an earth-work lined with

infantry." The Confederacy, of course, had no monopoly on such suicidal grandeur. About sixty Union regiments suffered battlefield casualties in excess of 50 per cent in a single engagement. A Union soldier put it best: "This, then, is what an assault means—a slaughter-pen, a charnel-house, and an army of weeping mothers and sisters at home. It is inevitable."

And still the field casualties mounted. In truth, the generals had little choice but to bleed their armies. Their quest for a climatic victory dictated the use of mass assaults in an attempt to break the enemy's lines, and their lack of modern electronic communications meant that they could maintain a semblance of control over their troops under battlefield conditions only by concentrating the troops at relatively fixed points.

Fighting for two respective democracies, the generals also had to be responsive to popular expectations. The sanguinary stalemate that characterized so much of the war frustrated both sides, and both Lincoln and Jefferson Davis were under pressure to find some offensive key to a quick victory. While Davis usually had to be convinced by his generals to order an offensive, Lincoln was constantly urging his generals to attack. Slow to perceive the military realities of the war, Lincoln often made unreasonable demands. Oblivious to the decided advantage enjoyed by the defense, he could not understand why McClellan failed to take Richmond in the spring of 1862. Yet McClellan, the attacker, had less than a two to one manpower edge over Lee. McClellan needed nearly three times as many troops to equalize the odds against a defender armed with the new rifled muzzle-loaders. Lincoln was continually frustrated by what he felt were missed opportunities to deal a death blow to Lee's army after a Union victory, such as at Antietam or Gettysburg. In fact, very few Civil War battles ever resulted in a decisive victory for either side complete with the near destruction of the opponent's army. The cost of battle was almost as high for the victor as for the defeated. McClellan, often criticized for being overly solicitous of the welfare of his troops, was nonetheless correct when he noted that battlefield casualties alone did not measure the exhausted state of an army after a major battle. There would also be "many thousands unfitted for duty for some days by illness, demoralization, and fatigue."

The cost of conducting an offensive measured by the destructiveness of the minié ball was perhaps the prime factor behind the rather tortuous advance of the Union armies. However, political and logistical demands placed on the invading Union forces also slowed the offensive. As they moved into formerly Confederate territory, the Union armies had to disperse. Because their task of conquest meant occupation and pacification of rebel areas, federal troops had to be detached for garrison duty. Regiments were needed for patrol duty, to serve as provost guards, and to shield overrun areas from a counterattack by Confederate armies or guerrillas. Pacification required patience and the deployment of troops away from the combat cutting edge of the armies.

A Civil War army, especially a Union one, was a cumbersome amalgam of men, horses, and equipment, weighted down by columns of supply wagons in the ratio of 25 wagons for 1,000 troops. The necessity of securing and protecting lines of communication for the sustenance of the troops resulted in the continual growth of the armies' logistical umbilical cords. Through most of the war, generals accepted the axiom that an army could survive in enemy territory only by maintaining contact with a fortified base of supplies.

Although Grant in his Vicksburg campaign and Sherman in his march through Georgia provided spectacular examples of the ability of Union armies to live off the surrounding countryside, such exploits were rare, and feasible only in exceptional circumstances, Indeed, as Sherman often noted, his Georgia campaign was possible only because the Louisville and Nashville Railroad had supplied his army as it marched from Chattanooga to Atlanta.

Depending upon the war's theater, the Union armies relied on various combinations of river, rail, and wagon transport. Railroads were most often the logistical key, but they were as vulnerable to Confederate raids as they were indispensable to any prolonged Union occupation. Grant's description in the fall of 1863 of the condition of the Memphis and Charleston Railroad between Memphis, Tennessee, and Corinth, Mississippi, summarizes the difficulties endemic to federal use of the Confederate railroads: "The bridges had all been destroyed by the enemy and much other damage done; a hostile community lived along the road; guerrilla bands infested the country, and more or less of the cavalry of the enemy was still in the west." Rebuilding, maintaining, and protecting the rail supply lifelines consumed an inordinate amount of manpower. By the final months of the war, Grant estimated that the combined effect of occupational and logistical duties had cut the front-line combat strength of the Union armies by at least half.

As much as the offensive capabilities of the Union armies were reduced by casualties and guard and garrison assignments, the immense number of soldiers immobilized by disease was a crucial and often overlooked factor in the military sluggishness that so exasperated Lincoln. To be sure, both armies suffered from grossly inadequate medical services, the Confederates probably more so, but the military impact was usually greater on the army that consistently had to assume the offensive.

For every battlefield death in the Civil War, two soldiers died of disease. Through disease nearly half of the effective strength of a regiment was lost in the first year of its existence; without fresh recruits, regiments tended to vanish as a result of illness alone within three years, by which time they would have been consolidated or discontinued. No wonder General William T. Sherman told his wife, "Our armies disappear before our eyes. [They] are merely paper armies."

Disease struck in two waves. The first was an epidemic of the childhood diseases, measles and mumps, which broke out as rural recruits were brought together in the central training and distribution camps. The soldier might develop immunity to these diseases, as well as to typhoid, but the second wave of camp diseases—diarrhea, dysentery, and malaria—would continue to debilitate him throughout the war. In the Union army alone, 1.7 million cases of diarrhea-dysentery occurred. Nearly every soldier contracted the illness, and the death rate increased during the war, from 4.2 per 1,000 mean strength in 1861 to 21.3 in 1865. The chronic cases, numbering in the hundreds of thousands, were pathetic. A soldier in the 3rd Wisconsin Regiment recalled that "the poor victim, with a face like shriveled parchment, lips bloodless, and nearly paralyzed with sheer muscular weakness, was an object pitiful to see." Diarrhea

and dysentery were the greatest scourges, followed by malaria-
related diseases. Northerners had no immunity to malaria, and
even among those who contracted the disease recurrences were
common. Troops stationed in the lower Mississippi Valley were
especially hard-hit.

Of course, many saw that the armies were as unhealthy as
they were large. Charles Francis Adams, Jr., once described a
Civil War army as "a city without sewerage, and policing only
makes piles of offal to be buried or burned. Animals die as they
do not die in cities and, if buried, they are apt to be insufficiently so." Still, ignorance and loathing, as much as knowledge
and compassion, conditioned the responses of contemporaries.
Compassion because impossible for many who were in daily
contact with the diseased. A captain at a Union tent hospital
in Atlanta in 1864 could not hide his revulsion: "The hundreds
of those disgusting sick patriots that creep around these grounds
form a sight that I loathe with every power in me."

The ill were reduced to such a miserable state because no one,
including the medical officers, understood the microbial origins
of disease. Without this knowledge and without the bulldozers
and gasoline used by twentieth-century armies to bury or destroy
their organic wastes, the Civil War armies bred their own disease.
The fecal stench around the camps, described by one Union
colonel as a "patriotic odor," had none of the glamour of a
clash of arms, but the ignorance that permitted it to hang in
the air fully rivaled an opposing army as a mass killer.

The military cost of disease in loss of efficiency, demoralization,
straggling, and absences without leave was tremendous. Sherman's
complaint regarding paper armies was valid because, at any given
point during the war, the effective strength of the armies was
only one-third to one-half of its paper strength. This loss held
in both the camps and the field.

As the Union Army of the Potomac and the Confederate
Army of Northern Virginia trained for the upcoming Peninsular
campaign in the fall and winter of 1861–62, a constant average
of one-third of both armies was hospitalized because of sickness,
which eliminated individual units and even entire armies as a
military factor. The 4th Ohio Regiment, sent to reinforce
McClellan, disembarked at Harrison's Landing on July 2, 1862,

with more than 800 men. On July 10 the unit was hit by a prostrating epidemic of diarrhea; within six weeks 600 cases had been reported. By November 10 the regiment was down to 120 men fit for duty, yet combat losses had been only 1 dead and 10 wounded. The initial federal effort to take Vicksburg in the spring and summer of 1862 was aborted primarily by malaria. General Thomas Williams, in command of the Union garrison at Baton Rouge, reported in mid-July that only one-quarter of his 3,200 troops were fit for duty. Malaria had killed or hospitalized most of the other 2,400 men.

Even when the losses were not so spectacular, the result was still a continual loss of combat efficiency. The straggling of those too weak to stand a hard march, the details of soldiers necessary to nurse and service the sick, and the puzzling, often paralyzing, problems of the generals in trying to cope with the chimerical size of their forces—all dulled the fighting edge of the armies.

Clearly, as Lincoln had begun to appreciate in the fall of 1862, the military dimensions of the war were complex and unprecedented. Still, generals who understood this war had to be found, and it is no accident that they emerged from the Western theater.

Union commanders in the West had two critical advantages over their Eastern counterparts. Perhaps most importantly, they had the time and independence to learn their craft. The Western armies were never the public's or the politicians' armies to the same extent as the Army of the Potomac, which was everybody's concern. The proximity to Congress and to newspaper correspondents, the simultaneous need to protect Washington and to capture Richmond, and, above all, the glaring publicity and high expectations that made this army the focus of attention subjected its commanders to unrelenting pressure.

Political interference from Washington plagued the Eastern armies. It was Lincoln who ordered the premature advance that ended in the rout at First Bull Run, and it was Lincoln who handicapped McClellan on the peninsula by leaving him in doubt as to the availability of General McDowell's corps of forty thousand. When Lincoln, reacting to the threat to Washington and the Baltimore and Ohio Railroad posed by Stonewall

Jackson's Shenandoah Valley campaign in the spring of 1862, finally held back McDowell's corps for defense in late May, McClellan was in a precarious position. He had divided his army north and south of the Chickahominy River in expectation of McDowell's arrival. His northern wing was to cover the junction with McDowell; the southern wing was to maintain the advance on Richmond. Confronted with Lee's savage counterattacks, McClellan was able to reunite his army in one of the war's tactically most difficult maneuvers. But the opportunity to take Richmond was lost.

Lincoln was well aware of the incalculable political importance of protecting Washington, and he was very sensitive to the Northern demand for a quick victory. Impatient with McClellan, he ran through several generals for the Army of the Potomac before he settled on Grant. In each case, a general had been promoted beyond his capacity. Whether it was John Pope, fresh from his victories on the Mississippi River, or Ambrose Burnside and Joseph Hooker, competent corps commanders in the Army of the Potomac, these men were simply overwhelmed by their new responsibilities. George Meade, in command at Gettysburg, was acceptable but too slow and methodical, to Lincoln's way of thinking. Although Lincoln cannot be blamed for his excessively close supervision of the main Eastern army, the result was often, as a Maine soldier put it, that "the farther our armies are from Washington the better success they have."

In the West, Grant and Sherman, each of whom began the war as colonel of a volunteer regiment, were able to learn from their mistakes. Promoted step by step in accordance with their ability, by 1863 they had emerged as truly outstanding leaders. Yet it is doubtful whether the Grant who was surprised at Shiloh in April, 1862, and who took the better part of a year to seize Vicksburg by July, 1863, would have survived in the hothouse atmosphere of the East, where McClellan was expected to capture Richmond within a few months. Similarly, the Sherman who feuded with the press and failed so badly in the assault on Chickasaw Bluffs in the Vicksburg campaign of December, 1862, might well have become a scapegoat in the East.

Conditions in the Western theater were strategically and tactically more favorable to the Union offensive than was the situation on the Eastern front. The sheer scope of the Western theater, plus the Union advantage of control over the rivers, gave the federal commanders an offensive advantage and room to probe and attack that were lacking in the East.

Over the objections of Lincoln, who preferred the direct land approach from Washington to Richmond, McClellan based his Peninsular campaign on Union naval supremacy. Although McClellan's army was safely placed by water transport on the tip of the Yorktown peninsula to the rear of Richmond, it was difficult to utilize any naval advantage in the actual campaign, because the rivers and inlets of the Virginia coast were too concentrated. There were no broad avenues of penetration such as there were in the West. The Tennessee and Cumberland rivers controlled the access routes to the mid-South corridor via Kentucky and central and eastern Tennessee. Once the Confederacy lost these rivers, with the fall of Forts Henry and Donelson in February, 1862, the mid-South was laid open. Union gunboats could follow the Tennessee River into northern Alabama and the Cumberland to Nashville, Tennessee.

In immediate danger of being isolated and outflanked, the Confederate armies had to retreat and reconcentrate in northern Mississippi. Despite a massive counterattack at Shiloh in the spring of 1862 and Braxton Bragg's invasion of Kentucky in the fall of the same year, the Confederacy was never able to right the strategic imbalance in the mid-South. The corridor to Atlanta and the industrial-munitions complex of eastern Tennessee and northern Georgia and Alabama was permanently exposed.

The loss of the Mississippi was equally disastrous for the South. The upper valley had been opened up by the Union in early 1862, just before New Orleans fell to Admiral David Farragut's fleet in April. Vicksburg and Port Hudson, the last two Confederate strongholds on the river, were taken in the summer of 1863, giving the Union undisputed control of this critical north-south axis. Foodstuffs from the trans-Mississippi region and blockade-imported war materials from Mexico continued to be smuggled across the river in small amounts, but the Confederacy had been effectively cut in two.

The Davis government did not have much more success in protecting its rail communications in the West. The Memphis and Charleston Railroad, running along the northern borders of Alabama and Mississippi, was the main east-west link for the Confederacy. Its loss by mid-1862 meant reliance on a slow, circuitous route, which dipped as far south as Mobile on the Gulf Coast. The redeployment of troops, the transfer of supplies, and the regaining of strategic initiative were all rendered immensely difficult by the Union's control of communications.

Federal successes in the West were a product of geography and technology as much as of the leadership capabilities of Northern generals. The Union gunboats were steam-driven and hence fast enough in most cases to maneuver out of the range of Confederate batteries. Moreover, these boats were armed with the new, heavier rifled guns, which rendered obsolete the traditional masonry and earthwork fortifications encasing the shore batteries.

Not only did the Confederacy lack the industrial and naval facilities to neutralize the Union gunboats with fleets of their own, but its entire Western defense was thin and porous. From the battle of Mill Springs in January, 1862, which forced the Confederates out of eastern Kentucky, to the fall of Port Hudson in July, 1863, the Confederacy had neither the men nor the matériel to defend its land mass between the Mississippi and the Appalachians. In early 1862, at the start of the great federal offensive, the Confederate general Albert Sidney Johnston was attempting to protect a 300-mile frontier across Kentucky with forty-three thousand troops. His men were scattered, his communications were inadequate, and the two linchpins of the defensive line, Forts Henry and Donelson, were undermanned, badly constructed, and highly vulnerable to any determined federal push.

Once these forts fell, the Confederate defenses began to crumble in a domino effect. As essential areas of political, military, and logistical support were lost, the defense of the remaining regions became more difficult. Federal armies, astride the major rivers and railroads, had secure bases from which to launch raids, to outflank Confederate armies, and eventually to initiate major offensives.

Finally, the comparative freedom of the Union generals to

shape their own operations should not be overlooked. Grant's successful Vicksburg campaign rested upon a daring gamble. After transporting his army downriver from Vicksburg in order to place it on high, dry ground on the Mississippi side of the river, he cut loose from his intended base of supplies at Grand Gulf. In a brilliant campaign of maneuver and deception, he defeated the surprised and scattered Confederate armies in separate battles and besieged Vicksburg from the rear. Although a similar expedient had been successfully employed by Scott in Mexico, Grant knew that this flaunting of military tradition —isolating oneself in the enemy's territory—would not have been approved by the Washington authorities. But, as he shrewdly noted, "The time it would take to communicate with Washington and get a reply would be so great that I could not be interfered with until it was demonstrated whether my plan was practicable."

Along the same lines, it is pertinent that the Western theater that Lincoln felt had the greatest political importance, eastern Tennessee, with its predominantly Unionist population, was that portion of the Western front where the federal effort most often bogged down. Lincoln devoted an inordinate amount of his attention to the region. In 1863 he was even arguing that its occupation would be comparable in importance to The Victory at Gettysburg. Anxious to create a loyalist government in the heart of the Confederacy, Lincoln was constantly ordering offenses into eastern Tennessee. But his desire for a political victory often conflicted with sound military judgment. The terrain of eastern Tennessee, with its mountains and deep valleys, negated the greater size of the Union armies by making maneuver difficult and logistics cumbersome. Ignoring the logistical realities that dictated that a large army could be supplied only by rail transportation via Nashville and water transport via the Tennessee River Valley, Lincoln insisted on an invasion by Don Carlos Buell in 1862 before communications had been secured. Buell failed, in large measure because of the logistical problem. The same problem in late 1863 almost put the armies of William Rosecrans and Ambrose Burnside in a cul-de-sac before they were rescued by the relief columns of Grant and Sherman.

The victories of the Union armies in the West more than

counterbalanced the Eastern stalemate. They dramatically demonstrated that a war of conquest was possible. At the same time, the limitations of the South's war of maintenance were painfully revealed.

Necessity forced the South to adopt the defensive. Strategically, an offensive policy was out of the question because of a lack of manpower and industrial resources to sustain an invasion of the North. Logistics also ruled out such a policy. An invading army in the North had to be supplied by either rivers or railroads, neither of which the South controlled. Lee did cross the upper Potomac on two occasions in 1862 and 1863, but his actions were more large-scale raids than prolonged offensives.

In formulating what defensive posture would characterize its military strategy, the Confederacy, while commissioning partisan rangers and resorting to partisan warfare wherever necessary, nonetheless intuitively rejected a full-scale guerrilla resistance. Although the need to keep open a lifeline to the outside world through blockade runners for war supplies was certainly an important factor, especially in the first two years of the war, rejection of partisan warfare was rooted even more in the nature of Southern society.

The guerrilla has to be extremely patient and willing to surrender large chunks of territory to the enemy while he retreats back into the interior. Unable to meet the enemy on the enemy's terms in modern warfare, the guerrilla must pick his time and terrain for the irritating and unsettling counterattacks that sap his adversary's will to continue the war. To function at all, however, the guerrilla must be protected and supplied by the agrarian masses. In the phraseology of Mao Tse-tung, "guerrillas must swim like fish in the sea of the people." Here was the crux of the Confederate problem. In the Deep South nearly half the people were slaves whose support could not be relied upon. True, the slaves did not rise up in mass rebellion during the war, but they fled to Union armies at the first opportunity and provided those armies with invaluable scouting and intelligence sources. Without complete popular support, Confederate guerrillas would have been severely handicapped.

The class outlook and social values of Confederate war leaders also made unthinkable a defense limited to guerrilla resistance. To have retreated into the mountains would have meant yielding not only the lush lowlands and black prairies that sustained plantation agriculture, but also most of the slaves. The South would have been sacrificing the very racial controls and way of life for which it was fighting. The twentieth-century guerrilla can make such sacrifices because his land and society are already controlled by an imperial outsider. In the South the situation was reversed, and the would-be guerrillas were not landless peasants but a mature, property-holding elite.

Thus, the real Southern debate hinged on whether it would conduct a passive or an aggressive defense (also known as an offensive-defense). The former course was favored initially by Jefferson Davis. By waiting for the North to attack, the South could reap the benefits of the 3 to 1 advantage enjoyed by the defense. Since federal armies had in the aggregate but a 3 to 2 manpower edge over the Confederate armies, the North conceivably could have been bled white in an exhaustive war of conquest. Morever, the South would have had the propaganda benefit of casting itself as the assaulted and injured party in the conflict. Early in the war Davis explained that "the Confederate government is waging this war solely for self-defense." Not a war of aggression but a war to defend the right of self-government was the Confederacy's self-defined mission.

Yet, a passive defense was politically untenable. Davis could not emulate George Washington's strategy during the American Revolution of withdrawing his forces into the interior and leaving open vast stretches of uncontested territory to the enemy. Washington could conserve his army in this manner because the American rebels were not accustomed to the security and protection of their own central government. Southerners, of course, were, and they bitterly resented any policy that smacked of leaving them alone to face the federal invaders without the protection of a Confederate army. Faced with this political reality, Davis attempted to salvage his passive defense by scattering his armies along a wide defensive perimeter. When the inevitable federal break-throughs occurred, first in the western Virginia mountains and along the South Atlantic seaboard, and then, in early 1862, across the Kentucky-Tennessee line, Davis was receptive to the demands of his generals and the public for a more aggressive strategy.

Robert E. Lee was the most persistent and brilliant Confederate general in his application of the aggressive defense. He argued persuasively that the Confederacy had to choose either inaction, and the constant danger of being outnumbered wherever the Union decided to attack, or a bold policy of seizing the initiative by concentrating troops to meet the enemy at chosen points. The federal troops could be prevented from invading everywhere only by being pinned down and forced to fight at a time and a place selected by the Confederacy. Concentration, maneuver, and the climactic battle—these were the essence of Lee's conception of warfare, and his Virginia campaigns until 1864 were masterful examples of swift, unexpected offensive strokes that paralyzed the enemy and exploited his divided forces.

Lee, more than any other individual, exemplified this dominant theme of Confederate strategy—the concentration of armies through the use of the railroad and telegraph for surprise counterattacks against the exposed salients of the multiple federal lines of advance. It was this strategy that blocked the Union forces in the East throughout most of the war and at least slowed their advance in the West. Despite its apparent success, however, the aggressive defense could not stave off Confederate defeat. On the contrary, the inability of nearly all Confederate generals, Lee included, to accent defense rather than the offense, hastened the Southern collapse.

Strategically, the Confederacy rarely assumed the offensive. Its most audacious offensive foray was also its most commonly overlooked, the New Mexico campaign of 1861–62. An outlet for slavery and access to the gold and seaports of California were the Confederate objectives in a brutal campaign that met with temporary territorial gains before the successful Union counteroffensive. Fewer than 2,000 returned from the main army of 3,700 men that had invaded New Mexico from Texas. It was such larger, and ultimately irreplaceable, losses that the aggressive defense was supposed to avoid. But in eight of the first twelve major battles of the war, the Confederate armies were tactically the aggressor. Their losses in these eight battles were 97,000 men (20,000 more than the Union suffered), a testimony to the folly of sustained assaults. During the same period, roughly the first twenty-seven months of the war,

Southern armies lost some 175,000 men. Attrition alone would force Confederate generals to be more defense-minded and conservative of their soldiers after 1863, but by then Southern manpower had already been irreversibly destroyed.

Popular frustration and anger over having the war fought on Southern soil, the inability of the generals to adjust to the destructiveness of the new minié-ball rifles, and the frantic desire to knock the North out of the war in one great battle—all reinforced the obsession with offense. Even Lee, for all his brilliance, succumbed. His stated objective was not merely to check or defeat the Army of the Potomac but to destroy it in Napoleonic fashion. In pursuit of this unattainable goal, he could be reckless with manpower, as during the Seven Days battles in front of Richmond in June, 1862, when he stubbornly attacked fortified positions. Failing to destroy the enemy's army, Lee took as his objective victories on Northern soil. The results were his bloody repulses at Antietam in September, 1862 (11,700 casualties), and at Gettysburg in July, 1863 (22,600 casualties). Lee's army which would confront Grant in Virginia beginning in May, 1864, already had been drained of its offensive power.

The South lacked more than the self-restraint necessary for a successful, long-range application of the aggressive defense. It also lacked the means of effectively coordinating its armies and command structure for concentration against the weakest points of the federal advance. Full exploitation of the aggressive defense required the close cooperation of scattered armies. This was hampered by the administrative and organizational problems inherent in the Confederate departmental system.

In 1861 the Confederate government adopted a system of semi-autonomous military departments as the basic administrative structure within which to organize the war effort. During the war some thirty-eight departments and numerous other districts and subdistricts were formed. The need for such decentralization was manifest. The sheer problems of size and inadequate communications meant that the Confederacy had to be broken into manageable subdivisions, each of which was theoretically responsible for its own defense and economic mobilization. At least as important as military and logistical considerations was the political need. Dissenters had to be controlled, politicians demanding protection for their home districts had to be placated, and, above all, the semblance of political control over all territory claimed by the Confederacy had to be maintained.

In order to function at all, the departmental system had to rest on the discretionary authority of the various military commanders. But this was both the system's greatest strength and its greatest weakness. Individual commanders naturally resisted any interference from Richmond and were concerned most with the defense of their own departments. Therefore, the system tended to become self-defeating whenever rapid concentrations of armies across departmental lines were required, or whenever unity of command was essential to a military operation that involved more than one departmental commander. Bickering between Generals Braxton Bragg and Edmund Kirby Smith over ultimate authority hampered the 1862 invasion of Kentucky; the refusal of General Theophilus Holmes to transfer troops from his Trans-Mississippi Department for the defense of Vicksburg in the spring of 1863 contributed to the loss of the city and the closing of the Mississippi; and the concern of the Alabama-Mississippi Department with retaining troops as a shield against federal cavalry raids was largely responsible for Sherman's ability to march his army uncontested from Atlanta to Savannah in the fall of 1864.

By early 1864 the merits of the aggressive defense were all but academic. The South had run out of the time and space required for a patient delaying action. In addition, any general who appeared to give up territory without fighting would be subject to withering criticism.

Joe Johnston, virtually alone of the major Confederate generals, appreciated the advantages of stressing defense. In the spring and summer of 1864 his deliberate policy of defensive maneuver and slow retreat, while always keeping his forces concentrated and poised for a counterattack, enabled him to conserve his army and compelled Sherman to take more than two months to move from Chattanooga to the outskirts of Atlanta. Although Johnston had not won a battle, he had bought time, precisely what the Confederacy needed most in this war of attrition. As Grant observed after the war, "I think that his policy was the best one that could have been pursued by the whole South—protract the war, which was all that was necessary to enable them to gain recognition in the end."

The rub was that Johnston did have to retreat, which by 1864 meant falling back into the ever contracting Confederate hinterland. Public opinion, sickened by the amount of territory already lost, demanded a more aggressive commander, which it got in John Hood, Johnston's replacement. Within half a year, Hood shattered his army by near suicidal assaults, first at Atlanta and then at Franklin and Nashville, Tennessee.

Although Hood's impetuosity accelerated the Confederate collapse in the mid-South, it is doubtful whether any policy could have saved the Confederate war effort by 1864. Most of the lower Mississippi Valley and the Upper South west of Virginia had been lost, and only a few seaports were still open to blockade runners. Not only was the Confederacy sealed off from its trans-Mississippi territory and vulnerable to an invasion via the Chattanooga-Atlanta corridor into the agricultural and munitions centers of Alabama and Georgia, but it was running out of manpower and military leadership. In the course of the war 55 per cent of the Confederate generals were to die in battle. Although it was on the edge of exhaustion, the Confederacy had not yet lost its will to defend itself. Within little more than a year, however, this will would be dissipated by the two foremost Union generals, Ulysses S. Grant and William T. Sherman. In these two generals from the Western theater, Lincoln had finally found the commanders who understood not only the nature of a total war, which the Civil War had become, but also what was required to deprive the Confederacy of any lingering chance for victory.

Appointed general in chief of the Union armies in March, 1864, Grant explained that his "general plan now was to concentrate all the force possible against the Confederate armies in the field. . . . Accordingly," he said, "I arranged for a simultaneous movement all along the line." Here was a sound, if obvious, strategy that Lincoln in fact had urged from the start of the war. The critical differences by 1864 were a Northern public more inured to accepting the heavy casualties that such a strategy necessarily entailed and a new command structure, which, while far from unified in the modern sense, nonetheless achieved a greater coordinated concentration of Union forces than had hitherto been possible. In criticizing the federal war effort prior to 1864, Grant noted that the various Union "armies had acted separately and independently of each other, giving the enemy an opportunity, often, of depleting one command, not pressed, to reinforce another more actively engaged." He added, "I determined to stop this." By applying massive, unrelenting pressure on the last two major Confederate armies, Lee's Army of Northern Virginia and Johnston's Army of the Tennessee, Grant kept the Confederacy from redeploying its troops for surprise concentrations and counterattacks.

The success of the offensive directed by Grant can easily be exaggerated. Lee still had sufficient cunning and manpower to stymie during most of 1864 the separate invasion armies advancing across West Virginia, through the Shenandoah Valley, and up the Yorktown peninsula. An integral feature of Grant's original plan, the occupation of Mobile, Alabama, to be followed up by a movement north toward Atlanta, was stillborn because the troops required were shifted to the politically inspired Red River campaign in Louisiana. Still, Grant's essential objectives, the destruction both of the South's two largest remaining armies and of its people's will to fight, were accomplished.

In Virginia, Grant, like a bulldog, clamped Lee's army in a death grip and chewed it to pieces. He was seeking victory not through some decisive battle but through the attrition of day-to-day battles. The entire Virginia campaign from May, 1864, to the end of the war was one continuous flanking action between two interlocked armies. Grant incessantly probed Lee's right flank and, in a series of rasping, brutal maneuvers, slowly forced Lee to extend it, until the flank was turned and the Confederate army was trapped in the entrenchments of Petersburg. For Lee the very worst had happened. He had lost his maneuverability and been forced to wage a war of attrition. As he had predicted to General Jubal Early, once he was besieged, it was a "mere question of time."

Grant succeeded, but at a terrible cost. In moving his army through the heavy forests and undergrowth north of Richmond known as the Wilderness to a base on the James River in May, 1864, he suffered fifty-five thousand casualties, the equivalent of Lee's total strength. Grant's response to the understandable charge that he was a butcher was simply that it was better to lose troops in a campaign to end the war than in a continuation of the prolonged stalemate that previously had marked the Virginia theater. And victory could be achieved, he concluded, only by undermining the morale of Lee's army "by desperate and continuous hard fighting." The elementary logic of Grant's position is undeniable, though it escaped most other Union generals. Lee's soldiers, however, had grimly appreciated what Grant was doing. George Cary Eggleston recalled:

> We had been accustomed to a programme which began with a Federal advance, culminating in one great battle, and ended in the retirement of the Union army, the substitution of a new Federal commander for the one beaten, and the institution of a more or less offensive campaign on our part. [But with the coming of Grant] the policy of pounding had begun, and would continue until our strength should be utterly worn away. . . . We began to understand that Grant had taken hold of the problem of destroying the Confederate strength in the only way that the strength of such an army, so commanded, could be destroyed.

While Grant was taking the Confederacy out of the war by destroying its most fabled army, Sherman was accomplishing the same end by the indirect means of demolishing economic resources and subverting civilian morale. The horror and fascination with which Sherman has always been regarded stem from the fact that he stripped warfare down to its basics. He had no illusions about modern warfare. Because well-equipped mass armies depended on home-front mobilization of economic resources and moral support, war clearly had become a contest between peoples just as much as, if not more than, between rival armies. To win such a contest, Sherman concluded, his armies "must make old and young, rich and poor, feel the hard hand of war, as well as the organizing armies." Readily admitting that this policy necessarily entailed cruelty and barbarity toward civilian populations, he still felt it to be the quickest way to achieve victory. As he pointedly told the citizens of Atlanta when he ordered the evacuation of their city as a military necessity,

"Now that the war comes home to you, you feel very different. You deprecate its horrors, but did not feel them when you sent car-loads of soldiers and ammunition, and moulded shells and shot, to carry war into Kentucky and Tennessee." In a letter to his wife Sherman was more succinct: Southerners "have sowed the wind and must reap the whirlwind."

Sherman's march in the fall of 1864 from Atlanta to Savannah and then up the coast into the interiors of the Carolinas was one extended exercise in destruction. His troops foraged liberally off the countryside, ransacked plantations, tore up railroads, and gutted factories and anything else of conceivable value to the Confederate war effort. A Georgia girl, Eliza Andrews, recorded in her diary what Sherman left in his track: "There was hardly a fence left standing. . . . The fields were trampled down and the road was lined with carcasses of horses, hogs, and cattle. . . . The dwellings that were standing all showed signs of pillage. . . . Hayricks and fodder stacks were demolished, corncribs were empty, and every bale of cotton that could be found was burnt by the savages."

With its main armies pinned down under constant poundings and with Sherman bringing the war home to civilians and leaving them nothing to fight for, the Confederacy was bludgeoned into submission by the early spring of 1865. The war, despite all earlier efforts to the contrary, had become a total war—in Lincoln's words, a "people's contest." Given the stakes involved, and the near-absolute involvement of the civilian populations, it could have become no less.

TOTAL WAR

"The greater and the more powerful the motives of a war, the more it affects the whole existence of a people. The more violent the excitement which precedes the war, by so much nearer will the war approach to its abstract form." Americans had to learn through bitter experience the relevance of this observation by Carl von Clausewitz, the German military theorist.

Until 1863 the North officially fought the war as a limited conflict with the objective of restoring the Union as it was. In this way, Lincoln sought to control the conflict and prevent it from degenerating, in his phrase, "into a violent and remorseless revolutionary struggle." He assured Southerners that he did not want to strike at the foundations of their society and that "the utmost care will be observed [consistent with saving the Union] to avoid any devastation, any destruction of, or interference with, property, or any disturbance of peaceful citizens in any part of the country." But implicit in Lincoln's policy was the assumption that the failure to suppress the rebellion through conciliation would necessarily lead to a harsher policy of punishment. "Such as may seem indispensable, or may obviously promise great efficiency towards ending the struggle, must and will come," warned Lincoln in March, 1862.

And still the war continued. McClellan's inability to take Richmond and the Confederate counteroffensives in 1862 hardened the Northern war spirit and dispelled the illusion that moderation would end the war. Lincoln, true to his vow that "I shall not surrender this game leaving any available card unplayed," began to sanction total war. In July, 1862, he authorized federal commanders to seize and use any rebel property, including slaves, that could be utilized for the Union war effort. In September he issued the seceded states an ultimatum: Either come back into the Union within one hundred days with slavery intact or face the loss of slavery as the price for continuing the war. After contemptuously rejecting this last effort at limiting the social impact of the war, the Confederacy interpreted the Emancipation Proclamation of January 1, 1863, as a demand for unconditional surrender. The war had become total for both sides.

Despite Lincoln's reluctance to declare emancipation as a war aim, the conflict could not be kept within its original bounds. By its very nature a civil war is very difficult to control, because it involves the fundamental issue of sovereignty, which, by definition, cannot be compromised. The rebels "cannot voluntarily reaccept the Union," remarked Lincoln; "we cannot voluntarily yield it." This ideological battle over absolutes was far different from most foreign wars, which are fought over fairly specific political or economic objectives. The comparison with a foreign war also highlights the inherent difficulties in undertaking peace negotiations during a civil war. A nation at war rarely denies the right of its foreign opponent to rule and hence has no compunction about recognizing its legal existence dur-

ing negotiations. But with whom could Lincoln or Davis negotiate when each rejected the other's claims to sovereignty? The
Confederacy denied the legitimacy of the Union's claim to rule
over the seceded states, and the U.S. government denied the
legitimacy of the Confederate claim to separate nationhood.

Had the Civil War not been fought between two democratic
societies and between two military organizations that still had
to call upon civilians for a wide range of vital support services,
the war conceivably could have been more manageable. As it
was, very few Americans, whether Unionists or Confederates,
soldiers or civilians, could escape involvement in the war. Both
sections shared a democratic culture that stressed the equal
right of all adult white males to participate in the governmental
decision-making process. Although this theoretical egalitarianism better describes the style and tone of politics than the
actual distribution of political power, the result was nonetheless
a striking, vibrant sense of individual identification with government. It was this feeling that the government in some real manner belonged to them that underlay the emotional identification
of Northerners and Southerners with their governments' respective war efforts.

Alexis de Tocqueville, perhaps the most perceptive of all
foreign commentators on nineteenth-century America, had
predicted that war would have a widespread impact on a
democratic society: "War, after it has destroyed all modes of
speculation, becomes itself the great and sole speculation, to
which all the ardent and ambitious desires that equality
engenders are exclusively directed." As early as August, 1861,
Ralph Waldo Emerson could write that "The war . . . has assumed
such huge proportions that it threatens to engulf us all—no
preoccupation can exclude it, and no hermitage hide us."
Throughout the war this submergence of self was constantly
deepened. Indeed it was implicit from the very beginning because of the need of both sections to define their course as a holy
one. Although Lincoln laconically noted that "God can not be
for, and *against* the same thing at the same time," most Americans were not troubled by such truisms. They assumed, as they
were told by their ministers, that they were doing God's work,
whether in preserving the Union or destroying it, and they

sought to understand as manifestations of God's will the bloody
battles that were so exhaustively reported by the press.

Americans demanded to know about *their* war not only because
their sons were fighting in a holy cause but also because civilians
themselves contributed so much to the war effort. The noncombatant populations, free and slave, male and female, manned
the war-related industries, to be sure, or grew the crops that
fed the armies and the industrial laborers, but it was the
massive, voluntary response to the medical needs of the armies
that most dramatically marked civilian involvement.

Civil War armies, whether Union or Confederate, had to
depend on civilians for most of the food, clothing, and medical
supplies that their governments were unprepared or unable to
provide. With the exception of Southerners subject to intensive
foraging by both armies, civilian support was voluntary. Individual households, under the direction of women, fraternal
organizations, soldier-aid societies, and churches sent a stream
of clothing, food packages, and hospital supplies to the front.
In the North a major degree of centralization emerged with the
creation of the U.S. Sanitary Commission. An outgrowth of
various women's relief societies, the Commission was the largest
private relief organization of the war. Relying solely on private
donations, it rendered services worth about $25 million. The
Commission stockpiled huge warehouses in the major Northern
cities and had a small army of several hundred field agents who
distributed the supplies. Its other main functions included
policing sanitary arrangements in the army camps and maintaining soldiers' homes and convalescent centers. None of this would
have been possible had not countless farmers responded to
appeals for fresh vegetables, had not public schools held "onion
days" and "potato days," and had not thousands of women given
their time and services voluntarily.

Because so much of the South was itself the war front, a
correspondingly centralized organization did not emerge in the
Confederacy. But, for that very reason, the exposure of Southern civilians to the war was even more direct. With armies in
their backyard subsisting off of civilians and with battlefield
casualties having to be cared for on the spot, Southerners were
in the midst of the war's anguish. During the Peninsular

campaign in the late spring of 1862, the streets of Richmond were aptly described by a resident as "one vast hospital." The distinction between home front and battlefield dissolved as "ambulances, litters, carts, every vehicle that the city could produce, went and came with a ghastly burden. . . . Women with pallid faces flitted bareheaded through the streets searching for their dead or wounded." Churches, public offices, homes, any unused buildings, were thrown open to the wounded as makeshift hospitals.

Nothing brought the war home so indelibly as this personal involvement with death and the dying. Field hospitals after a battle were first and foremost the homes and barns of civilians in the surrounding area; bedding was often little more than straw gathered up from the nearby stables. The harried and under-manned medical staffs called on civilians as nurses and orderlies. Everyone was pressed into emergency service. A resident of Shepherdstown, Maryland, which served as a makeshift medical center for those wounded in Lee's Maryland invasion of September, 1862, recalled that "even children did their part."

After the initial shock had worn off, those who experienced the horrors of a field hospital with its screams and amputations were left both numb and embittered. A Union nurse, Mary Phinney, in remembering the men she cared for, said simply, "I'll never forgive the Rebels who kill[ed] them." Of course, even those Northern civilians distant from the battlefront were deeply affected by the casualties. "You could not forget the war, even if you had wished," noted Edward Dicey, an English correspondent writing from the North in 1862. "Every carriage on the railway trains was laden with sick or wounded soldiers, traveling homeward to be nursed, and, if I could judge their faces rightly, to die." Many Northerners undoubtedly agreed with Jefferson Davis when he argued late in the war that peaceful reconciliation was impossible because of a "sea of blood that freemen cannot afford to bridge."

Two political factors partially countervailed the absolutist tendencies of the war. Initially, and until well into 1862, Lincoln and many of his advisers assumed that the Confederate government did not represent the majority of white Southerners. No one clung to this belief longer or argued it more persuasively than Montgomery Blair of Maryland, Lincoln's Postmaster General. Fearing that the military wanted to wage a devastating war against the people of the South, he insisted that "the conspirators who have got arms in their hands under the color of state authority are scarcely more obnoxious to the North than they are to the great masses of people of the South." By the end of 1862 whatever plausibility Blair's proposition might originally have had was rejected by a majority of Northerners. The reality of the Confederate resistance, punctuated by counteroffensives into Kentucky and Maryland, had revealed the shallowness of his position and the weakness of Southern Unionism.

A more persistent factor in limiting the nature of the war until 1863 was Lincoln's approach to the ultimate objective of somehow, someday restoring the rebel states to the Union as permanent, peaceful members. Wanting to avoid not only the social disruption of forced emancipation but also the possibility of unending, debilitating guerrilla warfare, Lincoln sought in the first years of the war to have federal armies re-establish political harmony and social stability as they advanced. Although extremely patient in pursuit of this goal, he gradually realized that his hopes conflicted with political and military realities. The rebellion was too strong to permit any compromise based on the maintenance of the Union. Its strength clearly rested on the Confederate military, which, as Lincoln noted, "dominates all the country, and all the people, within its range." To destroy that army required federal advances, and if the Union armies were to protect themselves within Confederate lines, let alone advance, they had to be agents of chaos and destruction.

The point at which Union commanders decided that the Confederacy could be defeated only through total war varied with the individual commander. Some, such as George McClellan, never made the transition from limited war, and others, such as Colonel James Montgomery, were committed to a war of destruction from the very beginning. McClellan was a conservative states'-rights Democrat who clung to his belief that the war should be one of reconciliation waged within the confines of the Constitution. Property rights had to be respected, devastation held to a minimum, and slavery left untouched. As he lectured Lincoln in his Harrison's Landing letter of July 7, 1862, "It should not be a war looking to the subjugation of the people of any State in any event. It should not be at all a war upon population, but against armed forces and political organization." In direct contrast stood James Montgomery. He had entered the war from the merciless guerrilla warfare on the Kansas-Missouri border and not, as McClellan had done, from the comfortable office of a bank president in Cincinnati. He had no illusions concerning a gentlemanly war of maneuver for limited political objectives. In the words of one of his officers, Montgomery's rationale for burning the picturesque coastal village of Darien, Georgia, was brutally simple: "The Southerners must be made to feel that this was a real war, and that they were to be swept away by the hand of God, like the Jews of old."

The experience of most Union officers and soldiers, however, paralleled that of Grant. These men brought to the war no fixed ideas save the vague belief that after a few sound thrashings the Confederacy would see the folly of further resistance and capitulate. But when the supposedly decisive victories did not bring the expected outcome, when, on the contrary, the Confederacy fought back to regain what had been lost, the result was a new conception of the war and how it would have to be waged. For Grant, the turning point was the Confederate counterattack at Shiloh in the spring of 1862.

> . . . I gave up all idea of saving the Union except by complete conquest. Up to that time it had been the policy of our army . . . to protect the property of the citizens whose territory was invaded, without regard to their sentiments, whether Union or Secession. After this, however, I regarded it as humane to both sides to protect the persons of those found at their homes but to consume everything that could be used to support or supply armies. . . . Their destruction was accomplished without bloodshed, and tended to the same result as the destruction of armies. I continued this policy to the close of the war.

Throughout 1862 the rationale of total war gained momentum. Major General Henry W. Halleck, Lincoln's chief military adviser before Grant was brought East in 1864, cited 1862 as the year in which the character of the war had changed. In outlining Union military policy for Grant in March, 1863, Halleck insisted, "There can be no peace but that which is forced by the sword. We must conquer the rebels or be conquered by them." This was the same Halleck whose antebellum writings had always disdained a war directed at the enemy's civilian population and its resources. Such a policy, he felt, would lead to. a breakdown of military discipline and convert the noncombatants into embittered partisans. By 1864, however, he was urging on Sherman just such ruthless warfare. Mildness had resulted only in a nest of "spies and guerrillas in our rear and within our lines." Strip the countryside, he advised, and send the civilians deep into the interior to seek the protection of their own armies. The South's ability to wage war must be ended. "I would destroy every mill and factory within reach which I did not want for my own use."

Aside from the continued Confederate resistance, both the cause and the effect of the remarkable transformation in Halleck's theory of warfare was related to the enclave strategy of the North. Contrary to McClellan's expectations, Union armies did not advance in an irresistible forward movement that automatically re-established federal hegemony in the areas through which they passed. Rather, Union offensives typically were slow, grating processes that wavered back and forth over disputed territory. Such offensives were possible only after secure defensive positions, or enclaves, had been established. Once an enclave had been carved out, whether it was a point on the coast or a communications center in the interior, a continuous war of attrition was launched. The war became kaleidoscopic as Union raids into surrounding areas were answered by Confederate counterraids by regular troops or guerrillas. It was in this category of relatively minor actions, skirmishes, and raids that over 70 per cent of the war's some ten thousand military encounters occurred.

The enclave strategy provided the North with a militarily feasible method of conquering the South. Confronted with a Confederate land mass of roughly 1 million square miles and with the immense casualties that were the price of an offensive war, the North simply did not have the logistical or manpower means necessary for a systematic occupation of large areas. Although enclaves permitted actual control over only limited, strategic areas, they definitely gave the Union the military initiative. A beachhead with a defensive perimeter could be used as a base for further campaigns, as a central point from which to begin establishing control over contiguous territory, or as a base for disruptive raids.

Not knowing precisely what the federal armies would do, the Confederacy was forced to maintain a military presence in an enclave region in order to meet any contingency. Once the South, tired of having its troops pinned down, retaliated with efforts to expel the Union forces, they were fighting the kind of offensive war that would bleed them of their limited manpower. But despite counterattacks, the enclaves were not eliminated; at best, the Confederacy succeeded only in shifting them from one area to another. Meanwhile, the process of social disintegration continued. The enclaves represented an alien presence that gradually dislocated and demoralized Southern society as federal probes from the enclaves brought the war home to civilians. Indeed Sherman's conception of total war was a logical extension of the use of raids to throw a region into chaos. Sherman consciously avoided occupying territory, so that his army could concentrate on undermining civilian morale and stability.

The earliest and most dramatic example of the enclave strategy was along the South Atlantic coast, particularly the Sea Island region, between Charleston and Savannah. With the advantage of sea control, the North could land troops anywhere along the Confederate coast. Although well aware of its vulnerability, the Confederacy could do little except abandon its coastal fortifications and block its tidal rivers with obstructions. The coast could not be defended, because most of the earthwork and even masonry forts were helpless when attacked by steam-driven fleets that combined maneuverability with the offensive effectiveness of new, long-range, shell-firing guns.

In November, 1861, an amphibious Union invasion led by Commodore Samuel F. DuPont and General Thomas W. Sherman occupied Port Royal Sound, just to the south of Charleston. This Sea Island region offered several attractions to the Union:

a coaling depot in the finest deepwater harbor between Cape Hatteras, North Carolina, and Florida; an anchor point for the South Atlantic blockade; access to huge stores of cotton; and the immense satisfaction of striking directly at the most secessionist-minded aristocracy in the South. As slavery dissolved with the advent of federal forces, the Sea Island planters soon learned the unpalatable truth that, as the crusty old South Carolina Unionist James L. Petigru expressed it, "in a war with an enemy that is master of the sea [the slaveholders] are masters of nothing."

Federal forces were now in a position to place either Charleston or Savannah under siege. While twenty-five thousand Confederate troops, desperately needed elsewhere, had to be retained along the coast to meet this threat, the Union enclaves continually detached troops on incursions into the inlets to the north and south of Port Royal. By the end of 1862, the federal blockade-occupation stretched from Georgetown, South Carolina, to Jacksonville, Florida. With the exception of the abortive assault on the batteries guarding Charleston in the summer of 1863, the South Atlantic theater had no major military engagements, but these coastal areas had hardly escaped the impact of the war.

The basic federal tactic of sending slashing raiding parties supported by gunboats up the rivers and inlets of the Carolinas, Georgia, and Florida had exposed Southerners to a war of subjugation. The purpose of these marauding expeditions was painfully apparent. General David Hunter, at the time commander of the Federal Department of the South, explained in 1863 that they were designed to force the South to sue for peace or else withdraw its slaves from the region, thus abandoning one of the most fertile districts in the South. Mass destruction was clearly the means to achieve such ends. The June, 1863, Combahee River expedition in South Carolina was typical. The *New York Tribune* reported, "The soldiers scattered in every direction and burned and destroyed everything of value they came across. Thirty-four mansions known to belong to notorious Rebels, with all their rich furniture and rare works of art, were burned to the ground."

For over three years, rice mills, cotton gins, foodstuffs, and occasionally entire towns were burned. Slaves who had not already fled behind Union lines or who had not been evacuated by their owners were brought back to the Union bases. The Southern responses were helpless rage and a determination never to submit to what they saw as fiendish warfare. Many demanded that any captured Yankee soldiers be executed under state law for inciting slaves to revolt. A young aristocrat and lieutenant from Georgia, Charles C. Jones, Jr., believed that no other punishment was fitting for "the lawless bands of armed marauders who will infest our borders . . . subvert our entire social system [and] desolate our homes."

In the interior as well as along the coast, the presence of Union enclaves had a disruptive impact that would best be measured not by the battles won or lost but by the legacy of cumulative destructiveness and bitterness. For example, the Union campaign to take Vicksburg is usually regarded as a failure until the spring of 1863, when Grant cut loose from his base, crossed the Mississippi below Vicksburg, and attacked the city from the rear. However, the period of stalemate from the summer of 1862 until May, 1863, which preceded Grant's successful campaign, nevertheless resulted in the virtual collapse of slavery along the Lousiana and Mississippi sides of the Mississippi River.

As early as June, 1862, the Yankees, operating from bases north and west of Vicksburg, began seizing slaves to assist in military-related work. Throughout the summer federal raids increased in tempo; plantations were ransacked and often burned. Planters sent as many slaves as possible back to the interior bayous or as far away as Texas. By fall in 1862, the delta country from Madison Parish in northeastern Louisiana up to Vicksburg was abandoned. The desperation of the few rebels who remained can be sensed in the plantation journal of Kate Stone. She decried her family's "miserable, frightened" condition and a life of "constant dread of great danger, not knowing what form it may take, and utterly helpless to protect ourselves." Just before her family finally fled in late March, 1863, Kate accurately summarized the Vicksburg campaign up to that time: "The enemy have now been three months before Vicksburg doing nothing against the city, but scourging this part of the country."

The scope of this social dislocation was exacerbated by economic devastation. The Union garrisons had to supply themselves. Although a rail line had to be kept open to bring in foodstuffs, as well as replacements and war materials, the armies increasingly turned to the ready expedient of living off the countryside. In the first year of the war, efforts were made to keep this practice under control, but by 1862 federal commanders increasingly followed the example of General John Pope, whose much publicized order from northern Virginia in July, 1862, authorized his troops to forage for their supplies. Pope made a distinction between rebels and loyalists, with the latter group ultimately to be reimbursed. Even in 1862, however, this distinction was a hazy one that was very difficult to enforce. By 1863 it had lost all practical significance as applied to those civilians still behind Confederate lines, for the "Instructions for the Government of Armies of the United States in the Field," issued in April, 1863, had legitimized total war.

This general order declared that military necessity "allows of all destruction of property . . . and of all withholding of sustenance of means of life from the country," as well as "the appropriation of whatever an enemy's country affords necessary for the subsistence and safety of the Army." The military authorities in Washington had caught up with the kind of war that many of their field commanders had already been fighting. The main difference by 1863 was that the generals now had official sanction for extending the concept of the raid from a diversionary tactic or an attack on enemy communications to a systematic effort at destroying the agricultural and industrial resources of the Confederacy.

The first spectacularly successful Union raid was the expedition of General Benjamin Grierson in April, 1863. Grierson's cavalry traced a 600-mile diagonal from Memphis, Tennessee, across Mississippi into Baton Rouge, Louisiana. Although intended primarily as a diversion to confuse the Confederate defenders of Vicksburg, the expedition also exposed the soft underbelly of the Confederacy. Grierson's men destroyed several hundred miles of track, factories, industrial equipment, and whatever else they could get their hands on. They quickly learned how to raise pillaging to the level of an art. A year later, in July, 1864, a Southern woman recalled that in a raid of that summer Grierson's men "left me nothing to eat at all. They took *every solitary* thing I had, except one jar of lard and my salt."

In the last two years of the war small detachments of Union cavalry swarmed over the nearly exhausted Confederacy in quick-striking, ravaging expeditions. Most of these raids have been forgotten, but their cumulative impact was staggering. A single minor expedition into northern Alabama in the spring of 1863 destroyed 1.5 million bushels of corn, 500,000 pounds of bacon, and huge quantities of grains and fodder; wrecked numerous small industrial establishments; and brought out 1,500 slaves. The federal commander reported that his men had "left the country in such a devastated condition that no crop can be raised during the year." In the last major raid of the war, in the spring of 1865, three cavalry divisions under General James Wilson demolished the remaining industrial base of the Confederacy by razing the ordnance and foundry centers of Selma, Alabama, and Columbus, Georgia.

At the same time, moreover, the line between a raid and a campaign became increasingly blurred. Sherman's "March to the Sea" is the best example, but the same principles of total warfare applied to Philip Sheridan's Valley campaign in the last half of 1864. Grant's orders to Sheridan stipulated that the Shenandoah Valley, one of the major sources of foodstuffs for Lee's army and a corridor for Confederate feints toward Washington, should be so devastated that "nothing should be left to invite the enemy to return." Sheridan was equal to the task. "This beautiful & fertile valley has been totally destroyed," wrote a Confederate general in October, 1864. "Sheridan had some of the houses, *all* of the mills & barns, every straw & wheat stack burned. This valley is one great desert."

Such warfare invariably spawned guerrilla resistance and, in turn, harsh retaliatory measures by federal forces. As could be expected, martial laws, fines, imprisonments, and the burning of houses and crops only stiffened resistance. How to cope with the guerrillas was an exasperating problem. The dilemma was epitomized by conditions in Missouri as late as February, 1865. "It seems that," Lincoln wrote, "there is now no organized military force of the enemy in Missouri and yet that destruction of property and life is rampant everywhere."

Guerrilla warfare characterized the fighting in at least three major areas: Missouri, West Virginia, and eastern Tennessee. Although the Unionists here were in the majority, the attitude of many was probably best captured by Mark Twain, who said of his fellow Missourians, "It was hard for us to get our bearings." There was "a good deal of unsettledness, of leaning first this way, then that, then the other way." Loyalties were divided, and both the Union and Confederacy tried to convert the undecided and win back those who had gone over to the other side. The guerrilla, whether a Confederate sympathizer in Missouri or West Virginia or a Unionist in eastern Tennessee, relied on harassment by means of ambushes and sniping attacks. These tactics, plus the response they provoked, resulted in a warfare that knew no rules save those of survival. The sickening brutality was measured by the smashed-in skulls and mutilated bodies of the ambushed soldiers, by the summary executions in reprisal, and by the efforts of both military authorities to depopulate regions of the enemy's sympathizers.

In the lower South, guerrilla resistance, while never the official policy of the Richmond government, was nonetheless pervasive. It was directed at slowing the federal advance and undermining the new sociopolitical order based on free labor that the Union armies were trying to impose after the midpoint of the war. Although this resistance was often organized by the military under the Confederate Partisan Ranger Act of 1862, much of it was a spontaneous civilian reaction. In either case, the enraged federal response intensified the war's destruction. Villages were burned in retaliation for raids on Union supply depots; property was seized to indemnify Unionists for guerrilla-inflicted losses; and, by 1864 in the lower Mississippi Valley, for every lessee of a federally leased plantation who was killed by partisans, a fine of $10,000 was levied, which was to be collected by confiscating property within a thirty-mile radius.

As the war ground to a conclusion, Southern civilians were as prostrate as their armies. For most, their commitment to the Confederacy had been as total as the Union war effort that finally vanquished them. But, in fact, neither army spared the civilians. To the Union commanders, Southern civilians were the unrepentant enemy who either fought as guerrillas or furnished the essential home-front support for the Confederate armies. To the Confederate commanders, the same civilians were their one sure source of supplies. Whereas federal armies increasingly stripped the countryside by design, Confederate armies did so by necessity. And both armies destroyed public and private property to keep it out of the hands of the other.

From the inception of the war the Confederacy accepted the need for a scorched-earth policy. When forced to abandon any property or facility of conceivable use to the enemy, the military ordered its destruction. Thus, in the summer of 1861, when federal forces were expanding their enclave around Fort Monroe at the tip of the Yorktown peninsula, the Confederate commander, John Magruder, had the village of Hampton, Virginia, burned by his cavalry. After the loss in November, 1861, of Fort Pulaski, which guarded the sea approach to Savannah, the Confederates burned the coastal town of Brunswick to prevent its use by the federal invaders. More commonplace than this self-immolation, however, was the standard procedure of destroying cotton stores and railroad equipment in all regions open to immediate federal occupation.

The generals usually had full political support for this harsh warfare. Not only did the Confederate Congress decree the destruction of all cotton and tobacco likely to be lost to the enemy, but state legislatures also resolved that entire Southern cities were to be reduced to ashes. The legislatures of Georgia and Alabama ordered the burning of Savannah and Mobile if their loss was unavoidable. When Galveston, Texas, fell in October, 1862 (it was soon retaken), only the resistance of the local citizens prevented the execution of Governor Francis Lubbock's order to burn the city and gut its water cisterns. For their efforts, the inhabitants of Galveston were branded as traitors by the newspaper editors in the interior of the state. It would be understandable that the generals were often all too willing to resort to a policy of self-destruction for the South. General Joe Johnston ordered the destruction of the rolling stock in central Mississippi after the loss of Vicksburg in the summer of 1863 rather than risk its capture by federal forces. Only the frantic last-minute intervention of Walter Goodman, president of the Mississippi Central Railroad, blocked the order and saved this equipment for subsequent use by the Confederacy.

To the extent that cotton was viewed as a rich man's crop and railroads and industrial property were owned by a small percentage of the population or by the government, their devastation did not directly touch or anger the common Southerners. But the widespread foraging of Confederate armies could not be ignored. The voracious armies despoiled the countryside. "I beleave [sic] our troops are doing as much harm in this country as the yankees would do with the exception of burning houses," wrote a Confederate soldier from Mississippi in 1863; "but our men steal all the fruit[,] Kill all the Hogs[,] & burn all the fence [sic] & eat all the mutton [and] corn they can camp in reach of."

Under the best of circumstances this foraging could not be controlled. Although the Confederate Impressment Act of 1863 attempted to regulate the practice by setting up legal machinery to purchase foodstuffs, its enforcement only intensified civilian resentment since purchase prices were well below market values. And the Impressment Act was of no use to a Confederate army in headlong retreat when the desperation of the soldiers left civilians especially vulnerable. William Watson, a Baton Rouge businessman who enlisted in the Confederate army, was in a small detachment of troops that followed in the wake of the retreat of General Sterling Price's army after the Confederate defeat at Pea Ridge, Arkansas, in March, 1862. He noted that the track of the army was a swath of desolation: "Every house was deserted, and everything in the shape of food or forage was carried away, and a good deal of property seemed to have been wantonly destroyed." Few Southerners would have argued with his observation that "be that army friend or foe, it passes along like a withering scourge, leaving only ruin and desolation behind." By the last half of the war Southerners were complaining as bitterly over the depredations of their own armies as they were over the Yankees'.

The war truly had been a learning experience. Militarily, as well as ideologically, Americans discovered that there could be no middle ground. As much as Lincoln wanted to believe at the start of the war that the two sides were "not enemies, but friends," four years of bloodshed belied this idea. To win its war of conquest, the Union turned to a theory of war that made civilians as well as armies its target. To stave off defeat, the

Confederacy was increasingly willing to sacrifice almost everything. As the wife of a Georgia minister and planter expressed
it, "I can look extinction for me and mine in the face, but
submission never!" For both sides victory had been defined as
the continued existence of their respective nations. Defeat, no
less than victory, would be total in the people's war.

2

The Ideology of Victory

On April 12, 1861, a state senator announced to the Ohio legislature that Fort Sumter had just been fired upon. The reaction of stunned, painful silence was broken by the cry of "Glory to God," uttered by abolitionist Abby Kelly Foster. Mrs. Foster had immediately embraced the war as a divinely inspired opportunity to free the black man by the sword. A far more typical Northern reaction was that of Jacob D. Cox, a Republican politician in Ohio and a future Union general. For Cox, civil war "seemed too great a price to pay for any good [except for] yielding what was to us the very groundwork of our republicanism, the right to enforce a fair interpretation of the Constitution through the election of President and Congress."

Foster and Cox epitomized the fundamental problem facing Lincoln as he strove to unite the North. The majority saw the war's sole objective as the perpetuation of the Union; a small, and often despised, minority passionately believed that the Union must also be regenerated through the war. Military necessity finally convinced Lincoln that the Union could be saved only by transforming it. Only after he was so convinced could he formulate the North's rationale of victory.

CONSTITUTIONAL UNIONISM

The vast majority of Northerners had no intention of fighting a war to free the slaves. Indeed, the evidence overwhelmingly indicates that, had emancipation been proclaimed as a war aim in 1861 or early 1862, the unity essential to a Northern war effort would have been shattered. Lincoln, as astute a politician as any who ever occupied the White House, had no choice but to recognize this basic political fact. Slavery was sanctioned by the Constitution, and to attack the institution was to undermine that document, which Northerners were fighting to defend. Yet Lincoln noted on several public occasions that slavery was the "only thing which ever could bring this nation to civil war."

Here was the ideological conundrum that was translated into a halting and ambivalent military effort until the issuance of the Emancipation Proclamation—an attempt to win the war while leaving untouched its basic cause. The limits of the constitutional Unionism under which the war was originally fought would have to be breached before this conundrum could be resolved.

War had come over the issue of the permanence of slavery, not its immediate right to exist. Lincoln and his party had made it clear that, even had they desired, they could not touch slavery in the states, because the institution was recognized and protected by the Constitution. The expansion of slavery into the territories was an altogether different matter, and on this point the Republicans were adamant. The Constitution gave Congress full power to regulate all affairs concerning federal territories; a power that, as the Republicans insisted, necessarily implied the authority to prohibit slavery in these territories. To exercise such authority, the Republicans felt, was both morally and constitutionally defensible. Slavery was a sin and a national curse that ultimately had to be extinguished. Moreover, it was the basis of a political economy that directly conflicted with the aspirations of free white labor. The Republicans warned that the establishment of slavery in any region meant the monopolization of economic opportunity, political power, and access to the press and pulpit by slaveholding interests at the expense of free white labor.

Southerners quite logically interpreted the Republican program as an indirect assault upon slavery. They believed that plantation agriculture, if denied room to expand, would continue to exhaust the limited soil resources of the South until slavery became an unprofitable burden. As whites began migrating to new areas, the percentage of blacks within the slave states would rise until racial control became impossible and the flashpoint of a racial holocaust was reached. Even those Southerners who detested slavery could agree with Mary Chesnut, the wife of a leading South Carolina planter-politician, when she rationalized that the expansion of slavery would result in a gradual dissolution of racial tensions. "We want to spread [our slaves]," she wrote in her diary in the summer of 1861, "west and south, or northwest, where the climate would free them or kill them; would improve them out of the world as the Yankees do Indians."

Because neither section was willing or able to compromise its position on slavery in the territories, war resulted. Slavery, as approached in this peripheral manner, became the cause of the war. But to the extent that the definition of the problem looked to the future rather than the present, its relevance to the war at hand could be initially denied. The result was a fiction that was maintained until January 1, 1863: that the Union could be restored while avoiding a frontal assault upon slavery. The Republicans were constitutionally bound not to interfere with slavery where it existed; the same emphasis on adhering to the spirit and letter of the Constitution as a national convenant was also the justification for the Republican program of preserving the Union by force. A restored Union with slavery intact appeared as nothing less than a constitutional mandate.

In Lincoln's first public policy statement after his election, his First Inaugural Address, on March 4, 1861, the concept of the Union overshadowed any references to slavery. Lincoln's major concern was to elucidate a theory of the Union as a permanent form of government whose forcible dissolution by any seceded states amounted to anarchy. Drawing upon Jackson's proclamation against nullification and the time-honored nationalism of such Whigs as Henry Clay and Daniel Webster,

Lincoln added the commonsensible observation that "no government proper ever had a provision in its organic law for its own termination." Even if the Union were but a compact between sovereign states, as the South contended, "can it," Lincoln asked, "as a contract, be peaceably unmade, by less than all the parties who made it?" Conflicts of interest would arise naturally in any government, but democratic redress required submission to majority rule. "A majority, held in restraint by constitutional checks, and limitations, and always changing easily . . . is the only true sovereign of a free people. Whoever rejects it," Lincoln continued, "does, of necessity, fly to anarchy or to despotism."

Lincoln's interpretation of the crisis that faced his administration concerned the nature and meaning of republicanism. Slavery was mentioned only briefly. Lincoln repledged himself to the protection of slavery in the states (offering no objections to a constitutional amendment permanently protecting slavery in the states from federal interference) and announced his willingness to support any workable fugitive slave act. He did admit that the "only substantial dispute" dividing the nation was that "one section . . . believes slavery is *right,* and ought to be extended, while the other believes it is *wrong,* and ought not to be extended." But even here he refused to draw any ominous conclusions. The existence of a moral barrier was mollified by Lincoln's reference to the legal bridge of compliance which he felt had characterized Southern acceptance of the law suppressing the African slave trade and the Northern acceptance of the Fugitive Slave Act.

Lincoln's skill at gauging public opinion became evident when the free states reacted to the Confederate firing on Fort Sumter. A wave of indignation, sparked by a shared sense of betrayal to the Union, swept over the North. The slavery issue was all but forgotten as Northerners pledged themselves to defend the Union. This remarkable outpouring of popular enthusiasm derived from one common source, the belief that secession was equivalent to anarchy. In permitting itself to be cast in the role of aggressor at Fort Sumter, the Confederacy had transformed the secession crisis from a debate over constitutional theories into a violent test of the ability of a free government to maintain itself. It was the sense that secession abrogated the most fundamental American right of all—the right to the peaceful settlement of issues by majority rule, as protected and sanctioned within the framework of a constitutional Union—that initially energized the Northern response in the spring of 1861 and sustained the war effort until victory was won.

Antebellum Americans, far more than those of today, were able to identify in a personal and direct manner with their government. In part, this reflected the strongly held notion that public offices should be available and responsible to their constituents. "Accessibility seems the especial and universal attribute of American statesmanship," noted the English visitor Edward Dicey. It was also a product of the acquisitive openness of a society that, by European standards, blurred the distinction between private and public spheres of action with the leveling tendencies of egalitarianism. However, in the final analysis, this identification occurred because the government so often was the people themselves. There was no federal bureaucracy to speak of, aside from thirty thousand scattered postmasters. Individual self-rule, within the context of the local community, was not merely cherished in the abstract as an American birthright; it was also put into daily practice. Whether engaging in constitutional conventions (there were, for example, fifteen in the fifteen years preceding the Civil War), in competition for political office, in voting, or in the literal creation of communities as they settled the frontier, Americans were experienced in government-making. Local home rule was seen as both an administrative necessity and an essential mechanism to protect the individual from the potential encroachments of centralized authority.

Because Americans were so intensely, almost obsessively, proud of their experiment in self-government, they were acutely sensitive to any action, such as violent secession, that seemed to reject the central tenet of their democracy, the concept of majority rule. If the South renounced the majority's decision, as constitutionally expressed in a national election, what was to prevent other sections, states, or individuals from doing the same? Without a strong monarchic government, or without the submission to authority built into a society divided along rigid class lines, how could a local community, to say nothing of a national republic, maintain law and order unless all abided by the will of the majority? To most Northerners the answer was obvious enough. "For this year," editorialized the *New York Tribune* on April 17, 1861, "the Chief business of the American People must be proving that they have a Government, and that Freedom is not another name for Anarchy."

The instinctive rallying of Northern public opinion behind constitutional Unionism was carefully nurtured and amplified by Lincoln. Indeed, one of Lincoln's greatest strengths was his ability to express the hopes and fears of Northern society in such a way as to convert the war effort into a metaphor of the common man's devotion to the Union.

In his message to the special session of Congress called in the summer of 1861, Lincoln began the crucial task of sustaining the ideological consensus behind the Unionist cause. The federal rout at First Bull Run had badly shaken Northerners' confidence that they faced a short and relatively mild war. Lincoln, after calling upon the states for four hundred thousand more troops and Congress for $400 million in additional war financing, flatly denied the legitimacy of the Confederate claim to national self-determination. Here, Lincoln was careful to distinguish betwen secessionist politicians, whom he accused of an "insidious debauching of the [Southern] public mind," and the great mass of Southerners, who possessed "as much of moral sense, as much of devotion to law and order . . . and reverence for . . . their common country, as any other civilized, and patriotic people."

It was essential that this distinction be made, at least at the start of the war, for without it the original constitutional justification for preserving the Union would have collapsed. Lincoln's war policy rested on the assumption that secession, the sophistical maneuvering of a conspiracy of slaveholders who did not represent the Southern majority, was illegal. This belief was widespread in the North until the end of 1862, because it resolved the paradox of coercing a people back into a "free" government. If Southerners had never really left the Union, coercion involved only the overthrow of their unrepresentative leaders, not the subjugation of an entire people.

On a more positive note, Lincoln then both broadened the Unionist cause and identified it with the immediate aspirations of the North's free labor society. "On the side of the Union, it is a struggle for maintaining in the world, that form, and substance of government, whose leading object is, to elevate the condition of men . . . to afford all, an unfettered start, and a fair chance, in the race of life."

Throughout the war Lincoln would return repeatedly to this same point: that the defeat of the Confederacy as an illegal, elitist government verging on despotism would be a victory for republican economic and political liberties. In his annual message of December, 1861, he denounced the rebellion as a "war upon the first principle of popular government—the rights of the people." He argued that Southern Unionists were deprived of their civil liberties, and then brought up the *bête noire* of an egalitarian democracy: "Monarchy itself is sometimes hinted at as a possible refuge from the power of the people." The common man was warned that the Confederacy represented an "effort to place *capital* on an equal footing with, if not above *labor,* in the structure of government." The inference was clear: If the Confederacy survived, a hierarchical society in which labor was either directly owned or held for life in a subordinate position would become permanent in America. And the existence of such a society would mean a concomitant loss in the mobility and opportunities for advancement of free labor.

Ultimately, Lincoln insisted, the Confederacy posed a direct threat to continued Northern progress. In December, 1862, he pointedly reminded the Unionists of the great Midwestern heartland that their prosperity and even their economic survival depended upon access to world markets through ports on the Gulf of Mexico or on either coast. Such access was assured in a united nation, but if the rebellion succeeded no one could gauge the disruptive impact of trade regulations across an international border. To the entire Union Lincoln stressed that the antebellum expansion and progress of America had been the envy of the world. Inevitably, such expansion and progress would be hindered by a balkanized America. "While it cannot be foreseen exactly how much one huge example of secession, breeding lesser ones indefinitely, would retard population, civilization, and prosperity, no one can doubt that the extent of it would be very great and injurious."

The Unionist theme was essential to creating and maintaining

Northern unity. It received Congressional sanction in the Crittenden Resolution of July, 1861, which stipulated that the North was waging a limited war whose objective was "to defend and maintain the *supremacy* of the Constitution, and to preserve the Union." Slavery was to be left untouched. Yet, paradoxically, an unwavering adherence to constitutional Unionism could be self-defeating. Implicit in the doctrine was the obligation of acting only in accordance with the Constitution, and it was by no means apparent that the Constitution was a source of strength in putting down the rebellion. On the contrary, many believed that the Constitution itself was a prime factor in the paralysis at the nation's center during the secession winter of 1860–61.

What contemporaries recognized was that the inherent ambiguities of the Constitution relative to federal-state relations had been indispensable to the development of the secession crisis. Was the Union but a confederation of sovereign states that had delegated limited, specific powers to the federal government, or was it a true nation in which ultimate sovereignty rested with the federal authorities as the spokesmen for all the people? Only four years of war could answer the question. In the meantime, Southerners logically could turn to the Constitution and be as sincere in believing secession to be legal and constitutional as Northerners were in believing the opposite.

Moreover, the same ambiguities had provided a rationale for the successful prewar efforts of Southern politicians aimed at stifling the emergence of any tradition of, or experience with, effective national governmental power. By enforcing an interpretation of the Constitution that mandated states' rights, strict construction, and dual federalism, the South had converted the Constitution into a strait jacket that precluded the use of centralized power. In particular, the last three antebellum presidents, Millard Fillmore, Franklin Pierce, and James Buchanan, were acceptable to the South because they voluntarily abdicated many of the potential powers of their office. These men saw themselves as the custodians of those limited powers that the states permitted the federal government to exercise. This meant, in practice, that the president's role was a supervisory one over the direction of foreign policy, Indian affairs, export trade, and perhaps some minor public works.

Once power had been surrendered by the chief executive as the price of holding office, it was understandable that the response of a Buchanan to the secession crisis would be tantamount to a loss of will. Buchanan's own reading of the Constitution handcuffed him. He admitted that secession was unconstitutional and revolutionary, but he simultaneously asserted that he had no constitutional authorization to cope with the crisis. In December, 1860, he simply threw the whole matter into the lap of Congress. He would try to execute the laws, "as far as this may be practicable," but aside from that, "the Executive has no authority to decide what shall be the relations between the Federal Government and South Carolina. . . . Any attempt to do this . . . would be a marked act of usurpation."

Nothing better dramatizes the contrast between Lincoln and Buchanan than the forthright manner in which Lincoln cut the knot of constitutional restrictions that had so immobilized his predecessor. Upon assuming office, Lincoln was immediately faced with the disastrous consequences of the constitutionally imposed theory and practice of limited national government. After handling the Fort Sumter crisis in such a way that if war resulted, the South would be branded the aggressor, he reacted by insisting that the nation had but one choice: "to call out the war power of the Government; and so to resist force, employed for its destruction, by force, for its preservation."

In mobilizing this power Lincoln made one key decision that led to a radically new and expanded version of executive prerogatives. He did not call Congress into special session for more than ten weeks after the firing on Sumter. Well aware that the Constitution had provided no guidelines under which Congress could formulate an affirmative policy of action during the secession winter, and fearful that the riddle of nationalism versus states' rights might once again hamstring Congress, Lincoln turned to an untapped and unencumbered source of constitutional authorization, his powers as commander in chief. Acting in this capacity, he assumed sweeping powers in the spring of 1861. He proclaimed a blockade of the Confederate ports, an act synonymous in international law with a declaration of war; he enlarged the regular military forces and treated the militia as a volunteer army; he suspended the writ of habeas corpus in numerous localities and authorized the military arrest of civilians "deem[ed] dangerous to the public safety"; and he pledged the credit of the government to the amount of $250 million and sanctioned the payment for military supplies of $2 million in unappropriated Treasury funds to individuals unauthorized to receive it.

Only after Lincoln had acted did he ask for Congressional authorization. In his message of July 4, 1861, he argued that he had done nothing that Congress could not subsequently constitutionally ratify. Beyond that, however, he claimed the war powers solely for the executive. The President, he reasoned, had the constitutional responsibility of giving "practical shape and efficiency" to the war effort; the role of Congress was virtually restricted to that of providing the "legal sanction" to a *fait accompli*. As to the legality of his actions, Lincoln said simply, "Whether strictly legal or not, [they] were ventured upon under what appeared to be a popular demand and a public necessity, trusting then, as now, that Congress would readily ratify them."

To many Americans Lincoln always remained the gangly country lawyer, but shrewder observers noted that he had stamped himself as a forceful leader. In his unprecedented exercise of executive powers, he had shown that he would be limited only by his own conception of his office. Although the Supreme Court in the Prize Cases of 1863 would endorse his interpretation of war powers, and although Lincoln would temper his actions with magnanimity and charitable self-restraint, his measures had obviously moved beyond the traditional boundaries of the Constitution.

Lincoln's actions were attacked as dictatorial and became the focal point of a whole cluster of Northern doubts and anxieties over the direction of the war. These fears were concentrated in the Democratic party, a coalition of localistically minded Americans who equated the sum total of good government with the preservation of local independence and individual rights against any interference from the federal government. Arbitrary arrests, military rule in civilian areas, suspension of the writ of habeas corpus, and occasional crackdowns on the press were interpreted by Democrats as dangerous signs of an unconstitutional centralization of power. They charged that in his conduct of the war Lincoln was undermining the constitutional Union that he claimed to be restoring.

For the Democrats despotic centralization was most evident in the Republican antislavery program. Throughout 1862 it was apparent that the Republican-dominated thirty-seventh Congress was slowly dismantling slavery. In March Union commanders were expressly forbidden to return fugitive slaves to their masters. Congress emancipated the slaves in the District of Columbia in April and by June had prohibited slavery in the territories. The capstone of Congressional action came in July with the Second Confiscation Act, which declared free the slaves of all those who supported the rebellion. This, on paper at least, was far more sweeping than the First Confiscation Act, of the previous summer, which had limited emancipation to those slaves actively used in the Confederate war effort. With the distinct possibility of total emancipation in the near future, the Democrats now had an issue the appeal of which transcended war weariness and the conduct of the war. They could now claim that white supremacy in the North was endangered by the potential massive infusion of freed blacks out of the South.

Before the war, majority sentiment in the North had tolerated slavery on the constitutional grounds that any national interference with the institution was a threat to states' rights and local autonomy. Following the lead of Stephen Douglas, Northern Democrats were opposed to the extension of slavery, but they were confident that local initiative as expressed through popular sovereignty would effectively bar slavery from the territories. They also favored local control as a buttress for white supremacy.

Democratic voters tended to be drawn from the lower socioeconomic strata of Northern society, the recently arrived immigrants in the Eastern cities and the farmers of Southern extraction in the poorer agricultural sections of the Midwest bordering the Ohio River. Of all Northerners, these groups were most susceptible to a racist ideology. The status of the immigrants was of the lowest and their job security precarious; what jobs and status they did possess had been gained only after bitter competition with free blacks. Farmers in the lower Midwest, viewing the Ohio River as a barrier that sealed them off from the degrading presence of blacks, fully shared the racial mores of their Southern kinfolk.

Democratic orators exploited the racial fears of their constituents by luridly depicting a contamination of white society and politics through a huge influx of inherently inferior blacks. The economy would suffer whether or not blacks were willing or able to work in a free society. If they infiltrated the labor market, the wages of whites allegedly would be depressed and job competition brutalized; if, as was often asserted, blacks were too lazy to work, the white community would be taxed to support a class of thieves and inveterate paupers.

Racial control would collapse, warned the Democrats, once the blacks discovered that they had a strong political ally in the Republican party. Republicans were accused of favoring amalgamation, that is, a mixing of the races that would result in a contemptible hybrid race and a deterioration of the white stock. Moreover, stressed the Democrats, white dominance in the North hitherto had been possible because the number of blacks had been kept at a socially acceptable low level, less than 1 per cent of the total population in most states. Blacks were too few and too isolated to prevent enforcement of laws barring them from voting, holding office, serving on juries, and attending school. But now, with the expected northward migration of freedmen, the sheer increase in black population would force a commingling of the races to the detriment of whites.

In the Congressional elections in the fall of 1862, the Democrats skillfully combined racial fears with the growing disenchantment over a seemingly stalemated war into an appeal that charged the Republicans with waging an unconstitutional war for abolitionism. By carrying the belt of six states stretching from Illinois eastward to New Jersey, the Democrats reduced by half the Republican majority in the House of Representatives. Republicans, especially from the Midwest, singled out Negrophobia as the major factor in their party's poor showing. Many felt that Lincoln's Preliminary Emancipation Proclamation in September had turned the tide. A defeated Republican candidate for Congress from Ohio wrote Secretary of the Treasury Salmon P. Chase, "I had thought until this year the cry of 'nigger' & 'abolitionism', were played out but they never had as much power & effect in this part of the state as at the recent elections."

Lincoln was far too astute a politician not to have foreseen the political dangers of having his administration identified with an emancipation policy. Any votes that such a policy might win his party in New England would be more than counterbalanced by a Democratic resurgence in the Middle Atlantic and Midwestern states. In addition, the Unionist slave states on the northern rim of the South might well be driven into allegiance with the Confederacy. Consequently, Lincoln would turn to emancipation only with great reluctance and only after he had convinced himself that he could minimize its impact on the racial and constitutional sensibilities of his fellow Americans.

Lincoln's initial policy consisted simply of reassuring the slave states, whether in the Union or not, that he had no desire to disturb slavery. Had the rebel states taken Lincoln at his word, he undoubtedly would have permitted them to return with slavery intact. But in a repetition of its antebellum behavior, the South proved to be its own worst enemy. The Confederacy spurned reunion and continued a war that Lincoln had warned would inevitably erode slavery. By 1862 Lincoln concluded that to win this war some solution had to be found for the inseparable problems of slavery and race adjustments. His answer was a pragmatic blend of concessions to racism and appeals to the voluntarism that was the bedrock of constitutional Unionism. At the same time, however, he never abandoned the option of resorting to forced emancipation if military necessity dictated such a measure to ensure victory.

As in so many other areas of the war, the Constitution was a poor guide for Lincoln as he formulated his stand on slavery. Because he believed that the legality of secession was nothing but a pernicious abstraction, it followed that the seceded states were still within the Union and under the protection of the Constitution. Therefore, at the start of the war Lincoln ordered the enforcement of the Fugitive Slave Act.

Some Union generals, especially George McClellan, fully agreed with Lincoln's policy. Fearing that the old Union of 1860 could never be restored if slavery were threatened, McClellan pleaded with like-minded conservative Democrats in the fall of 1861 to "Help me to dodge the Nigger—we want nothing to do with him." However, most Union commanders were loath to return to the enemy manpower that would be used in the Confederate war effort. Their problem, as defined by one army officer, was how "to elude the Constitution by Constitutional evasions."

General Benjamin Butler at Fort Monroe, Virginia, provided a solution in May, 1861, when he began defining slaves who entered his lines as contraband of war. Butler reasoned that, by employing runaways as military laborers, he would be adding to the strength of his army while subtracting from that of the enemy's. Besides, as he coyly added, "the Fugitive Slave Act did not affect a foreign country, which Virginia claims to be." Military necessity, as well as a Northern public opinion generally hostile to the use of Union troops as slave-catchers, supported Butler's evasion of the Constitution. Civil and military leaders had to adjust to the wartime realities.

Although Lincoln, in McClellan's judgment, was "really mild on the nigger question" at the beginning of the war, he reversed his position on fugitive slaves by 1862. Conflicts between U.S. marshals and the commanding general of the District of Columbia over the return of fugitive slaves who had fled to Washington were a constant source of irritation for Lincoln during 1861 and 1862. When, in the spring of 1862, the situation had degenerated to the point where the civilian and military authorities were resorting to armed force against each other in retaliation for either enforcing or not enforcing the Fugitive Slave Act, Lincoln intervened. He worked out a compromise under which only the runaways of Unionists were to be returned. Officially, Lincoln held to this position, but his advice to worried loyalists throughout the Border states offered little hope for the return of their slaves. In a letter of November, 1862, to a Kentucky Unionist (which apparently he never sent), Lincoln bluntly stated his case: "Do you not know that I may as well surrender this contest, directly, as to make any order, the obvious purpose of which would be to return fugitive slaves?"

In 1862 Congress finally settled the vexing issue by ratifying what had become the standard practice of most field commanders. As of March, Union naval and army forces were ordered not to return any fugitives, and beginning in July the slaves who came into Union lines were declared free if their masters were rebels.

The difficulties and consequent temporizing that beset Lincoln over the fugitive-slave issue were mild compared to the complexities of dealing directly with slavery. Again the Constitution presented legal and conceptual barriers. Slavery was a domestic institution the regulation of which the Constitution left solely to the states. Any action against slavery, such as emancipation, without the consent of the states involved was equivalent to declaring that the federal government was not legally bound by the Constitution. This was true whether the slave states were Unionist or Confederate. The former were clearly still within the Union, and the latter, Lincoln insisted, had never left in any legal sense. Apparently, any federal move against slavery would require abandonment of either the Constitution or Lincoln's belief in a permanent Union.

At the start of the war, the Northern public did not question slavery's constitutionally privileged position. The Constitution was revered as the touchstone of American liberties and the main bulwark against the excesses of an unrestrained democracy. To attack slavery was to undermine the constitutional liberties of all Americans. Reinforcing this respect for the rights of slaveholders was the North's original conception of the war. It was widely believed that the war would be short. Southerners would soon come to their senses *unless* they were faced with the loss of slavery. Once the South was faced with subjugation and a forced revolution in its racial and class structure, all hope of reconciliation would vanish. It was feared that the loyal Border states would be alienated and that Southern Unionists, whom Northerners confidently expected to take the Confederacy out of the war, would turn against the Union with a vengeance.

The exigencies of war soon revealed that slavery's apparent sanctity was an illusion. The war was not ended quickly, and the North realized by 1862 that Southern Unionists were too few and too divided to lead the seceded states back into the Union. Northern soldiers discovered that the Unionism of even a loyal Border state such as Kentucky had been greatly exaggerated. "There is no such thing as unionism in Kentucky," wrote Colonel William Utley of the 22d Wisconsin Volunteers. In the same letter to a friend in November, 1862, he added that "all Kentuckeyans were either d——d trators [sic] or cowards, that there was no loyalty in the state, that you might put it all in to one end of the scales, and a nigger baby in the other end, and Loyalty and unionism would go up with a rush." What particularly had embittered Utley were his difficulties with Kentucky state authorities over his refusal to enforce the Fugitive Slave Act. But his conclusion that unconditional Unionism was a mirage was reached by most Union soldiers when they learned that their presence in the South only stiffened Confederate resistance.

Northern civilians also were coming to the conclusion that the Union and slavery were incompatible. Horace Greeley, editor of the *New York Tribune,* though eccentric and occasionally flighty, was nonetheless respected by Lincoln as a sounding board for Northern public opinion. Greeley cautioned Lincoln in March, 1862, that the patience of the North on the slavery issue was limited. Northerners had to feel that in the war *"things are going ahead.* The stagnation of the grand Army has given life to all manner of projects which would be quiet if the War had been going vigorously on." The stagnation to which Greeley was referring was broken by McClellan's Peninsular campaign. However, the end result of this campaign, the sense of a stalemated war, was just as frustrating for Northerners to accept. Throughout the summer of 1862, Lincoln was warned of Northern concern over the seeming aimlessness of his war policy and his refusal to deal firmly with the rebels. One letter in the *New York Tribune* concluded with the disturbing question, "Does this mean that [Lincoln] does not care what becomes of the country —that he is ready to play conservative to the ruin of the Nation?"

Northern religious leaders also were urging that Lincoln take a strong stand against slavery. The Reverends William W. Patton and John Dempster, representing several religious denominations in Chicago, presented Lincoln in September, 1862, with a petition for emancipation. The ministers spoke for what was rapidly becoming the consensus in many areas of the North, especially those of Republican mass support. The war, they said, was divine punishment for the national sin of slavery. If further providential retribution were to be avoided, this sin had to be expurgated. Secession followed slavery, and to strike at the former while ignoring the latter would only prolong the bloodshed. Divine justice and public opinion alike demanded emancipation. "The struggle has gone too far, and cost too much treasure and blood, to allow of a partial settlement."

The combined pressure of military events and Northern public opinion was pushing Lincoln toward emancipation, a policy that he felt would produce the greatest crisis of his administration. Before he committed himself, however, he had to be convinced of the failure of his efforts to cope with the slavery issue within the confines of constitutional Unionism.

The outlines of Lincoln's plan were first made public in his December, 1861, annual message to Congress. Interpreting the anticipated results of the First Confiscation Act of August, 1861, as a forfeiture to the federal government of the legal claims of rebel owners to their slave property used in the rebellion, Lincoln recommended that these blacks be declared free by Congress with the proviso that immediate steps be taken to colonize them "in a climate congenial to them." He hoped that the individual states would follow this precedent. The states, after assuming legal ownership of confiscated slaves, could turn them over to Congress "in lieu, *pro tanto,* of direct taxes, or upon some other plan to be agreed on with such States respectively."

At this stage of the war, Lincoln assumed that any program of emancipation, however mild, would be rejected by a white-supremacist society unless it were linked with the expatriation of blacks. He suggested that those blacks already free might be induced to leave America voluntarily. As for the racist rejoinder that appropriating funds to acquire territory for colonization would benefit only blacks, he shrewdly reasoned that black emigration would result in just that much more social and economic opportunity for whites. Above all, Lincoln defended his colonization proposition as a war measure essential to preserving the Union. If the war could not be kept within manageable bounds, and if the nation as a whole had to face the unprecedented problem of a mass emancipation, he feared that the Union could not be perpetuated.

In March, 1862, after no state had responded to his proposal, Lincoln urged Congress to adopt a joint resolution calling for voluntary, federally compensated emancipation. Congress passed such a resolution in April and supported its word by appropriating funds for compensation and colonization when it emancipated the slaves in Washington, D.C. An additional $500,000 in colonization funding was made available in July, when Congress freed slaves in the hands of Union military forces.

Lincoln now had a specific national commitment to use as a bargaining point with Border-state congressmen. Throughout 1862 he exhorted them to seize this constitutional offer, which he believed would shorten the war and free the Upper South of both slaves and the concomitant race problem. Voluntary emancipation, Lincoln asserted, would soon achieve the war's overriding political objective of restoring the Union. In freeing its slaves the Upper South would be divested of any desire to aid or join the Confederacy, while the rebels would give up any hope of eventually winning over sister slave states. "Break that lever [of slavery] before their faces," Lincoln told the Border-state representatives on July 12, and the Confederacy "can shake you no more forever."

Either help end the war now, Lincoln added, or receive nothing for your slaves. If the war continued much longer, slavery would be "extinguished by mere friction and abrasion—by the mere incidents of the war. It will be gone, and you will have nothing valuable in lieu of it." Here, then, was a concrete offer, in Lincoln's words, "to sell out" and obtain a fair value for a form of property that almost certainly would not survive the war. As he crudely stated his case to a Maryland congressman, "Niggers will never be higher." Furthermore, Lincoln continually stressed that the ex-slaves would not remain. He was confident that abundant land for blacks in Central or South America could be obtained cheaply and that once a successful start had been made toward colonization, other free blacks would be eager to leave.

Finally, Lincoln reminded the Border states that he was under increasing abolitionist pressure to support a far more radical solution. The abolitionists did not want to pay for slaves, he warned, and they would leave the South straddled with a large free black population. "By conceding what I now ask, you can relieve me, and much more, can relieve the country, in this important point."

And yet the Border states would not concede. In an incredible testimony to the tenacity with which whites would desperately cling to slavery as an institution for racial control, every loyal state of the Upper South rejected Lincoln's offer. Their congressmen and state legislators responded that the free states would not permit themselves to be taxed to provide compensation to slaveholders, that emancipation in the Upper South would only intensify the Confederate resolve not to surrender, and that, once a precedent was set, the emancipation of 3 million slaves in the Lower South was but a matter of time. Underlying all these arguments was the specter of social revolution. Even as the institution of slavery was crumbling in their midst, the Border states were immobilized by fear of black equality.

Lincoln was puzzled and angered by this intransigence. Still, he would not abandon the essentials of his plan. Realizing by the middle of 1862 that an executive proclamation freeing the slaves in Confederate-held territory was rapidly becoming a military necessity, he redoubled his efforts to convince influential black leaders to support foreign colonization for their race. Success in this would minimize the impact of an emancipation proclamation on a racially tense North and might yet rally nonslaveholders in the Upper South behind his voluntary plan for emancipation.

In August, 1862, a committee of free blacks, headed by Edward M. Thomas, president of the Anglo-African Institution for the Encouragement of Industry and Art, was invited to the White House. Introduced to Lincoln by the Reverend James Mitchell, the federal Commissioner of Emigration, the committee was there to hear the president's arguments for black colonization. Waiving the question of right or wrong, and implying that blacks were as much at fault as whites, Lincoln pointed to the long-standing and apparently permanent antipathy between the races. Each race, in his opinion, suffered from the presence of the other. Not only were the vast majority of blacks held as slaves, but even free blacks were not treated as equals by white men, nor could they ever expect to be. "The aspiration of men is to enjoy equality with the best when free, but on this broad continent, not a single man of your race is made the equal of a single man of ours." Overlooking the inability of his own race to confront the reciprocal problems of slavery and racism, Lincoln then blamed the blacks for the fact that whites were "cutting one another's throats" in a civil war. "But for your race among us there could not be war, although many men engaged on either side do not care for you one way or the other."

Physical removal seemed the best solution. Urging blacks to

emulate George Washington's sacrifices during the American Revolution, and asking for colonization leaders "capable of thinking as white men," Lincoln painted a glowing picture of the attractions of founding a colony in Central America. The region Lincoln had in mind, a site on the Isthmus of Chiriqui in the Caribbean, was far closer to the United States than the original black colony of Liberia in Africa. The site was thought to contain rich coal deposits that would provide jobs for the black settlers and profits for the white speculators who had an interest in these mines. In what he hoped would clinch his case, Lincoln told his audience that there would be no prejudice against blacks in racially mixed Central America and that the climate would be beneficial to what whites assumed was the peculiar biological adaptability of blacks to the tropics.

However logical, though wrenching, an answer to America's racial dilemma (and the political needs of the Republican party) was furnished by colonization, the movement was stillborn. Most blacks understandably felt that they had at least as much right as whites to remain in America; the speculators in Chiriqui over-extended themselves; and the neighboring nations of Honduras, Nicaragua, and Costa Rica threatened to use force to prevent what they saw as a clever scheme of Yankee imperialism.

In his annual message to Congress in December, 1862, Lincoln again brought up the colonization issue and argued, almost wistfully, that perhaps blacks might yet be convinced of the wisdom of voluntarily emigrating. Indeed, the main emphasis of the message was an attempt to allay Northern racial fears by linking colonization with a package of constitutional amendments that represented Lincoln's last effort to find a constitutional Unionist solution to the emancipation problem. Lincoln insisted that slavery and the racial question could still be compromised through mutual concessions by the friends of the Union. His proposed constitutional amendments included (1) the issuance of federal bonds to compensate those loyal states that abolished slavery before 1900; (2) legal recognition of the freedom of all slaves "who enjoyed actual freedom by the chances of war," with compensation for their owners, if loyal; (3) a federal pledge to provide funds for colonization by blacks.

Lincoln defended his proposals as the last best hope for restoring the Union in terms of mutual reconciliation. If his amendments were approved, Border-state conservatives would be assured that no constitutional objections could be raised against federally compensation emancipation. Racial adjustment could be minimized because each state was free to choose whatever gradual plan of emancipation it desired. Lincoln even hinted that dismantling slavery by degrees would leave room for control over the blacks through apprentice systems of labor. Unionists were told that paying for the slaves would be far cheaper in the long run than fighting to free them. Lincoln had already sent Congress detailed fiscal charts that revealed that one-half of the daily expense of the war would pay for Delaware's slaves at the rate of $400 per head and that eighty-seven days of the war's cost would cover the slaves in the loyal Upper South. Besides, the fiscal burden would be spread over the next thirty-seven years and would be lightened proportionately by the expansion of America's population.

Slaves were offered the dubious advantage of remaining under the paternalistic direction of whites. His plan, said Lincoln, "saves them from the vagrant destitution which must largely attend immediate emancipation in localities where their numbers are very great; and it gives the inspiring assurance that their posterity shall be free forever." The Northern whites who had responded to the racist appeals of the Democrats in the recent congressional elections were reassured that emancipation would not threaten white supremacy. The anticipated voluntary emigration of some freedmen would certainly raise the wages of all labor by reducing competition. Even without removal, Lincoln maintained that most ex-slaves would remain in the South. Previously, blacks had fled to the North to escape bondage and poverty. But once they were free, their former masters would naturally turn to them as their chief labor supply. Assuming the worst—that large numbers of freedmen would migrate to the North—Lincoln noted that they would still comprise only one-seventh of the total population if distributed equally among the states. Surely, Lincoln contended, this did not represent an insurmountable problem for white control. "And, in any event, cannot the north decide for itself, whether to receive them?"

Lincoln stressed that neither the war nor the soon to be issued

Emancipation Proclamation would be stayed by the mere recom-
mendation of his plan. Still, "Its timely *adoption,* I doubt not,
would bring restoration and thereby stay both." He pointed out
that in addition to the five loyal Border states, two more slave
states would have to ratify his proposed amendments in order to
meet the constitutional requirement of concurrence by three-
fourths of the states. Such approval, he felt, by laying the slavery
issue to rest, "would end the struggle now, and save the Union
forever."

Despite his high hopes, the momentum of the war had by-
passed Lincoln's experiment in constitutional statecraft. The
Confederacy would not yield a single point in its drive for independence. Conservatives in both the Democratic and Republican parties feared he was moving too far and too fast, and the
mainstream of Republican sentiment feared he was moving too
slowly and too cautiously. The war could neither be contained
nor won within the traditional confines of the Constitution. Constitutional Unionism had confronted Lincoln with a dilemma
that could be resolved only by turning to revolutionary
Unionism.

REVOLUTIONARY UNIONISM

Lincoln's commitment to forced emancipation had been foreshadowed by his repeated warnings that he would resort to any
expedient necessary to save the Union. "The truth is," he wrote
in the summer of 1862 to a Louisiana loyalist worried over the
impact on slavery of the federal occupation of New Orleans,
"that what is done, and omitted about slaves, is done and
omitted on the same military necessity."

Earlier he had revoked the emancipation orders issued by two
of his commanders because he thought such measures were premature, politically dangerous, and an infringement on his own
prerogatives. When General John C. Frémont's proclamation of
August 30, 1861, ordered the confiscation of the slave property
of Missouri rebels, Lincoln acted quickly to quiet the fears of
Unionists in the Border states. He countermanded the order on
the grounds that Frémont had overstepped his authority by making a purely political decision that would drive the Border South

out of the Union. With the loss of these states, Lincoln felt the game was up. "We would as well consent to separation at once, including the surrender of this capitol," he confided to Senator Orville Browning of Illinois. A more sweeping military emancipation order had been issued in May, 1862, by General David Hunter, commander of the Department of the South. Stating that slavery and martial law were incompatible, Hunter declared free the slaves in Georgia, Florida, and South Carolina. Again, Lincoln's reaction was swift, but he now suggested that he, as commander in chief of the army and navy, might very well have the power that had been denied to Hunter. Lincoln reserved solely for himself the decision to exercise such supposed power, and he would be governed by whatever was "indispensable to the maintenance of the government."

By the summer of 1862 Lincoln's patience, and that of his Northern constituency, had about run out. Tired of waging a war in which he felt the Union was staking everything and the enemy nothing, frustrated by the stalemate in the Eastern military theater, and prodded by Congress with the passage of the Second Confiscation Act, Lincoln told his cabinet on July 22 of his intention to issue an emancipation proclamation. With the exception of Montgomery Blair, the Postmaster General from the Border state of Maryland, cabinet reaction was favorable. On the same day, and also in response to the Second Confiscation Act, Lincoln authorized the executive order empowering the military seizure of any Southern property, including slaves, that could be of use in the Union war effort.

Following the advice of William Seward, his Secretary of State, to await a military victory before issuing his proclamation, Lincoln held off public announcement of his new policy. Indeed, his actions from late July to mid-September suggest that his decision was still not irreversible. In his famous letter to Horace Greeley in August, he reiterated, "My paramount object in this struggle *is* to save the Union, and is *not* either to save or to destroy slavery." He debated with the emancipationist ministers from Chicago who visited the White House in early September whether an emancipation proclamation would have any practical effect. He pointed out that he had been powerless even to prevent the capture and sale into slavery by the Confederacy of some

black laborers who had been sent to the battlefield of Second
Bull Run to help in the retrieval and burial of the bodies of
Union soldiers. Besides, he asked, what could be done with the
blacks if masses of them were freed? Not only would they place
a burden on the Union armies for their upkeep, but "if we were
to arm them, I fear that in a few weeks the arms would be in the
hands of the rebels." And, as always, Lincoln expressed concern
over the effect of emancipation upon the loyal Border states. He
told the ministers that he could not yet risk the defection to the
Confederacy of the fifty thousand Union troops from the Upper
South.

Lincoln's pessimism in this interview may well have marked a
shrewd attempt to probe the depths of the increasing Northern
commitment to emancipation. But, in all likelihood, it was also
a hangover of the intense gloom he experienced after John
Pope's army had been humiliated by Lee at Second Bull Run in
late August. Edward Bates, his Attorney General, reported that
after this federal loss, so close to Washington, Lincoln "seemed
wrung by the bitterest agony—said he felt almost ready to hang
himself."

The victory Lincoln needed to rekindle his spirits and to give
the impression of dealing from strength was provided by Antietam
in the middle of September, when McClellan turned back Lee's
invasion of Maryland. On September 22 the Preliminary Emancipation Proclamation was issued.

The Proclamation, for all its revolutionary implications, revealed the limits of Lincoln's conversion to revolutionary Unionism. The proposed emancipation was still legitimized in constitutional terms. Believing that Congress had no power over
slavery in the states, a conviction largely responsible for his non-
enforcement of the Second Confiscation Act, Lincoln cited his
responsibilities as commander in chief as the legal source for
whatever measures were necessary to preserve the Constitution.
As he had told the Chicago ministers, and as John Quincy
Adams had foreseen twenty years earlier, the war powers of the
executive included "a right to take any measure which may
best subdue the enemy." Despite an unprecedented application of
executive power, the façade of constitutionalism had been retained.

Moreover, any slave state could escape forced emancipation by accepting Lincoln's offer to return to the Union by January 1, 1863. The criterion for readmission would be whether a majority of the qualified voters in any previously rebel state elected representatives who would be seated in Congress by that date. In the meantime, Lincoln repledged himself to committing Congress to a program of financial assistance for any state that would voluntarily embark upon emancipation.

Lincoln did redeem his pledge in his December message to Congress. He would also be so anxious to avoid the charge of waging a war for abolitionism that he would waive the preconditions for readmission he had set back in September. The final version of the Emancipation Proclamation, issued on January 1, 1863, applied only to Confederate-held territory. It excluded from emancipation not only the loyal slave states, which had always been represented in Congress, but also those areas under federal occupation. None of these specified occupied regions—Tennessee, New Orleans and its surrounding parishes, Norfolk and the Eastern shore of Virginia, and West Virginia—was represented in Congress by members elected by a majority of the qualified voters. Aside from the explosiveness of the slavery issue, Lincoln wanted to avoid any policy that would impede his reconstruction plans in these regions. Expediting their readmission, even if it meant leaving in abeyance the question of slavery, was justified on the grounds of undermining Confederate morale and adding to the slim Republican majority in the recently elected Congress. As the Democrats were quick to note, the restored states would undoubtedly ally themselves with the party to which they owed their very presence in Washington.

Clearly, the Emancipation Proclamation was but a promise of future action. It would be implemented only to the extent that federal armies could overrun the Confederacy. Seward's reported comment that "we show our sympathy with slavery by emancipating slaves where we cannot reach them, and holding them in bondage where we can set them free" summarized the disappointment of many Northerners. The legal status of slavery after the war was left open. As a war measure, the Proclamation, Lincoln felt, would be declared inoperative by the courts once the fighting had ended. Whether the Proclamation would apply to those slaves who had not actually entered Union lines during the war and whether it would cover the children of present slaves were fundamental questions still to be settled.

Yet, the Proclamation was undeniably the turning point of the war, the dividing line between the efforts to restore the old Union of 1860 and the reluctant commitment to forge a new Union. The lingering hopes of the Confederacy for foreign recognition were shattered once the antislavery majority of Europeans saw that Unionism had become firmly equated with an extension of freedom. In terms of the military effort, Union commanders now had an ideological prop for conducting a total war. They had both a legal justification for destroying the foundation of Southern society and executive sanction for tapping the black manpower pool. The Emancipation Proclamation had authorized the enlistment of ex-slaves for naval duty and "to garrison forts, positions, stations, and other places."

This decision to accept blacks for military service represented another major policy shift. Blinded by their racial prejudice, Northerners initially declared that the black man's role in this, a white man's war, was to be a purely passive one. The leading Republican newspaper in Indiana, the *Indianapolis Journal*, spoke for the dominant Northern sentiment when it expressed the hope in November, 1861, that "we may never have to confess to the world that the United States Government has to seek an ally in the negro to regain its authority." Racial slurs depicted blacks as a weak, cowardly race incapable of the courageous self-reliance demanded of the soldier. According to the logic of white supremacy, arming the blacks would not only be a military blunder and a confession of white failure, but it would also imply that blacks had achieved a measure of equality that whites were not yet willing to grant.

Any move toward a combat utilization of blacks, whether those already free or those to be emancipated during the war, would have to evolve out of compelling war needs. The prejudice in the military, which resulted in the consensus that the use of black troops would demoralize white soldiers and cripple their combat efficiency, would have to be broken down, or at least modified, by the recognition that in a total war no potential sources of support could be ignored.

Union commanders first assumed that the only military service blacks could render would be that of camp laborers. The fugitives who flocked behind federal lines were forced to work as teamsters, cooks, and construction hands on fortifications. The use of blacks for such duties freed white soldiers for the front and reinforced the white belief that blacks were fit only for supervised common labor. But then, as the Union armies drove deeper into the Southern black belts, they discovered that their best allies, and often their only ones, were slaves. Acting as spies, scouts, and informers, the blacks performed essential intelligence services. General O. M. Mitchell telegraphed Washington in May, 1862, from northern Alabama that "I shall soon have watchful guards among the slaves on the plantations . . . , and all who communicate to me valuable information I have promised the protection of my government." He added that if this policy were disapproved, "it would be impossible for me to hold my position."

Slowly, a grudging respect emerged for the military capabilities of the blacks. At the same time, Northern soldiers came to realize that black labor was indispensable to the Confederacy. "The niggers are the backbone of the rebellion," concluded P. E. Holcombe, a Vermont captain stationed in the lower Mississippi Valley in the spring of 1862.

> [The Confederacy] can put twice as many men in the field, for having the niggers to cultivate the crops. What's the use to have men from Maine, Vermont and Massachusetts dying down here in the swamps   you can't replace these men, but if a nigger dies, all you have to do is to send out and get another one.

This rather chilling logic was commonplace in the Union armies by the middle of the war. The military necessity of stripping the Confederacy of its basic labor supply and using it for the Union war machine had become self-evident. The question of whether these blacks would be used in a combat capacity remained, but the war weariness and lagging volunteer enlistments that so worried Lincoln by the summer of 1862 gradually convinced military and civilian leaders in the North that the proffered black assistance could no longer be refused.

As with emancipation, Congress, rather than Lincoln, took the initiative. In July, 1862, the Second Confiscation Act authorized Lincoln, in deliberately vague language, "to employ as many persons of African descent as he may deem necessary and proper for the suppression of this rebellion." In the same month, Congress more specifically endorsed black enlistments by passing a new militia act, which repealed the "white only" provisions of the 1792 law.

Although black regiments had been organized previously, in South Carolina by David Hunter and in Kansas by James Lane, the War Department refused to sanction them. With the change in Northern opinion as registered by Congress, the Department for the first time authorized black troops in August, 1862. General Rufus Saxton was directed to raise five black regiments, to be officered by whites, from among the freedmen on the South Carolina Sea Islands. Lincoln's official attitude was still one of disapproval, and this initial mobilization was probably intended as a trial balloon to gauge public reaction in the North as well as to offer proof to skeptical whites that blacks could be efficient soldiers.

The experiment with the Sea Island blacks was pronounced a success in the official dispatches of the Union commanders. Convinced now of the military urgency and feasibility of arming the blacks, Lincoln approved the policy in the Emancipation Proclamation and moved rapidly to implement it in the winter and spring of 1863. The Democratic press played on the themes of executive tyranny and racial treason. Many in the military continued to grumble. "Instead of this nigger question," wrote Major William Watson, a surgeon in the Army of the Potomac, "if the administration with Congress will devote itself entirely to our financial affairs and the vigorous prosecution of the war the rebellion will be suppressed in less time than it will take to organize, equip and dicipline [*sic*] the niggers."

But Lincoln would not reverse his policy. Aware that the Emancipation Proclamation, to an extent, would have a negative impact on the Unionist cause, he was determined to accentuate the positive advantage of increasing military manpower. "What is evil in effect we are already enduring," he wrote General Nathaniel P. Banks in late January, 1863, "and we must have the

counterpart of it." This was Lincoln's rationale for reinstating
Benjamin F. Butler, who had had previous experience with black
troops, to organize the mobilization of blacks from southern
Louisiana. "The colored population is the great *available* and
yet *unavailed* of force for restoring the Union," Lincoln told
Andrew Johnson, the Unionist war governor of Tennessee, while
urging him in March to consider the possibility of enlisting
blacks.

The Northern governors were instructed to accept blacks in
fulfilling their state troop quotas, and commanders in the South
were ordered to mobilize as many blacks as possible. The federal recruitment drive centered in the lower Mississippi Valley,
the source of nearly half of the some 180,000 black troops who
fought in the war. Intense prejudice against the blacks remained,
and many white soldiers were never reconciled to the use of
black troops. Still, Lincoln in truth could claim success for his
policy. He constantly reminded frightened conservatives that the
combat role of blacks was shortening the war and conserving
white manpower. Every ex-slave in the Union armies was one
laborer fewer to support the Confederate armies. Moreover, blacks
were stationed as garrison troops in the malaria regions along
the Mississippi River in order to save the lives of white soldiers.

Emancipation, coupled with the arming of the blacks, had been
a calculated gamble on Lincoln's part. In reviewing these measures for Congress in December, 1863, he noted that they "gave
to the future a new aspect, about which hope, and fear, and
doubt contended in uncertain conflict." Because of this uncertainty, he felt that the Emancipation Proclamation had precipi-
tated "the crisis of the contest." The crisis had been faced in
1863 and successfully weathered. Lincoln had stretched the Constitution without breaking it, and he had intensified the racial
fears of white Northerners without driving apart the Unionist
coalition.

THE NEW NATIONALISM

The Proclamation, however, remained but a means to an end,
namely, the restoration of the seceded states to what the North
regarded as their proper place in the Union. Because the Found-

ing Fathers had not provided for an eventuality that they had not anticipated and contemporary Unionists differed among themselves as to the legal status of the rebel states, the entire problem took on an extraconstitutional quality. Although Lincoln and Congress would interpret certain constitutional provisions in such a way as to sanction their own control over the reconstruction process, their dilemma was so unprecedented that constitutional Unionism had to be jettisoned if for no other reason than that it was irrelevant.

The central premise of constitutional Unionism was the unquestioned control of each state over its internal affairs. This premise could be reconciled with the reconstruction of the Union only if the majority of the citizens in each seceded state were indeed Unionists. Once Unionist strength in the South was shown to be negligible, Lincoln and Congress were driven to the necessity of instituting direct federal control. Lincoln turned to his role as commander in chief. He imposed military governments on Union-occupied areas and appointed hybrid civil-military governors who exercised a wider latitude of powers than any other executives in American history. Republican congressmen, citing the constitutional obligation to guarantee a republican form of government to each state, maintained that they could set terms for readmission. In either case, the antebellum concept of states' rights was abandoned.

The impact of this new nationalism on Southerners was in direct proportion to their commitment to the Confederacy. If any state had voluntarily decided to return to the Union by January 1, 1863, and if the credentials of its representatives elected in federal elections had been acceptable to Congress, in all likelihood the state could have escaped its impact entirely. Until the Emancipation Proclamation went into effect, Lincoln placed no conditions upon readmission and Congress had yet to agree upon any. The terms of readmission that Lincoln outlined for Louisiana in late July, 1862, were a model of simplicity and leniency. "Let [the people of Louisiana], in good faith, reinaugurate the national authority, and set up a State Government conforming thereto under the constitution." Federal forces would be withdrawn once they were no longer required to protect the Unionist government and "the people of the State can then upon the old Constitutional terms, govern themselves to their own liking."

Although Lincoln had made it as easy as possible, only one region under initial Confederate jurisdiction was brought back into the Union during the war. The citizens of the northwestern counties of Virginia, physically and psychologically isolated from slavery, and resentful of the dominance of state politics by the slaveholders on the other side of the Alleghenies, were detached from the Confederacy early in the war. Although Congress temporarily recognized the Unionists of western Virginia as the legitimate representatives for the entire state, this fiction was soon dropped, to be replaced by a movement for separate statehood. On June 20, 1863, West Virginia formally entered the Union.

Even this reconstruction of sorts was made possible only by dodging the Constitution. The necessary legal consent of the parent state, Virginia, was nominally obtained by declaring that a state legislature in Wheeling, composed almost entirely of representatives from the districts in the northwest, was the "restored" government for all Virginians. After conceding to his cabinet in December, 1862, that the majority of the qualified voters in Virginia did not participate in the separate statehood movement, Lincoln sidestepped the issue by arguing that precedent had established that it was "the qualified voters, *who choose to vote*, that constitute the political power of the state." He added that he would not become ensnarled in constitutional abstractions. "Can this government stand, if it indulges constitutional constructions by which men in open rebellion against it, are to be accounted, man for man, the equals of those who maintain their loyalty to it?" Although troubled by this highly unorthodox, if not downright illegal, division of a state, Lincoln was confident that it could not serve as a precedent for peacetime. Even if it did amount to a sanctioning of secession, there was a difference, he concluded, between secession in favor of the Constitution and secession against it.

West Virginia was an anomalous case that could hardly serve as a guide for reconstruction. Nonetheless, in rationalizing what they had done, both Lincoln and Congress foreshadowed much of their future handling of reconstruction. Lincoln now had a constitutional argument for holding that the loyal people of a state, no matter how few in number, could be recognized as constituting a valid government. The principle of majority rule was replaced by that of loyal rule. On the other hand, Congress had exercised its right to dictate terms for readmission. As a condition for statehood, the constitution of West Virginia had to provide for gradual emancipation. Beyond this step, however, Congress established that it would act under the exigencies of war whether or not it had a specific constitutional mandate. As Thaddeus Stevens, a Republican congressman from Pennsylvania, expressed it, "I will not stultify myself by supposing that we had any warrant in the Constitution for this proceeding" of admitting West Virginia.

This pattern of simultaneously following and ignoring the Constitution characterized all reconstruction policy. Both Lincoln and Congress recognized the inherent difficulties of structuring a program given the constitutional confusion. Lincoln's answer was to react separately to each problem as it emerged, thereby retaining a maximum number of options. Congress strove to find a solution applicable to all rebel areas. Although friction was generated, it did not result in a break between Lincoln and Congress, because both were moving in the same direction —toward instituting nationalistic controls.

The first reconstruction measure that received the support of Republican congressmen was the Ashley bill, reported out of committee in March, 1862. The organizational principle of the bill was territorialization, the concept that the seceded states had reverted back to the status of territories. Citing the practical necessity of setting up loyal governments in the areas regained from the Confederacy and the inadequacy of relying upon military governments, the backers of the bill argued that territorialization was a constitutionally valid method for establishing plenary federal power in occupied regions. This power was expressed in provisions for emancipation, disqualification from political privileges of lawyers, ministers, and former federal officials who supported the rebellion, and confiscation of rebel property and its distribution to loyal citizens, black or white. The bill's failure to prohibit blacks from voting or serving on juries under the territorial government signified a tentative effort toward instituting a biracial democracy in the South.

The Ashley bill was far too radical for nearly all Democrats and for the conservative minority of the Republican majority. This coalition tabled the bill in March over the opposition of the majority of the Republicans. The notion of territorialization frightened many. Some argued, with Lincoln's approval, that the bill amounted to a virtual recognition of secession because it admitted that the Union was not perpetual. The minority report from the Committee on Territories, issued by the Border-state Democrats, labeled the bill "revolutionary, unconstitutional, and monstrous, if not palpably treasonable." What especially alarmed these Democrats was the recognition that the old Union of 1860, if ever restored, was on the verge of being transformed. They sought refuge in the Constitution by asserting that any prescription of regulations and terms for readmission would "alter the whole form and construction of the American Union as at present organized."

Lincoln responded to his party's pressure from the left in two ways. Abandoning the assumption that local Unionists could bring their states back into the Union without the active intervention of the federal government, he applied to reconquered areas the same military protection that had been used to hold the Border states in the Union. In Maryland secessionist members of the legislature had been arrested; in Missouri federal forces reconvened the state legislature in order to force the re-establishment of a Unionist government; and in Kentucky, whose request to be treated as an armed neutral was rejected by Lincoln, military arrests and intimidation were instrumental in ensuring Unionist election victories. Lincoln had used whatever combination of military power and political patronage was necessary to maintain Unionism in the Border region. He extended this policy in the spring of 1862 by establishing provisional military governments in Arkansas, North Carolina, Tennessee, and Louisiana. The governors of these areas were appointed directly by Lincoln. In fashioning this alternative to territorialization, Lincoln still held to the theory of state indestructibility, but he had also seen the need to create interim governments under his control that would protect the Unionists until they were strong enough to restore their old state governments.

Lincoln's second reaction to the Ashley bill involved taking a more decided stand against slavery. Beginning in March,

1862, he pushed his plan of voluntary, compensated emancipation as a substitute for congressionally dictated emancipation. This shift toward a position that implied that not all of the pre-existing powers of the seceded states would necessarily be upheld in the restored Union was finalized with the issuance of the Emancipation Proclamation. Now, at the very least, the price of readmission included the loss of slavery, although Lincoln would still permit the returning states to dismantle slavery as slowly as they saw fit. As he explained on January 8, 1863, to the Democratic politician and general John A. McClernand of Illinois:

> Even the people of the states included [under the Proclamation], if they choose, need not to be hurt by it. Let them adopt systems of apprenticeship for the colored people, conforming substantially to the most approved plans of gradual emancipation, and, with the aid they can have from the general government, they may be nearly as well off, in this respect, as if the present trouble had not occurred.

Until December, 1863, when Lincoln issued his Proclamation of Amnesty and Reconstruction, no plan of reconstruction had been offered to the Confederate states. Congress saw the need for some definitive statement but was unable to agree on any program. By 1863 Congress dropped the territorialization issue, in part because of the unrelenting opposition of conservatives who feared it would provide a pretext for revolutionary change, and in part because military emancipation had rendered it less important as an antislavery device. A bill introduced by Senator Ira Harris of New York in February, 1863, embodied the new approach of Republicans to reconstruction. The bill called for provisional civil governments under the control of Congress. Based not on any territorial status of the ex-states but on the constitutional duty of Congress to guarantee a republican form of government in each state, the bill pledged the provisional governments to respect the states' laws at the time of secession with the exception of those pertaining to slavery. Former Confederate military and civil officers would lose the privileges of voting and holding state office, and the rebel war debts would have to be repudiated, but the South was assured through racial qualifications that only white men's governments would be established.

The Harris bill represented both the best opportunity for active cooperation between Lincoln and Congress and the most moderate terms that the seceded states could expect from a Republican-controlled Congress. Territorialization, confiscation, and black suffrage had all been dropped by the Republicans, who now rested their case on creating state governments whose constitutions would enact the conditions of the Harris bill. Ironically, it was the Democratic party that defeated the bill. As strict states' righters, Democrats defined republican government as simply self-government. They argued that the emancipationist provisions of the Harris bill, which they singled out for criticism, violated republicanism by denying local control over slavery and by ignoring the prior existence of home rule in the South.

Whether or not Lincoln would have signed the Harris bill is a moot point, but his Proclamation of Amnesty and Reconstruction was intended to align himself more closely with his party as well as to accelerate the sluggish program of reconstruction he had initiated under his military governors. For the first time Lincoln publicly made emancipation a precondition of returning to the Union, although he did not insist that it be written into new state constitutions. A loyalty oath, calling for future allegiance to the Union and compliance with the wartime measures against slavery, was required of all who wanted to participate in reconstruction. However, leading Confederate officers were excluded from the presidential offer of amnesty.

In what is regarded as the most lenient feature of the Proclamation, Lincoln pledged to recognize any Unionist government that was approved by as few as 10 per cent of the qualified voters of 1860 who took the loyalty oath. The loyalty of Southerners, not whether they necessarily constituted a majority, was the foundation of Lincoln's plan, and in this context, what is striking is not the plan's apparent leniency, but its adroit attempt to hasten reconstruction by flatly denying that republican government must rest on the will of the majority. The prime concern was to use reconstruction as a means of shortening the war by offering Southerners a practical alternative to Confederate rule. Here, in Lincoln's words, was "a plan . . . which may be accepted by them as a rallying point, and which they are assured in advance will not be rejected here."

Initially, Lincoln's outline for reconstruction was favorably received by Republicans. By the summer of 1864, however, widespread opposition had emerged. Republicans were increasingly worried by what they saw as unwarranted military control over government decisions that had been left traditionally and constitutionally to civil authorities. They noted that in Louisiana Lincoln had given General Nathaniel Banks a free hand to direct reconstruction. Fearful of the unsettling effects of calling a constitutional convention, Banks had ordered an election for state officers on the basis of the old constitution and then nullified by military decree the proslavery sections of that constitution. Military force and coercion were no substitute for a free government, insisted the Republicans, and military decisions might well be overturned by the courts at the conclusion of the war. Moreover, Lincoln's party critics were angered over the lack of any guarantees for the rights of either Unionists or freedmen. Under conditions of war Lincoln could control his reconstructed states as pocket boroughs because they were beholden to him for their existence, but once peace was established, what would prevent former rebels from regaining power and ignoring the rights of those who had remained loyal to the Union?

Republican opposition crystallized in the Wade-Davis bill. Resting upon the republican guarantee clause of the Constitution, the bill included the now familiar three conditions that would have to be met by a constitutional convention and ratified by a majority in each state—emancipation, political disqualification of leading rebels, and repudiation of Confederate war debts. Under the bill, reconstruction would not begin in any given state until the majority of its citizens took an oath of future loyalty, and only those able to swear to past allegiance in an iron-clad oath could vote for, or be members of, the required constitutional convention. Blacks were offered the minimal protection of having the writ of habeas corpus extended to those freedmen who might be deprived of their liberty by Southern whites.

Lincoln pocket-vetoed the Wade-Davis bill in July, 1864, out of a pragmatic desire not to be committed to any single plan of reconstruction. In particular, he did not want to overturn the governments he already had created in Louisiana and Arkansas. Careful to avoid recognizing any ideological gulf between himself and the majority of Republican congressmen, he suggested that any Southern state was still free to choose the terms of the Wade-Davis plan.

Lincoln was still hoping for a compromise with Congress, and one last opportunity was presented in the winter of 1864–65, when a revised Wade-Davis bill was debated in Congress. The revisions limited the emancipation requirement to those areas covered by the Emancipation Proclamation and cited the Proclamation as the source of Congressional authority. In the key concession, Lincoln's 10 per cent Louisiana government was excluded from the bill's provisions. In return, Congress added the stipulation that those blacks who had served in the federal military would be enfranchised and permitted to participate in reconstruction.

After Lincoln had indicated that he would approve such an amended bill, the expected compromise collapsed when the House Committee on the Rebellious States overplayed its hand by recommending that Louisiana and Arkansas be forced to comply with the conditions of the bill and that a guarantee of black civil rights be written into the constitutions of the reconstructed states. Moderate Republicans rallied behind Lincoln and voted down the bill. Meanwhile, a Senate filibuster led by Charles Sumner of Massachusetts, who was alarmed over the lack of a black-suffrage clause in the Louisiana constitution, forced an indefinite postponement of the recognition of the Louisiana senators elected under presidential reconstruction.

Lincoln never reached agreement with Congress on a plan of reconstruction. But it would be a mistake to exaggerate their differences. From the perspective of the constitutional Unionism of 1860, both had embraced a radically new concept of nationalism. By the middle of the war, Lincoln and Congress were united in the conviction that the slaves had to be freed and armed in order to preserve the Union. Despite their different approaches to reconstruction, both still had sanctioned an extension of federal power over the internal affairs of states that would have been unthinkable in 1860. Both had tentatively broached the explosive issue of black political equality by going on record as favoring some limited form of black suffrage in the South, especially for those who had fought for the Union.

Although the actions of the Republicans would be couched in constitutional language, many Unionists felt, as Ralph Waldo Emerson put it in 1862, that "all our action is new and unconstitutional." The point that Emerson missed was that the Constitution was used to provide a rhetorical cushion for unprecedented policies that were extraconstitutional. Lincoln and the Republican-dominated Congresses had acted on the only assumption consistent with the exigencies of victory, namely, that the necessity of preserving the Union and the Constitution made legal what otherwise would have been unconstitutional. Only in this way could they forge the North's ideological equivalent of the total war being waged by Union armies.

3

The Confederacy: A Society at War

The organization and maintenance of the Confederacy were testimony to the skill of the slaveholders in reacting under stress. Major structural shifts occurred in the economy of the South, and manpower was used to the utmost. The mobilization and total war effort in the South, far greater than that required in the North, was achieved because of the leadership capabilities of a planter class accustomed to command. The slaves had no choice but to accept this leadership, and the poorer whites did so because they equated the South's defeat with emancipation and with their own subsequent loss of status and identity through economic competition and social amalgamation with the freed blacks.

THE COMMITMENT TO VICTORY

The Confederacy embraced a society that eventually consumed itself in the pursuit of independence. The energy and passion that sustained the Confederate war effort flowed from a common sense of persecution that united Southerners against the Northern enemy. Steeped in the tradition of states' rights and conditioned by a generation of increasingly bitter sectional disputes to view the free states as a source of dangerous and fanatical abolitionism, Southerners always insisted that secession was a legal and neces-

sary act of self-defense. "Have not fifteen [slave] states a right
to govern themselves and withdraw from a compact or constitution disregarded by the other states to their injury and (it may
be) their ruin?" So wrote the Reverend Charles C. Jones, an
esteemed minister and planter in Liberty County, Georgia,
in a letter to his son on the eve of Lincoln's election in 1860.
Throughout the war Southerners would fall back repeatedly on
the same refrain. "Ours is not a revolution," maintained President Jefferson Davis in a public speech in October, 1864. "We
are a free and independent people, in States that had the right
to make a better government when they saw fit."

Southerners naturally turned to the political tradition that
was consistent with their self-image as an injured and oppressed
people, the doctrine of constitutional conservatism. Convinced
that Northerners had violated the original constitutional compact
by disregarding the concept of mutual forbearance for sectional
differences, Southerners first contended that the old Union was
gone, destroyed in spirit if not in form, even before South
Carolina touched off the secession movement in December, 1860.
Then, as if to prove to the outside world and to themselves
that they were the true conservatives and the rightful inheritors
of the constitutional mantle of the Founding Fathers, Southerners adopted a constitution closely modeled after the federal
document. Most changes were ones of degree, not of kind.
The Confederate president was limited to a single six-year term,
appropriations in a congressional bill were subject to a separate
executive veto, and national funding for internal improvements
in the states was prohibited, as were bounties and protective
tariffs. In an omission that Lincoln was to jump on and use to
taunt the South, the Confederate Constitution contained no
reference to the presumed right of secession.

In one fundamental area, slavery, the Confederacy departed
significantly from the federal Constitution. Slavery became a
thoroughly nationalistic institution under the Confederacy, whose
Congress was prohibited from passing any law that would
impair the rights of slaveholders and was enjoined to recognize
and protect slavery in any acquired territories. Furthermore,
slaveholders were specifically guaranteed the right to travel or
sojourn with their property in any state of the Confederacy.

The nationalistic safeguards that encased slavery expressed the persistent Southern willingness to ignore states' rights on matters relating to the institution that was the core of their society. Even while the metaphysics of states' rights was being employed to legitimize secession in the winter of 1860–61, Southern congressmen who lingered in Washington were demanding an extension of federal power on behalf of slavery. Led by Senator Robert Toombs of Georgia, these congressmen wanted not only a more stringent and rigorously enforced Fugitive Slave Act that would deprive the alleged fugitives of the protection of jury trials and habeas corpus writs, but also Congressional legislation to punish anyone who was to aid a slave insurrection or "commit any other act against the law of Nations, tending to disturb the tranquility of the people or government of any other State."

As the Toombs proposals revealed, states' rights were means to an end—the perpetuation of slavery. Jettisoned whenever they hindered the defense of slavery, states' rights were a beguiling abstraction that ultimately fooled no one as to the true nature of the cause for which Southerners would fight. In a famous speech delivered in Savannah in March, 1861, Confederate Vice-President Alexander Stephens stated this cause. Attacking Northerners for favoring racial equality (by which Stephens meant simply that they apparently wanted to free the slaves), he praised the Confederacy for anchoring itself to the opposite idea of innate black inferiority. "Our new government is founded upon . . . the great truth, that the negro is not equal to the white man; that slavery—subordination to the superior race—is his natural and normal condition."

Pride, the desperate yearning to quell forever the slavery agitation, the desire to vindicate slavery and Southern morals to a reproachful outside world, and a certain blunt honesty were all involved in Stephens's assertion that slavery was the "corner-stone" of the Confederacy. Nearly all Southern whites agreed. Their class structure, agrarian economy, and mechanisms for racial control, indeed the very rhythm and tone of their daily lives, were intimately related to the black man's bondage. Prodded for a generation by their political and religious leaders to view the institution as a positive good, a Southern consensus had emerged that accepted slavery as both a practical necessity and a Christian obligation.

Not knowing how to disentangle themselves from slavery and, in many instances, having lost the will to do so, Southerners reacted to the growing antislavery movement with righteous indignation and interpreted it as nothing less than a direct threat to their safety and well-being. As a result, they overlooked much that was conservative and racist in the Northern attitude. Abolitionists, Republicans, and eventually all Northerners were portrayed as unreasoning fanatics who would force emancipation and then racial equality on the South.

Southerners equated emancipation with a loss of racial control and an unavoidable debasement of the white race. This fear cut across class lines and produced a South united behind the Confederacy. While the planter would fight to protect his slave investment, his plantation profits, and his class leadership, the nonslaveholder was militantly committed to maintaining the legal and fixed subordination of the blacks as the surest sign of his own status and racial superiority. As Lincoln's Postmaster General, Montgomery Blair, pointed out, "It was by proclaiming to the laboring whites who filled the armies of rebellion that the election of Mr. Lincoln involved emancipation, equality of the negroes with themselves, and consequent amalgamation, that their jealousy [of caste] was stimulated to the fighting point."

Southerners went to war secure in the knowledge of having enlisted in a holy cause—holy, on the one hand, because they were defending their homes and their sacred right to self-government as enshrined in the Declaration of Independence, and, on the other hand, because they alone had been entrusted with the divine mission of uplifting and civilizing the African through slavery. In the summer of 1861 an anonymous contributor to *DeBow's Review,* the leading journal of the South, summarized how slaveholders had assumed the ideological offensive: "The Southern labor system is not only moral, in the highest sense of the word, but it is a holy cause. It is the cause of humanity and civilization." After crediting slavery with taming and disciplining the wild savages of Africa, the same author proudly asserted that the products of slave labor —cotton, rice, and sugar—"feed the poor and clothe the masses of the civilized nations of the earth."

Southern leaders accepted an image of themselves as an innocent, aggrieved people because this image provided the most direct means of relieving themselves from any self-doubts over secession. But, more than just reinforcing their confidence, this image also conformed to the Protestant morality that molded and defined Southerners' conceptions of themselves and their society. The Southerner was acutely conscious of standing alone. His values had been attacked for so long that they could be defended only by denying the moral authority of his critics. Abolitionism, therefore, became a heresy. One minister, the Reverend W. M. Cunningham of LaGrange, Georgia, explained that it was *"an ever-contracting iron band* around the soul that squeezes out and kills all the charity of piety and the humanity of our nature from the heart." How then, asked Cunningham in reference to the abolitionists, could Southerners "maintain Christian fellowship with such traitors and *unnatural monsters*"?

Other Southerners, particularly the wives of planters, likened their duties to those of a Protestant missionary. Daily they attended to the needs of their slaves and instructed them in the Christian responsibilities of a civilized life. Such a role had its rewards, to be sure, in the labor and obedience of the black pupils, but it demanded an intimate contact with an inferior race that Southerners scornfully felt would have repelled Northern whites. "Think of these holy New Englanders forced to have a Negro village walk through their houses whenever they see fit, dirty, slatternly, idle, ill-smelling by nature," mused Mary Chesnut. "These women I love have less chance to live their own lives in peace than if they were African missionaries."

All the offended sensibilities of Southerners found an outlet in the Confederate cause. The press and the pulpit hammered away at the theme that truth, justice, and God were on the side of the South. First secession and then military enlistments led to a community involvement that bordered on a celebration. Volunteers rushed to war; women sewed uniforms, molded cartridges, and packed boxes of food; ministers invoked God's blessings; and entire communities turned out to send their Christian warriors to the front. "An universal spirit of rivalry pervaded the people," noted the English newspaper correspondent Samuel P. Day in the late spring of 1861. "All were anxious to do or sacrifice something for the general weal."

The brash, unrestrained ardor of the early months of the war, of course, could not be regained. However, the war spirit would be sustained as the initial enthusiasm gave way to a grim determination to accept whatever sacrifices were required for victory. "We have nothing before us," wrote the Reverend Charles C. Jones in the fall of 1861, "but self-sacrifice and devotion to a cause which exceeds in character that of our first revolution—and an unshaken trust in the righteousness and goodness of God."

As the war unfolded, the original image of the Yankee as a ruthless enemy intent on the destruction of slavery was constantly reinforced. The North had to be the invader. The very presence of Yankee soldiers on Southern soil confirmed expectations that Lincoln would unleash un-Christian hordes intent on destroying property, burning homes, and inciting slaves to revolt.

Beginning early in the war, a public message of Jefferson Davis was not complete without a long list of uncivilized abuses charged to the Union armies. "Rapine and wanton destruction of private property, war upon noncombatants, murder of captives, bloody threats to avenge the death of an invading soldiery by the slaughter of unarmed civilians" were, according to Davis in August, 1862, "some of the means used by our ruthless invaders to enforce the submission of a free people to foreign sway." Davis explained such violation of civilized rules of warfare in terms of Northern "perfidy," "madness," and "the malignity engendered by defeat."

While Davis was rallying war sentiment by depicting the Yankee as an implacable enemy with whom compromise was impossible, Confederate generals were also preaching total commitment. In a typical exhortation from the military, General Albert Sidney Johnston assured his troops before the battle of Shiloh that they were fighting "for all worth living or dying for," and he urged them to "march to a decisive victory over the agrarian mercenaries sent to subjugate and despoil you of your liberties, property, and honor." It is doubtful if the troops needed such prodding. They intuitively interpreted the war as a struggle over slavery in which the enemy was quite literally an abolitionist who would plunge the South into racial and economic chaos. A Union major, John A. Connolly of Illinois, was surprised to learn in March, 1862, that captured Confederates whom he interviewed believed that the Northern war effort was an antislavery crusade. "They thought our army was coming down there to carry off all the 'niggers'; they told me they thought none but abolitionists were in our army, and that they were surprised when they found there were more Democrats than abolitionists in it."

The war that the Confederacy assumed it was fighting all along, one over the preservation of slavery, became a reality with the Emancipation Proclamation. Southerners now rededicated themselves to the war, for they were assured that they had not misread the intentions of the Republicans. In his message to the Confederate Congress on January 12, 1863, Davis could not refrain from a note of self-congratulation: "The people of this Confederacy, then, cannot fail to receive this proclamation as the fullest vindication of their own sagacity in foreseeing the uses to which the dominant party in the United States intended from the beginning to apply their power." After noting that the Proclamation put to rest any talk of a reconstruction of the Union or even of establishing close political ties with the North, Davis concluded that the Confederacy was faced with three alternatives: Either the slaves would be exterminated if they made a foolhardy bid for freedom, whites would flee the South rather than coexist with freed blacks, or Southerners would recommit themselves to winning final and complete separation from the United States.

The passage in the Emancipation Proclamation that urged slaves "to abstain from violence unless in necessary self-defense" particularly alarmed Southerners. In a revealing commentary on the anxieties generated by living in the midst of a large slave population, Southerners interpreted the passage as a call for a slave rebellion. Davis, citing it as proof positive of the insidious, diabolical nature of the Yankee mind, branded the entire Proclamation as the "most execrable measure recorded in the history of guilty man."

Lincoln was convinced that the military and moral effect of emancipation would be negated if it resulted in a general uprising of the blacks. Anxious both to avoid a political backlash in the North and to minimize disruption in the South, he made certain that the combat use of blacks was a controlled process under the leadership of white officers. Still, although no indiscriminate slaughter of whites occurred, the arming of blacks was in itself sufficient provocation for Southerners to expect the very worst. With all the suppressed guilt and exposed fears of a master class confronted with part of its servile population armed and turned against it, Southern whites saw the war as a revolutionary struggle to the death once blacks were actually sent into combat. "The Yankees know they make it ten times worse for us by sending Negroes to commit these atrocities," wrote Kate Stone upon hearing of a raid by black troops in northeastern Louisiana. "The Paternal Government at Washington has done all in its power to incite a general insurrection throughout the South, in the hopes of thus getting rid of the women and children in one grand holocaust."

The official Confederate reaction to the Northern use of black soldiers was a harsh policy that soon became self-defeating. On April 30, 1863, the Confederate Congress authorized the execution, or other suitable punishment ordered by military tribunal, of white officers captured while commanding black troops. Black prisoners were to be turned over to state authorities to be dealt with according to state laws that stipulated the death penalty for any blacks engaged in insurrection. In response, Lincoln announced on July 30, 1863, that a Confederate prisoner would be executed for every murdered Union prisoner, white or black, and one would be sentenced to hard labor for every black prisoner returned to slavery.

To avoid retaliation upon its own soldiers, the South had to temper its policy, though it was often none too subtle. In August, 1863, the Confederate Secretary of War, James A. Seddon, told General Kirby Smith, commander of the Trans-Mississippi Department, that public execution of white officers would be unwise. Rather, he suggested, they "had better be dealt with red-handed on the field or immediately thereafter." After sanctioning murder under the guise of battlefield conditions, Seddon then revealed the typical Southerner's inability to credit the black man with having the same drive and ambition as a white. Any captured blacks should be treated, in Seddon's words, "as deluded victims of the hypocrisy and malignity of the enemy [and] received readily to mercy, and encouraged to submit and return to their masters."

In practice, Confederate policy toward black soldiers and their officers wavered between extreme brutality and a grudging acknowledgment that these troops were protected by the laws of war. White officers were treated humanely if captured, and the majority of the black prisoners were not executed or enslaved but imprisoned in war camps. However, the Confederacy could not bring itself to exchange black prisoners on an equal basis with Confederates held in the North. This entailed a recognition of equality repugnant to Southern mores. Primarily because of the black issue, the exchange cartel between the Union and Confederacy broke down in the summer of 1863. As was so often the case during the war, Northern moralism and military needs reinforced one another. The Confederacy would be hurt more by shutting off prisoner exchanges, because it had a much smaller initial manpower pool. Although it would mean untold suffering for the prisoners in both sections, there was no gainsaying Grant's argument in April, 1864, against any further exchanges: "Every man we hold, when released on parole or otherwise, becomes an active soldier against us at once[,] either directly or indirectly."

By 1863 the evolution of the war relative to emancipation and black troops had reinforced for Southerners their original motives for going to war. As a result, Northern peace overtures based on the maintenance of the Union were stillborn. Having rejected Lincoln's offer to return to the Union with slavery before January 1, 1863, Southerners saw no reason to return under Lincoln's 10 per cent plan of reconstruction that made emancipation in some form a precondition. "Mr. Lincoln's rule that the just powers of the government are derived from the consent of *one tenth* of the governed is as much a perversion of the principles of the Declaration of Independence," noted Governor Joseph Brown of Georgia, "as his abolition proclamation is a violation of the Constitution."

Moreover, Southern leaders immediately saw that presidential reconstruction was an attempt to divide and conquer the Confederacy. "Our newspapers treat it with derision," reported Robert

Kean, the Head of the Confederate Bureau of War. Still, Kean respected the cleverness of Lincoln's approach. As he read the 10 per cent plan, it was intended to set off the masses and the rank and file of Confederate officers from those in a position of power. The first two groups would be granted the amnesty denied to the third and would be used to consolidate the Union conquest of overrun states.

The fusion of the slavery issue with the war effort also debilitated any peace movement within the Confederacy. The one sizable block of Confederates most disposed to reaching an agreement with the North was the Whig Unionists who had reluctantly followed along in the wake of secession. Headed by Vice-President Alexander Stephens and supported by some urban merchants, planters in the older, more established plantation regions, and the yeomanry in the mountainous interior, these Whigs always had a more qualified commitment to independence than the Democratic secessionists. But their opposition, undisciplined by any institutionally sanctioned two-party system in the Confederacy, most often took the form of carping, petty criticism directed at President Davis. They could not structure a peace program capable of serving as a bridge back into the Union, because, for all their disdain of Davis and the rabid Southern nationalists, they agreed with the Davis administration and the Democrats that military victory would have to be the precondition for any peace negotiations.

Most Whig leaders never wavered in their conviction that victory meant a guarantee of the preservation of slavery. Alexander Stephens concurred completely with the dogmatic assertion of Benjamin H. Hill of Georgia, a states'-rights Whig and Davis supporter in the Confederate Senate, that "none of the states of the late U. States can ever have peace or good government until the whole idea, spirit, policy and body of abolitionism is crushed out and destroyed." However, far from being weakened by the war, abolitionism was on the verge of its greatest triumph. As the impact of the war made it clear that a reconstructed Union would by definition exclude slavery, the Whig Unionists were denied any potential peace plan acceptable to both the Union and the Confederacy.

Another crippling problem for Southern Unionism was the

conflict of emotions intrinsic to any civil war. As he passed through the quasi-reconstructed regions of Tennessee in late 1862, Edward Dicey noted that the continuance of the war was precluding any expression of unqualified Unionism. "Men may grow convinced of the folly of Secession, may even wish for the triumph of the Union; but their hearts must be, after all, with the side for which their kinsmen and friends are fighting." Torn between irreconcilable commitments and unable to give complete allegiance to either side, Southern Unionists were captives of a war they could neither control nor terminate.

Although an increasing number of Southerners would question whether independence was worth the price of the war, most remained loyal to the Confederacy until the end. Exhorted by their ministers to endure the war's burdens as a providential purging of the spirit, many Southerners accepted their hardships as a penance for sins. "We needed as individuals and as a nation chastisement to bring us to a sense of our sins and of our many and great shortcomings," wrote Lieutenant Charles C. Jones of Georgia to his minister father. Jones was confident that Southerners, after being "purified by fire," would be rewarded by God with victory. For others, the sheer number of Southern dead was a sacrifice that could be redeemed only by victory. Anything less would besmirch those who had fallen.

The Richmond government embodied and directed the Confederate war spirit. It was so committed to victory that it failed to make any provisions for defeat. In attempting to arrange a *de facto* armistice in the first week of April, 1865, John A. Campbell, the assistant secretary of war for the Confederacy, explained to Union authorities that no Confederate officer had legal authority to negotiate. These officials, he pointed out, "don't understand how [they] can negotiate for the subversion or overthrow of their [government]."

Only President Davis was empowered to enter into peace talks, and his initial impulse, once Lee's lines had been broken, was to flee with his cabinet and continue the war from interior bases. At a war council in Abbeville, South Carolina, in late April, 1865, Davis insisted that the cause was not yet lost. "Even if the troops now with me be all that I can for the present rely on, three thousand brave men are enough for a nucleus around which the whole people will rally when the panic which now afflicts them has passed away." The generals in this refugee entourage brought Davis back to reality. As related by General Basil W. Duke, they reminded their president that "the people were not panic-stricken, but broken down and worn out. . . . all means of supporting warfare were gone. . . . We would be compelled to live on a country already impoverished, and would invite its further devastation."

Bowing to the inevitable, Davis relented. His last concession to the Confederate cause and to his own pride was to permit himself the questionable dignity of being captured, rather than surrendering.

Nationalism and Mobilization

However much the Confederacy was dedicated to the proposition that it was better to be destroyed than to submit to Yankee rule, any commitment to victory had to be sustained by a mobilization effort that would compensate for the material advantages enjoyed by the Union. The Confederacy would have to mobilize its resources earlier and more completely than the North if it were to have any chance for victory.

In rejecting the alternatives of waging a guerrilla resistance or retreating into the interior and conserving manpower in the fashion of George Washington during the Revolution, the Confederacy implicitly accepted warfare on the North's own terms of a massive, total effort supported by the economic and technological resources of the civilian population. At first glance, this decision by the Confederacy appears suicidal.

In accessible white manpower of military age, the Union had an advantage of three and a half to one. In industrial production, the Confederacy entered the war with no more than 15 per cent of the national output. To cite just a few industries indispensable to the war effort, a single county in Connecticut manufactured firearms whose value in 1860 was more than ten times that produced in the states of the Confederacy. The nation's forges and rolling mills were concentrated in Pennsylvania and New York. With the exception of the Tredegar Iron Works in Richmond, the Confederacy initially did not even have a cannon foundry or a heavy-ordnance center. The economic superiority of the Union also covered logistical support. The North had two-thirds of the nation's railroads and nearly twice as many of the horses and mules needed to transport troops and supplies. As it was, more than a third of the draft livestock in the South was in Kentucky, Tennessee, and Texas, states beyond the effective reach of the Confederacy for most of the war.

Despite its seemingly overwhelming inferiority, the Confederacy sustained a mobilization effort that ultimately succumbed only to the North's practice of total war. The military manpower disadvantage was redressed in part by the demands placed on the Union forces. The attacker needed odds of three to one to wage a successful offensive war, and at no time during the war was the North able to field much more than twice as many troops as the Confederacy. But, even when allowance is made for the garrison duties of Union soldiers, it is apparent that the Confederacy deserves much of the credit for reducing the odds against itself.

In order to field armies even half the size of the Union's, the Confederacy had to mobilize virtually all of its available white manpower. Out of the approximately 1.25 million Southern whites between the ages of seventeen and fifty who were subject to military service, the Confederacy mobilized from 750,000 to 1 million. Once deductions are made for the attrition resulting from the natural death rate, exemptions for physical disabilities or work in war-related industrial and agricultural production, and the loss of recruiting areas such as eastern Tennessee, the totality of the Confederate effort is even more evident. In contrast, only about half of the available Northern manpower went into the Union armies.

The South put its population to military use earlier, as well as more completely, than the North. In April, 1862, the Confederacy passed the first comprehensive conscription act in American history. Intended to stimulate volunteering and to prevent the original twelve-month enlistees from going home, the act placed in the direct service of the Confederacy all white males between the ages of eighteen and thirty-five, except those with special exemptions.

Having created a national army through an unprecedented use of centralized power, the Confederate Congress then tightened the conscript system during the rest of the war by closing loopholes and by extending the draft to include whites between the ages of seventeen and fifty. In December, 1863, conscripts were prohibited from sending substitutes, and in February, 1864, all previous grants of exemptions were canceled and a new list was drawn up that halved the original number of exemptions. For the last year of the war, exemptions were limited to the physically unfit, government officials, mail carriers, various professional groups such as physicians and editors, overseers in charge of at least fifteen slaves, hospital and railroad workers, and those industrial laborers detailed to military assignments under presidential authorization.

Although debates over the constitutionality of conscription were rampant, the Confederate draft was rigorously enforced. The generals demanded that every fit man be sent to the front. Lee's correspondence with Davis was insistent on this. In January, 1864, Lee emphasized that unless every present soldier was retained in the army and "all fit for effective service be sent to it promptly . . . , we must rely for deliverance from our enemies upon other means than our arms."

Responding to this pressure, Richmond strictly administered the draft through a Bureau of Conscription that employed 2,800 officers by early 1864. Exemptions were kept to a minimum. They totaled 87,863 in the states east of the Mississippi as of February, 1865, and this sum comprised mostly Confederate bureaucrats and essential industrial workers. The thoroughness of the conscription agents can be gauged from a report issued by the Bureau of Conscription in January, 1864. "The results indicate . . . that fresh material for the armies can no longer be estimated as an element of future calculation for their increase." Indeed, as early as the summer of 1863, Robert Kean of the War Department had noted that, relative to draftable manpower, "we are *almost exhausted*."

The draft legislation was the first major indication that Confederate leaders would not be bound by the dogmas of states' rights. Confederate armies were not an amalgam of state militia units under the control of their respective governors but a national force under the centralized direction of the Richmond government. The *Charleston Mercury* of Robert Barnwell Rhett spoke for all alarmed Southern localists when it pointed out that the Confederate government through its conscription acts "claimed omnipotence over the States and its citizens, including the officers of the States in its military resources."

This Confederate violation of states' rights is all the more remarkable when set against the Northern legislation on conscription. Lincoln did not feel confident enough to push for a Union draft until the spring of 1863, a full year after the Confederacy had acted. Even then, Lincoln had to face an explosion of resentment in the New York City draft riots of July, 1863, an act of organized resistance without parallel in the Confederacy. Moreover, the Northern draft was more limited in scope. It was restricted to men between the ages of twenty and forty-five and was applied only in areas that had not fulfilled their assigned troop quotas. No Northerner was placed in the federal service until selected by the draft. In contrast, eligible Southerners were technically part of the army once the draft legislation had passed Congress; the task of the military authorities was simply to sweep into the army all draft-age residents of the Confederacy who had previously escaped military service. Measured by its direct effectiveness, the Southern draft was far more thorough. The 177,000 Confederate conscripts constituted about 18 per cent of the troops, whereas the 162,000 Union conscripts accounted for but 6 per cent of the federal armies.

The speed with which the Confederacy nationalized its manpower was related not only to the overriding factor of military necessity but also to the leadership qualities and innovativeness of the elite who controlled the Confederate government. Nearly all of the 267 members of the three separate Confederate congresses were slaveowners, with 40 per cent in the planter status of owning twenty or more slaves. These congressmen represented a socio-economic elite, as is shown by the fact that a little more than half reported estates whose value was at least 600 per cent of the average in their home congressional districts. The military leadership also reflected the South's hierarchic class structure. The roster of generals and other top-ranking commanders was dominated by the very best of Southern families. The Confederacy, thus, had a prior existing group of trained leaders to whom it naturally turned.

In legislating and directing a war effort, these men had the advantage of the habit of command. As members of a master class, expecting deference from blacks and poorer whites, they assumed that their orders would be obeyed. These Confederates knew what they were fighting for, a way of life grounded in slavery and their idealization of that social order. Having too much at stake to be hamstrung by the shibboleths of states' rights, they demanded that other Southerners sacrifice for the war, and they ultimately compelled them to do so.

This elite, under no illusions that all Southerners shared its intense commitment to independence, was brutally frank in assessing the need for conscription. Lieutenant Charles C. Jones was intensely proud of his volunteer company, the Chatham Artillery. The company was an exclusive one that initially admitted new men only if their "character, blood, and social position" were approved by a four-fifths vote of its members. On special duty in the summer of 1862 to obtain conscripts for his company, Jones was contemptuous of the draftees. His aristocratic sensibilities had first been affronted by the location of the state conscript camp in Calhoun, Georgia. "Like all the little towns in Upper Georgia," Jones wrote his father, "it is not remarkable either for the cleanliness of its inhabitants or for anything else of an attractive character except the clear, cold water." Convinced that the draftees were shiftless, unpatriotic skulkers, Jones nonetheless conceded that the Conscription Act was accomplishing its purpose of "filling up our decimated ranks." Although he did not feel that brave soldiers were being added to the army, he concluded that "they will answer as food for powder and understand how to use the spade."

Once having fielded a national army, the Confederacy had to feed it. Despite the fact that the South was an overwhelmingly agrarian society with more livestock and corn per capita than the North in 1860, the production, acquisition, and distribution of foodstuffs to the military were major problems that were never adequately solved. The *Augusta* (Georgia) *Southern Cultivator*, a leading agricultural newspaper, summarized the dilemma in the spring of 1861 by arguing that "we labor under a greater deficiency than the want of arms. IT IS THE WANT OF BREAD." After citing the extensive drought that had cut food production in 1860, the paper added that the fundamental difficulty was the unwillingness of planters to forgo the profits from raising cotton for a more balanced agriculture. It was for this reason that in 1859 over $5 million of Western foodstuffs had been shipped to Atlanta from Chattanooga on the Western and Atlantic Railroad.

In one respect the pessimism of the *Southern Cultivator* was misplaced. Southern agriculture did shift to food provisions during the war. Cotton production steadily declined from 4.5 million bales in 1861 to fewer than 300,000 in 1864. Planters had no incentive to raise a crop they could not market because of the Union blockade, and they voluntarily responded to the public demand for putting acreage into food crops in order to meet the needs of the army and civilians. When the voluntary controls started to break down as some planters eyed the immense profits to be gained from an illegal trade with the advancing Yankees, the states intervened. The legislatures of Alabama, Arkansas, Georgia, and South Carolina set limits on cotton production or acreage that were enforced by fines, imprisonment, and prohibitive taxes.

The combined effect of voluntarism and state coercion between 1860 and 1863 was to double the acreage in the Confederacy devoted to corn, wheat, and potatoes. However, food production did not keep pace, because yields per acre dropped throughout the war. For example, corn output in South Carolina declined from 15 bushels an acre in 1861 to 9 by 1863 and to 6 by 1865. Confederate agriculture lacked the manpower, tools, and livestock necessary to maintain the prewar level of farm efficiency.

Virtually all the able-bodied white males were in the army. As early as September, 1861, Lieutenant Jones noted of the village of Bath, Georgia, "This little retreat is deserted of its male inhabitants. Most of them are in Virginia." By the summer of 1864 the comments of a resident of Egypt, Mississippi, were echoed throughout the Confederacy. "There are not men enough left to bury the dead. The people are subsisting on the un-

gathered crops, and nine families out of ten are without meat."
The women, old men, boys, and invalid soldiers left to manage
the typical farm had to rely on a dwindling supply of agricultural implements that could be neither repaired nor replaced. The antebellum South had imported most of its farm
machinery from the North, and now the local shops capable
of producing even items as basic as a plow were engaged in
purely military work. Both the quality and the number of livestock deteriorated markedly. Military demand was a constant
drain on draft animals, and the few that remained on the farms
suffered from being overworked and underfed. Further hamper-
ing meat production were the ravages of hog cholera and a
severe shortage of the salt needed to preserve pork and beef.

Hit hardest by the dislocation of Confederate agriculture were
the families of the yeomanry, those without slaves who had to
depend on their own manual labor. The yeomanry had no protection from the draft, because rural exemptions were geared to
the largest producers. One man was exempted for every 20
(lowered in 1864 to 15) slaves on a plantation, and 1 man for
every 500 cattle or sheep or 250 horses or mules. These exemptions were intended to ensure protection for women and children in black-belt regions and to maximize the output of
plantations. Every exempted planter or overseer had to post a
bond guaranteeing that his supervised slave labor would produce 100 pounds of meat per slave to be sold, along with other
agricultural surpluses, to the Confederacy at government-fixed
prices. Nevertheless, these exemptions were attacked as class
legislation favoring the rich. The yeomanry were further embittered by the realization that they lacked the capital, credit, and
political connections that the planters fell back on to partially
cushion the war's impact.

About the only recourse open to the yeomanry was holding
out for the highest prices for its farm produce. Faced with spiral-
ing costs for the goods and supplies it needed, the yeomanry
was reluctant to sell provisions to the army when currency
depreciation was raising prices daily and speculators were out-
bidding the military. The result was a major crisis for the military by the autumn of 1862. Frank C. Ruffin of the Confederate
Bureau of Subsistence wrote in October, "With the whole Con-

federacy completely exhausted of supplies, we have only meat rations for 300,000 men for twenty-five days." A month later the Secretary of War, James A. Seddon, was alarmed by "an almost universal repugnance on the part of producers and holders to sell at any price, except under compulsion."

Legal compulsion was insituted in March, 1863, with the passage by Congress of "An Act to Regulate Impressments." The Confederate government met the problem of transferring farm goods from private hands to the public service by direct intervention in the economy. The former haphazard army practice of seizing provisions was regulated under a government bureaucracy that combined impressment with price controls. The act stipulated that, whenever the impressment agent and the producer could not agree on prices, local arbiters were to determine them, with an appeal by the Confederate officer to a state board. A further effort to hasten the procurement of agricultural supplies and to hold down prices was incorporated into the tax legislation of April, 1863. A direct tax of 10 per cent on farm produce, to be paid in kind, was extracted from the countryside after a reserve allowance was made for home consumption.

These acts, which overlapped similar legislation passed by the states, met the immediate need of supplying the armies, but they generated such intense opposition that civilian morale was sapped. Government impressment prices were well below what the open market would bring, averaging about one-third in the last months of the war. Many farmers persisted in hoarding their goods or selling them to speculators. Civilian resistance was partially overcome by ruthless enforcement procedures, which in turn intensified the popular dissatisfaction. A farmer in Calhoun County, Florida, asked his governor "if it is the law for these 'pressmen' to take the cows from the soldiers' families and leave them to starve." The farmers who rode into Athens, Georgia, in October, 1863, to vote on election day were infuriated when impressment agents surrounded the town and seized all of the horses fit for use by army officers.

The agricultural tithe was both cumbersome to administer and unevenly enforced. Moreover, the distribution of goods placed a tremendous strain on the transportation system of the Confederacy. Tons of supplies spoiled at depots while awaiting transshipment to the front. Out of $150 million of provisions collected under the tithe, over two-thirds never reached the armies.

Still, more than any other single factor, it was the inability of the Confederacy to defend its territory that handicapped its agricultural efforts. Even before the 1863 legislation was passed, the Confederacy had lost most of the prime grain and livestock areas of Kentucky, Tennessee, and Missouri. By the end of 1863 the lower Mississippi Valley and the trans-Mississippi region were in Union hands or otherwise inaccessible to the Confederate bureaucracy. The agricultural burden was thrown back on an ever contracting heartland that was subject to devastation. In June, 1863, the quartermaster general's office reported that it was possible to collect the tithe tax in all the counties of just two states, Georgia and South Carolina. At the same time, the shortage of manpower resulted in a constant shrinkage of the land under cultivation, and Union raiders destroyed much of what was cultivated.

Although a better transportation system would have distributed the available foodstuffs more quickly and uniformly, there simply was not enough food for both the civilians and the military. As Lucius B. Northrop, the harassed head of the Commissary Department put it in December, 1864, "The idea that there is *plenty for all* in the country is asburd. The efforts of the enemy have been too successful." As early as the winter of 1861–62, the legislatures of the Deep South passed relief acts and voted subsidies for the families of volunteer soldiers. Cries of imminent starvation, especially from town-dwellers on fixed salaries and the yeomanry in the upland regions, produced additional relief programs in the latter half of the war. Military rations were steadily reduced until the common soldier learned to live on the verge of starvation. For many hunger became the main enemy. "There was . . . no fear in the Confederate ranks of any thing that General Grant might do," recalled George Cary Eggleston in looking back on the Wilderness campaign in 1864, "but there was an appalling and well-founded fear of starvation, which indeed some of us were already suffering."

In the industrial sphere, the agrarian Confederacy was surprisingly far more successful in its economic mobilization.

Starting from scratch, the Confederacy organized an industrial program that supplied its armies with the materials of war. Despite the facts that most of the manpower was in the military, that transportation was slow and hazardous, that the currency was continually depreciated, and that a blockade worsened pre-existing shortages, the industrial war economy was steadily strengthened until it was smashed by the Union army. Josiah Gorgas, the head of the Confederate Ordnance Department, could well boast after the war was over of what the Confederacy had accomplished:

> We began in April, 1861, without an arsenal, laboratory or powder mill of any capacity, and with no foundry or rolling mill, except at Richmond, and before the close of 1863, in little over two years, we had built up . . . foundries and rolling mills, smelting works, chemical works, a powder mill far superior to any in the United States . . . , and a chain of arsenals, armories and laboratories equal in their capacity and their improved appointments to the best of those in the United States.

This successful industrial effort resulted from government controls that verged on state socialism and from an ability to develop techniques of self-sufficiency that rivaled the Yankee North in ingenuity. Through direct ownership, subsidies, and various regulatory devices, the Confederate government tightly controlled the economy. Wherever possible, substitutes were developed when shortages became severe, and a recycling process permitted a maximum use of resources.

Where industrial production was most critical to the war effort, as with munitions, ordnance, and gunpowder, the government often set up its own factories. Within three years a string of government arsenals and foundries was established in the interior along a wide arc between San Antonio, Texas, and Richmond, Virginia. This decentralization, which forced Union armies to attack along a broad front, was a concession to a transportation system incapable of delivering huge amounts of supplies to a few areas. It also enabled the Confederacy to take advantage of local markets for labor and raw materials.

However, a concentrated munitions complex was taking shape at the war's end. A Confederate powder factory in Augusta,

Georgia, containing storerooms, a refinery, and mills, was the largest on the continent. Beginning production in the spring of 1862, the factory was the government's major supplier and eventually manufactured more gunpower than was imported through the blockade. To the west were located the marine-machinery equipment of the Confederate Naval Ironworks in Columbus, Georgia, and the arsenal, powder factory, and ironworks that constituted the heavy-ordnance center of Selma, Alabama. The capstone of these government-owned industries would have been a central chemical laboratory at Macon, Georgia. Intended to ensure uniformity in the quality and dimensions of ammunition, the laboratory-factory was not quite completed by the spring of 1865.

The Confederacy also intervened directly in the procurement of essential raw materials. The Nitre and Mining Bureau, organized in April, 1862, was responsible for the production of nitre, iron, lead, copper, and other minerals, as well as industrial chemicals. No work performed by the Bureau was more crucial than its development of supplies of nitre, an essential component in the manufacture of gunpowder. The entire nitre-bearing region of the Confederacy was divided into districts under the supervision of officers from the Bureau. Caves were mined, and nitre beds, pits two feet deep filled with decomposing organic matter later strained with water to yield nitrogenous materials, were established in countless backyards. By converting the carcasses of dogs, human wastes, and animal manure into nitre, the Confederacy had a major source of saltpeter. Eventually, it relied on blockade runners for only half of its nitre supply.

Under the Bureau, the output of iron, copper, and lead greatly expanded. Mine owners were offered the same choice as other Confederate businessmen: Either operate at full production or surrender their property to the Confederate authorities. In return for cooperating with the Confederacy, the businessmen received subsidies through government loans and advances, access to transportation, and assurances of an unlimited government market and an adequate labor supply. These government services were part of the quasi-nationalization of the private sector of the economy. Prices were fixed at first at a 75 per cent, and later a 33⅓ per cent, profit over costs of production for all firms that employed draft-exempted labor. To guarantee an ample flow of nonordnance goods to the government, businesses were required to sell two-thirds of their production to the Confederacy. These regulations could be enforced because the Confederate government controlled the labor supply and the transportation facilities. By refusing to exempt workers from the draft or denying use of the railroads, the Richmond authorities could force any business to conform.

During most of the war Southern businessmen responded enthusiastically to forced industrialization under national controls. War profits were high, outstripping increases in the costs of labor and raw materials. The expansion of the Tredegar Iron Works illustrates the advantages of a close partnership with the Confederate government. Located just outside of Richmond, Tredegar was the South's only source of heavy industry in 1860. Indeed, it was one of the main factors in the removal of the Confederate capital from Montgomery, Alabama, to Richmond. During the war Tredegar was both the chief supplier of military ordnance and the seedbed for industrialization throughout the Confederacy. In addition to manufacturing torpedoes, a primitive submarine, plating for ironclads, and 1,100 cannons, Tredegar was the source of much of the machinery and skills needed for the newly created foundries.

By the middle of the war Joseph R. Anderson, the president of Tredegar, had fashioned an industrial empire that approached self-sufficiency. A Confederate loan of $500,000 had enabled him to acquire the blast furnaces and coal mines that ensured a supply of pig iron. To feed his labor force, which had tripled to 2,500, Anderson sent purchasing agents as far south as Alabama to buy foodstuffs; to clothe his workers he built a tannery and shoe factory and then bought a blockade runner to take cotton to Bermuda and return with cloth. Thomas C. DeLeon, a Confederate author and soldier, accurately noted of Tredegar that "it thrived so well on government patronage—[in] spite of sundry boards to consider if army and navy work was not paid for at ruinously low rates—that it greatly increased in size . . . , and, at the close of the struggle, was in better condition than at the commencement."

The government-directed war economy was more successful in

arming the military than in providing it with clothing and shoes. The much maligned Quartermaster Department had the lowest priority of the Confederate bureaus. As Jefferson Davis remarked, "For the infantry, men must first be fed, next armed, and even clothing must follow these; for if they are fed and have arms and ammunition they can fight."

The manufacture and allocation of cloth and leather were closely regulated, and both the Confederate and the state governments underwrote the expansion of clothing factories and tanneries. Convict labor was pressed into service with the result that, in the Trans-Mississippi Department, the main suppliers of textile goods were the state penitentiaries at Little Rock, Arkansas, and Huntsville, Texas. Problems in the Quartermaster Department arose not so much with production as with distribution. Because troops, munitions, and foodstuffs had first claim on the railroads, the shipment of shoes and textiles was delayed, and these goods rarely reached the army on schedule.

Foreign trade, as well as the domestic economy, was centralized under the Confederacy. Desirous of the profits previously garnered by the private blockade runners, and alarmed over the drain of specie and cotton used to purchase the predominantly nonmilitary supplies brought in through the blockade, the Confederate Congress virtually nationalized the export trade in February, 1864. In order to obtain clearance papers and permission to export, private shippers had to reserve one-half of their cargo space for the Confederate government. Freight rates were fixed by the government, with higher rates to go into effect if the Confederacy were granted two-thirds of the space on vessels. At the same time, the importation of all items except essential war goods and medical supplies was prohibited, and special presidential licenses were required for exporting most agricultural staples.

Although by 1864 the success rate in running the blockade was down to 60 per cent from the 1861 figure of 90 per cent, the Confederate government was still able to bring in huge amounts of supplies. In the last two months of 1864, an estimated 8.5 million pounds of meat and 3.5 million pounds of lead and saltpeter, in addition to hundreds of thousands of blankets and pairs of shoes, were imported through Charleston and Wilmington on the Carolina coast. These imports were financed by the

Confederacy's only negotiable asset, cotton. During the war the Confederate government acquired at least 500,000 bales. This cotton had been pledged in return for bonds under the various produce loan acts of 1861, 1862, and 1863, collected under the direct tax of 1863, or impressed by local army officers.

Often criticized for not exporting more cotton in the early years of the war, by 1864 the Confederacy nonetheless made effective use of its cotton by converting it into gold and military supplies. Cotton was the basis of a flourishing trade across both Union lines and the Atlantic. By monopolizing cotton exports for the government, the legislation of 1864 enabled the Confederacy to take maximum advantage of the war-inflated prices when the market value of cotton increased roughly tenfold in Union greenbacks.

At late as 1864, the Confederacy was able to export through the blockade nine-tenths of the cotton consigned to foreign purchasers. But the chief market for cotton was in the Union. New England textile manufacturers, faced with a 75 per cent drop in production by the summer of 1862, pressured Lincoln to bring out cotton. Lincoln obliged by issuing executive permits for private individuals of reputedly solid Unionist credentials to trade in cotton behind Union lines. By an executive order in September, 1864, he even allowed cotton sellers to import back through Confederate lines noncontraband merchandise equal in value to one-third the sale price of the cotton.

Despite a host of federal regulations and legal restraints, the cotton trade became a speculative bonanza that demoralized Union soldiers and contributed significantly to the Confederate war effort. Grant felt that cotton speculators robbed his army of one-third of its effectiveness, and another Union general, Edward Canby, estimated the military advantage of the cotton trade to the Confederacy as equivalent to an additional fifty thousand troops along both sides of the Mississippi. In a report sent to Lincoln in May, 1864, General Daniel Sickles stated that $500,000 worth of goods was being sent weekly through Memphis into Confederate territory.

> Boats loaded with supplies have had almost unrestricted opportunities for trade on the Mississippi, and some of its navigable tributaries, stopping anywhere along the river and dealing with

anybody. It is estimated that Memphis has heretofore been so reliable and constant a source of rebel supplies . . . as to secure for it a comparative exemption from attack by the enemy.

As Sickles noted, the lower Mississippi Valley was the center of the cotton trade. By the summer of 1864 this trade had earned the Trans-Mississippi Department of the Confederacy goods and credits worth $30 million in specie. The flow of cotton out of the region for Union or foreign supplies was regulated by a government Cotton Bureau, set up in August, 1863, by Kirby Smith, the military commander of the Department. Smith was later to boast, "I bought cotton through my Cotton Bureau at three and four cents a pound, and sold it at fifty cents a pound in gold. It passed in constant streams by several crossings of the Rio Grande, as well as through Galveston, to the agents abroad." In approving a cotton deal with a speculator with high connections in the U.S. Treasury Department, Smith said simply, "He represents a million of capital and brings the authority of the President and Secty. of Treasury of the United States for the transaction."

When the Confederacy could not monopolize the cotton trade directly, authorities tended to ignore, if not actually encourage, illicit trading with the enemy. In the last months of the war, a major source of supplies for Lee's army came from Union-licensed stores along the Virginia–North Carolina border. Local farmers bought cotton from Confederate officials, sold it at the Union stores for salt, foodstuffs, and greenbacks, and exchanged the surplus for more cotton. When complaints reached the Commissary General Lucius B. Northrop that the "unpatriotic" behavior of the farmers was demoralizing the Confederate populace, Northrop replied that the trade must be continued because of the "results in subsistence gotten for the army."

The Confederacy supplied itself from the Yankee soldier as well as the Northern speculator. "It is no exaggeration to say that a great part of the Confederate army has been equipped at the expense of the United States," remarked an anonymous English visitor in 1862. "From the blanket [the Southern soldier] sleeps on to the cartridge he shoots with, almost everything has been appropriated from the enemy at one time or another."

Stripping battlefields and Union soldiers of usable military material quickly became an organized part of the Confederate supply system. Field ordnance officers impressed labor to gather up military debris for eventual sorting and reprocessing. In this manner, the Confederacy acquired tons of lead, copper, clothing, and guns. In the first two years of the war 40 per cent of rebel firearms were of Union manufacture and had been taken from battlefields.

While availing itself of the largess of the well-stocked federal armies, the Confederacy continued to exploit all internal resources. The goal of self-sufficiency was never attained, but by developing substitutes for scarce items, reconverting consumer goods for military use, and forcing every unit of production to approach autarky, the Confederacy compensated for many of its economic weaknesses.

Ersatz products were important in the factory and on the farm. When petroleum lubricants and rubber for machine belts became unavailable, they were replaced in industry by lard and by cotton cloth soaked in linseed oil, respectively. A government fishery off the Cape Fear region of North Carolina served the double purpose of securing oil for machinery and food for the industrial work force. The women who worked the plantations rigorously economized and devised ingenious substitutes for the domestic necessities that were cut off by the blockade. Much of the salt used to preserve pork was later saved by boiling the residue of brine left in the curing barrels. Starch was made from the bran of wheat flour and a makeshift putty from a heated mixture of potatoes and flour. Roasted okra seeds served for coffee, and dyes were extracted from roots and barks.

Consumer products, especially those containing metal, were recycled for the war effort. According to Gorgas, one-third of the lead supply came from window weights and water mains. Bird-shot lead, manufactured under government contracts, was exchanged for scrap iron, which was melted down for bullets. The Confederate Iron Commission established in January, 1863, was empowered to purchase or impress track iron from secondary railroads for the construction of ironclad ships or redeployment on main military lines. The Commission was soon also impressing locomotives. When a Union raid in late 1863 closed the Duck-town copper mines in southeastern Tennessee, all available scrap copper was impressed. The major untapped domestic sources of copper, which was essential in the production of percussion caps, were turpentine and apple-brandy stills scattered throughout the Carolina and Tennessee mountains. Enough copper for rerolling was obtained from these stills to maintain the production quotas of percussion caps for the last year of the war.

Military, industrial, and agricultural units increasingly had to depend on their own resources. Soldiers with a skill were detailed to repair and manufacture shoes, clothing, and metal-wares. Many were furloughed to return home and bring back the necessary implements or raw materials. "In short," recalled a Maryland soldier, "recognizing the straits that the Confederacy was now put to in the furnishing of supplies, we aimed to save and eke out issues in every possible way." Businessmen set up their own packing houses in order to acquire meat for their workers and animal lard for use as an industrial lubricant. Meanwhile, plantations were becoming miniature factories turn-ing out clothing and blankets on hand looms. Without this household industry the supplying of the army would have been an insurmountable problem.

THE LAST SACRIFICE

In late 1863 Gorgas wrote, "We are now in a condition to carry on the war for an indefinite period. . . . we have war material sufficient—men, guns, powder—the real pinch is the Treasury." Most observers have agreed that finances were the weakest link in the Confederate war program, and the incredible inflationary spiral seems to prove that the Confederate Treasury had badly mishandled the war financing. Measured by its equivalent value in gold, the Confederate paper dollar was worth only 8 cents by the summer of 1863; by March, 1865, it was worth less than 2 cents.

In what apparently was the height of economic folly, the Con-federacy had attempted to finance the war by printing redundant issues of treasury notes, or paper money, that had no backing in gold. In contrast to the North, which relied more heavily on borrowing and taxation, consequently holding down the issuance of fiat money to 13 per cent of its total income, the Confederacy depended on paper money for almost 60 per cent of its war income. However, the massive Confederate inflation was as unavoidable as it was predictable.

During the entire war, the Confederacy never had more than $27 million in specie, a sum totally inadequate to pay for a war that cost, in equivalent gold value, $572 million by October, 1864. The inevitable inflation was certainly fueled by paper money issued by states, municipalities, and private businesses as well as the Confederate government, but soaring prices were caused by more than the increased stock of money. In the first three years of the war the money supply increased elevenfold, while prices shot up twenty-eightfold. What exacerbated inflation were the combined effects of the federal blockade and the structural weaknesses within the Confederate economy.

The blockade created severe shortages of those consumer goods such as coffee, salt, and leather that previously had been imported, thereby driving their prices still higher. At the same time, real output was declining and consumers were spending their money even faster in an effort to minimize the impact of inflation. Physical productivity dropped as slaves, women, children, old men, and wounded veterans supplanted the white manpower called off to the army. Labor inefficiency was worsened by the difficulties of repairing and replacing worn-out or defective machinery. Prices rose as Southerners competed for the fewer available goods and tried to get rid of their money before its value fell even further.

In attempting to combat inflation, the Confederate government was ruthless in claiming what specie was available. Nearly half of its gold and silver supply, $11.7 million, was expropriated under a sequestration act that legalized the government seizure of the funds and property of alien enemies. When the banks of New Orleans, which held the largest specie reserves in the South, transferred behind Confederate lines over $4 million in bullion before the city fell to federal forces, the Richmond government seized the specie and replaced it with treasury notes.

The government also turned, though belatedly, to a stringent program of taxation. In April, 1863, a comprehensive revenue act levied an 8 per cent tax on a variety of products, an income tax, and various licensing and sales taxes. Still, although a 5 per cent direct land tax was later enacted (with rebates), probably no more than 1 per cent of all Confederate income was derived from the cash payment of taxes. Very little specie was in private hands. Much more effective in financing the war were the direct taxes in kind and the impressment policy that legalized the seizure of foodstuffs at below their market value.

In a major effort to reduce the currency and raise its value, the Confederate Congress passed a Refunding Act in early 1864. The holders of treasury notes were obligated to exchange them for either 4 per cent bonds or new treasury notes at the rate of $3 in old money for $2 in new money. The penalty for failing to refund the old currency was an automatic monthly reduction of 10 per cent in its value until January 1, 1865, at which point it would be legally worthless. Although briefly effective, the Refunding Act ultimately compounded the currency crisis. The threatened repudiation of the old notes hastened their depreciation, and what little confidence remained in Confederate money was destroyed by the government's admission of bankruptcy implicit in its decision to erase one-third of the currency.

The failure of Confederate financing is often linked with the King Cotton theory—the widespread, but fallacious, assumption of Southerners that the withholding of cotton from England and France would produce an economic crisis in these nations that would result in their recognition of Confederate independence. The critics of the Davis administration have argued that the Confederate government, rather than denying cotton to England and France, should have purchased huge amounts of cotton in 1861 and 1862 and shipped it to Europe as future collateral. By drawing upon the cotton as needed, the Confederacy allegedly would have had a sound basis for its currency.

In all likelihood, this projected use of cotton would have been as unworkable as was the notion that England and France could be coerced into granting recognition by having their cotton supply cut off by the South. By the time the Confederate government was organized in February, 1861, most of the 1860 crop had already been sold. Public opinion, not the Richmond government, demanded that the remaining crop and that of 1861 be embargoed. Moreover, there were few ships available to carry abroad large amounts of cotton, and no foreign nation would risk war with the Union by sending over its own fleet.

However, even if cotton could have been stockpiled abroad in 1861 or 1862, it is doubtful that such a policy would have yielded the Confederacy more supplies and specie than did its subsequent actions. By 1864 the scarcity of cotton had greatly increased its price. Its export out of the Confederacy was now a government monopoly that netted the South far more for every bale than could have been obtained earlier in the war. In December, 1864, Lincoln explained what had occured:

> By the external blockade, the price of [of cotton] is made certainly six times as great as it was. And yet the enemy gets through at least one sixth part as much in a given period, say a year, as if there were no blockade, and receives as much for it, as he would for a full crop in time of peace. . . . this keeps up his armies at home, and procures supplies from abroad.

To a large extent the Confederacy had converted its cotton into white gold, but this was small solace for the vast majority of Southerners, who felt helpless in the face of massive inflation. Confederate paper money depreciated by an average of 10 per cent a month. By continually printing money, the government was abolishing its debt and forcing its citizens to contribute to the war effort. The result was a sharp drop in living standards and a decline in real wages by at least two-thirds. In effect, the inflation had compelled Southerners to pay for the war in the most direct possible way—by taxing them at the rate of 10 per cent a month for holding on to their money.

Inflation was but the most pervasive of the sacrifices endured by Southerners. The forced enlistment of manpower and goods through conscription, impressment, and direct taxes, as well as the occasional imposition by the Confederate authorities of martial law through the suspension of the writ of habeas corpus, was also a painful reminder of the cost of the war. As the staggering military casualties continued to mount, more and more Southerners began to ask, as did Mary Chesnut, "Is anything worth it? This fearful sacrifice, this awful penalty we pay for war."

The willingness of Southerners to accept the loss of their sons and their individual liberties was a function both of their initial commitment to secession and the impact of the war on their lives and immediate society. At the start of the war most oldtime Whig planters and businessmen agreed with Jonathan Worth of North Carolina, who "regarded the dissolution of the Union as the greatest misfortune which could befall the whole nation and the whole human race." Trapped between what they saw as the follies of both sections, such Whigs ultimately sided with the Democratic secessionists as the lesser of two evils.

With potential mass support from among the upland yeomanry, who were always prone to view the war as a rich man's struggle fought by the poor, the Whiggish former Unionists made a political comeback in the mid-war state and congressional elections of 1863. Now that war weariness had set in, the Whigs increased their representation in the Confederate Congress from 35 per cent to close to half. For the first time ever, Alabama and Mississippi elected Whigs as governors. Although not necessarily a propeace or reconstructionist vote, the 1863 returns did indicate a growing disenchantment with the war and an identification with those leaders who had been most reluctant to secede in the first place.

What was particularly striking about the 1863 Whig vote was its concentration in the mountainous and piedmont regions that had not yet been overrun or occupied by federal troops. The unoccupied, or interior, regions had to bear the brunt of the war effort because they alone were within the reach of the Confederate bureaucracy. The men, supplies, and taxes demanded by the war were extracted from a diminishing base. Moreover, these districts were hit especially hard by inflation. Confederate paper money was shipped out of occupied areas, where it was worthless and replaced by Union greenbacks, to the interior regions where it still had some value. Without the political unity fostered by direct contact with the enemy, and resentful over paying what seemed to be an unfair share of the war's cost, the yeomanry in regions free from invasion expressed its dissatisfaction by turning to the Whigs.

Conversely, the Democratic and proadministration congressmen who would force yet greater sacrifices from the populace were elected in disproportionate numbers from those areas of the Confederacy occupied or directly threatened by the Union army. Because soldiers and refugees were permitted to vote, phantom political districts were created around the shrinking area actually controlled by the Confederacy. Representing at best displaced constituencies, these districts returned solid majorities for the Davis administration. The Confederate army, as did the Union troops, voted for the incumbent administration, which promised to see the war through to a successful conclusion. Just as the soldiers naturally expected complete dedication from the civilians, so also did the refugees. These were the Southerners who often willingly had fled from the Yankee invaders and surrendered much, if not all, of their property and personal belongings in the cause of independence. Having already demonstrated their loyalty by sacrificing their homes and possessions, the refugees voted for war leaders pledged to demand the same sort of commitment from other Southerners and to push for an aggressive military policy to regain the lost territory.

Although the immediate political consequence of the creation of a large displaced class was a stiffening of Southern resolve, in the long run the refugee problem weakened the Confederate war effort. Eventually some two hundred thousand refugees were crowded into the compressed Confederate hinterland. Their presence placed a crushing burden on the already overtaxed civilian sector of the economy. For this reason, Union commanders, most notably Sherman at Atlanta in 1864, forcibly evacuated civilians as a war measure. As expected, the flood of refugees intensified shortages of food and housing. Both prices and the crime rate soared as refugees gathered in Southern cities, many of which doubled in population during the war. Food riots broke out in Richmond, Atlanta, and Mobile, and in most urban centers social control was on the verge of collapse.

Hostility toward refugees was widespread and grew worse as their numbers multiplied during the last half of the war. In the absence of a Confederate relief program, poorer refugees were unwelcome because their new communities in some way would have to support them. On the other hand, the wealthier refugees were snubbed as the renegade rich who were shirking their war duty. Class friction previously had been minimized by the lack of contacts between the rich and the poor and by the recognition of the sacrifices forced on all social groups by the war. But now, when the families of planters moved in among the common folk, and especially when they brought some slaves or a few luxury items, class envy was heightened. In apologizing to Mary Chesnut for not offering her some tea, a planter's wife who was a refugee in the North Carolina upcountry explained, "If [the townspeople] saw us with tea, they would not send us bread. They will not tolerate luxuries in pauper exiles. Our men-servants sauntering around the yard with cigars in their mouths brought us near starvation."

For their well-being and the sake of appearance, the wealthy refugees tried to conceal the contempt they felt toward their hosts. But among themselves the displaced planters were often savage in their denunciations. When invited to community barbe-cues, they debated whether the food was clean enough to eat or whether they should dine with plebeians. Kate Stone's refugee family in Tyler, Texas, once put in an appearance at a local masonic celebration "to see the animals feed," as Kate's mother put it. They left early to attend a party given by a Confederate officer for the refugees in Tyler.

The antipathy and not infrequent bitterness between the refugees and the communities in which they settled reflected in a more extreme form the polarization in Confederate politics between occupied and interior districts. On a more general level, it was a symptom of the growing social disintegration in the Con-federacy. However serious was the refugee problem, Southerners could at least convince themselves that it was temporary, a crisis to be endured only as long as the war lasted. What struck most Southerners as a far graver threat to social control was the question of arming and emancipating part of their slave popula-tion. By even considering such a revolutionary means of salvaging victory, Southerners revealed the incredible extent to which mili-tary necessity had forced a reassessment of their basic values.

At the start of the war, the Confederacy proudly proclaimed that slavery would be one of its greatest strengths. "It may be safely estimated," wrote an anonymous contributor to *DeBow's Review* in 1861, "that a population of twelve million, one-third of whom are slaves, are equal in time of war to a population of twenty million without slaves." Until 1863 slavery was an asset to the Confederacy because the use of slave labor freed whites for the military. But once the North committed itself to arming and emancipating the slaves, the Confederacy was placed in the paradoxical position of supplying manpower for the Union armies. Simultaneously faced with the need to replenish the depleted ranks of their own armies, many Southerners were driven to the obvious, but nonetheless heretical, conclusion that the Confederacy must arm the slaves before the Union did. The slaves, as the *Montgomery* (Alabama) *Weekly Mail* argued in September, 1863, "must be used for or against us. There is no alternative."

The debate over arming the slaves was initiated in Alabama, Mississippi, and Louisiana. By the summer of 1863 the citizens of those states understood firsthand how the war measures of the Union had converted slavery into a frightening weakness of the Confederacy. Large chunks of territory in those states had been overrun by federal armies with the aid of slave spies, and the lower Mississippi Valley was the center of the Union recruitment drive for black troops. After noting what had occurred in Alabama and neighboring states, the *Montgomery Mail* warned that the "enemy will seize the negroes everywhere, and organize them as soldiers, to burn and desolate the country, and extirpate their masters." To avert such a catastrophe, the Alabama legislature resolved in August, 1863, that the Confederate Congress should take whatever steps were necessary to mobilize slaves more effectively for the defense effort.

A young major general from the Western armies, Patrick R. Cleburne, was the first leading Confederate to argue that these steps must include the arming of the slaves. In a document that he circulated among the officers of the Army of Tennessee in January, 1864, Cleburne presented his case.

Citing the growing exhaustion and declining morale of the troops, he predicted that Confederate defenses would collapse within a year unless slaves were recruited as soldiers. He saw no other way to balance the military manpower between the sections. In addition to providing the advantage of enlarged Southern armies capable of taking the offensive, Cleburne reasoned that his plan would unify the Confederacy by restoring the confidence of slaveholders. As matters then stood, "wherever slavery is once seriously disturbed, . . . the whites can no longer with safety to their property openly sympathize with our cause." In order to save their property, such slaveholders soon took the oath of loyalty to the Union. However, Cleburne argued that if the slaves were promised their eventual freedom, and then armed, they would become staunch allies of their owners. Slavery would again be a source of strength.

Clearly, the emancipation of all slaves who actually fought was integral to Cleburne's plan, but so also was the freeing of all slaves who remained loyal to the Confederacy. He noted that arming the slaves would be suicidal for whites unless provisions were made for emancipation. Having freed the black soldier and his family, the Confederacy then would have to eliminate slavery completely. Otherwise security would be impossible. As Cleburne stressed, "The past legislation of the South concedes that a large free middle class of negro blood, between the master and slave, must sooner or later destroy the institution." By voluntarily sacrificing slavery, the Confederacy, Cleburne insisted, would cripple the Northern war effort. Blacks presumably would be deprived of any incentive to fight against the South, the antislavery sentiment that helped so much to energize the Union cause would be rendered meaningless, and European nations might yet intervene on the side of the Confederacy when they saw that it was no longer defending slavery.

Emancipation, of course, was the direct antithesis of the perpetual black bondage that nearly all Southerners had assumed was the fundamental social pivot of the Confederacy. Cleburne's proposals appeared not merely to subvert the very values on which the Confederacy was founded but to deny them completely. Understandably, Jefferson Davis not only rejected Cleburne's plan but also attempted to suppress all debate on the subject.

However, the subject could no more be ignored than could the onslaught of Union armies. Throughout 1864 the anguish of defeat acted as a solvent on the fears of Davis and other Confederates concerning a combat role for the slaves. Such a policy, coupled with emancipation, was indeed, as an associate of Cleburne's expressed it, "revolting to Southern sentiment, Southern pride, and Southern honor," but the alternative was seemingly certain defeat.

More than three years of war, by confirming for Southerners their worst expectations of the Yankees as an inhumane and unchristian enemy, had left the Confederacy a prisoner of its own fears. The will to resist was sustained by the image of complete subjugation and humiliation that would follow in the wake of a Yankee victory. In December, 1864, the Richmond *Sentinel* insisted, "Any sacrifice of opinion, any sacrifice of property, any surrender of prejudice—if necessary to defeat our enemies—is now the watchword and reply. Subjugation is a horror that embraces all other horrors and adds enormous calamities of its own."

This frantic appeal was part of the most open debate ever held in the South on slavery. Aided immensely by the public approval of the most renowned Confederate, Robert E. Lee, those who would sacrifice slavery for independence won a partial victory in early March, 1865. The Confederate Congress authorized Davis to call on the states for up to one-fourth of their male slaves "to perform military service in whatever capacity he may desire." No slaveholder was compelled to yield his slaves, nor was emancipation of those who fought expressly provided. Nonetheless, the Confederate government, by an extension of power unimaginable in 1861, was prepared to sanction emancipation. The subsequent regulations of the War Department accepted for armed service only those slaves granted freedom by their masters.

The Confederate Congress had moved dramatically beyond its earlier program of legalizing the impressment of slaves for noncombatant duty. Of course, many whites were horrified by the irony of the Confederacy offering freedom to blacks to win a war fought originally to keep blacks enslaved. "The two sections are vieing [*sic*] with each other in the work of emancipation," warned the Raleigh *North Carolina Standard* in January, 1865. "The negroes are to be armed, and society is to be not merely upset, but destroyed." For those Southerners who agreed with an unknown letterwriter to the *Macon* (Georgia) *Telegraph* that "every [Confederate] life that has been lost in this struggle was an offering upon the altar of African slavery," arming and freeing the slaves was in itself an admission of defeat.

The crisis confronting Southern conservatives had come full circle. Having initially viewed secession as a revolution likely to degenerate into anarchy, they supported the Confederacy in an effort to moderate the expected social disorder. But the revolution they so dreaded could not be checked. Once emancipation, however indirectly, had been sanctioned by the votes of Democratic congressmen, particularly those from occupied districts where slaveholdings were not extensive, the Whigs were convinced that the horrors of the French Revolution were about to be re-enacted. Defeatism became predictably virulent when the Whigs discovered that the Confederacy itself was to be the source of anarchy. "With such wild schemes, and confessions of despair as this," wrote William A. Graham, a Whig senator from North Carolina, in reference to Confederate emancipation, "it [is] high time to attempt peace."

Although most prevalent among wealthy, conservative Whigs, defeatism had cut across class and party lines by the last months of the war. The prestige and property of all slaveholders were directly theatened by the move toward converting their slaves into soldiers and free men. The taunts of an anonymous Southern white quoted in March, 1865, by the South Carolina planter James Chesnut were a statement of the loss in status about to be incurred by the wealthy: "They will have no Negroes now to lord it over! They can swell and peacock about and tyrannize now over only a small parcel of women and children, those only who are their very own family."

As debilitating to the Confederate cause as was the increasing defection of the wealthy, the desertions from the armies were an even more alarming symptom of impending defeat. Desertion became a critical problem beginning in late 1864; and its major cause was the poverty of the families left behind by the soldiers. Whereas the rich were faced with the loss of a comfortable way of life, the common Southerner was struggling simply to survive after the midpoint of the war. The destruction by both armies, the seizures of Confederate impressment officials, and the lack of manpower on the home front had reduced non-slaveholders to pitiful straits. Despite efforts by governors to hoard supplies and of state legislatures to enact relief programs, impending famine became a fact of life for many families.

The desperation of their families made extraordinary demands on the Confederate soldiers. General Joseph Johnston summarized their dilemma: "Those soldiers of the laboring class who had families were compelled to choose between their military service and the strongest obligations men know—their duties to their wives and children." Not only did the desertion rate accelerate late in the war, but there also was an understandably marked correlation between counties of greatest destitution and the number of deserters who gathered there. For these soldiers and their families the war was over. The will to fight was gone when a North Carolina woman could write of her soldier husband, "He has nothing to fight for[;] I don't think that he is fighting for anything[,] only for his family to starve." More and more soldiers were reaching the same conclusion. "We want the ware stopt [*sic*] for the sake of our little ones at home" was how a North Carolinian put it in the summer of 1864.

Although the collapse of the Confederacy was obviously hastened by the defeatism that permeated all classes by early 1865, this should not blind us to what was still an incredible over-all war effort. Even given the increased desertion at the end, the Confederate rate of desertion was but 1 man per 9 enlistments as opposed to a ratio of 1 to 7 in the Union armies. Many, perhaps most, Confederate soldiers believed in eventual triumph as they would in a religious dogma. Only through such faith could they endure the hardships of the war. Conditioned by religious revivals that swept the armies after the middle of the war to fight for a providential victory, some preferred death to a recognition of defeat. By 1864 soldiers in Lee's army, as described by George Gary Eggleston, suffered from a gloomy fatalism. "Believing that they must be killed sooner or later . . . many became singularly reckless, and exposed themselves with the utmost carelessness to all sorts of unnecessary dangers."

This near-fanatical unwillingness to submit to Yankee rule enabled the Confederacy to survive for four years, and this survival was itself a major accomplishment. Confederate leaders had forced sacrifices well beyond what the Union asked of

Northerners, and most Southerners responded with a virtually complete commitment. The mortality rate among Confederate soldiers was double that of the Union armies, just as the per capita indebtedness in the Confederacy to finance the war was twice that experienced in the North. The economy was industrialized and converted to war production through nationalistic controls far more stringent than any other in American history. States' rights were an irritant in the Confederate war effort, but their impact was overshadowed by the seminationalization of all resources.

The Confederacy finally succumbed to the limitations of its economy and to the hammerings of the Union armies. When war weariness set in by 1864, it was directly traceable to both Union military successes and to the sacrifices demanded by the Confederate government, sacrifices that impoverished the majority of Southerners and threatened the existence of slavery. By 1865 Confederate subjugation was imminent because the North had learned how to use its military force systematically to destroy the social and economic fabric of Southern society.

Still, even at the war's end, there would be many Southerners who shared the disbelief of Kate Stone on hearing of Lee's surrender: "Such terrible news if true, but we cannot believe it. . . . God spare us from this crushing blow and save our dying country." At least defeat, as inevitable as it was unacceptable, would be the last sacrifice demanded of Confederates.

4

The Black Man's War

The Civil War reversed, at least temporarily, the enforced passivity of blacks in white America. Just as the presence of blacks in America was the root cause of the war, so also was their active support essential if either the Union or the Confederacy were to achieve victory. "The Negro is the key of the situation," noted the great black leader Frederick Douglass, "the pivot upon which the whole rebellion turns."

Much to the chagrin and even disgust of many whites, the military assistance of blacks was necessary to preserve the Union. "Drive back to the support of the rebellion the physical force which the colored people now give, and promise us," wrote Lincoln in September, 1864, to one of his critics over the enlistment of black troops, "and neither the present, nor any coming administration, *can* save the Union. Take from us, and give to the enemy, the hundred and thirty, forty, or fifty thousand colored persons now serving us as soldiers, seamen, and laborers, and we can no longer maintain the contest." In addition to the two hundred thousand blacks who eventually fought for the Union, half a million slaves undermined the Confederate war effort by fleeing behind Union lines, where they worked as noncombatants.

Although the slaves did not revolt and most Southern blacks were held as slaves until the end of the war, those blacks who did fight against slavery or flee from it demonstrated that their race was no longer merely an object to be manipulated as whites saw fit. But it was military necessity alone that induced white Americans to accept black assistance. Blacks soon discovered, even while the Confederacy was being defeated, that white supremacy was by no means a casualty of the war.

From Pawn to Unionist

At the onset of the war few Northerners foresaw that the despised pawn of the Union, the black race, would become its savior. Enslaved in the South and degraded in the North through the humiliating restrictions of Jim Crow legislation, blacks were denied their humanity and rights of citizenship throughout America. "Here, as elsewhere," observed Edward Dicey of his visit to New York City, blacks "form a race apart, never walking in company with white persons, except as servants."

Northern blacks, to say nothing of Southern slaves, had no elevated expectations of their future in America. The presidential election of 1860 left them but a sterile choice. After reviewing the four candidates in the field—John Bell of Tennessee for the Constitutional Union party, Stephen Douglas of Illinois for the Northern Democrats, John Breckinridge of Kentucky for the Southern Democrats, and Abraham Lincoln of Illinois for the Republicans—a black abolitionist, H. Ford Douglass, announced, "So far as the principles of freedom and the hopes of the black man are concerned, all these parties are barren and unfruitful; neither of them seeks to lift the negro out of his fetters, and rescue this day from odium and disgrace."

The *New York Anglo-African* charged in March, 1860, that the major parties differed only in their means of subjecting blacks. "The Democratic party would make the white man the master and the black man the slave, and have them thus together occupy every foot of the American soil." The Republicans, declared the newspaper, offered blacks but an empty guise of morality. Their stand against slavery was not motivated by any humanitarian concern with the plight of blacks but solely with the self-interests of white labor. It amounted to a declaration that slavery should not be forced on whites who did not want it. The Republicans "oppose the progress of slavery in the territories [but] their opposition to slavery means opposition to the black man—nothing else."

The bitter indictment by the *Anglo-African* was understandable. The only major party that went so far as to argue that the federal government had a constitutional right and a moral duty to checkmate the spread of slavery was the Republicans. But Lincoln's party left no doubt that it wanted the territories reserved for white laborers alone. "We want them for homes of free white people," proclaimed Lincoln during his 1858 debates with Senator Stephen Douglas. "This they cannot be, to any considerable extent, if slavery shall be planted within them." True to their word, Kansas Republicans prohibited the immigration into their state of free blacks, as well as slaves.

Moreover, as we have seen, the Republicans were pledged to protect slavery in the states, and they did not demand a repeal of the Fugitive Slave Act. Their stand on black civil rights, while more enlightened than that of the Democrats, was still ambiguous and subject to the pressure of vacillating public opinion. For example, in 1860 the Republican legislature of New York passed and put on the state ballot a constitutional amendment that would have repealed the state's $250 property qualification for black suffrage. Despite the courage of party leaders in backing such a change, most Republican speakers and newspapers either qualified their support or ignored the amendment during the election campaign. Although what votes it did receive came from Republicans, suffrage change was defeated by a two to one margin because many rank-and-file Republicans joined with Democrats in opposition to any weakening of white supremacy. Lincoln had carried New York, but blacks had further evidence that his party could not be trusted.

Republicans encompassed a wide spectrum of opinion from virulent racists, who pushed for segregationist black codes, to abolitionists, who were anxious to expose the myth of innate black inferiority. The majority of Republicans, however, probably shared Lincoln's ambivalence in racial matters. Lincoln believed that the physical differences between the white and black races precluded their ever living together in social or political equality. However, as he told an audience in Charleston, Illinois, in 1858, he could "not perceive that because the white man is to have the superior position the negro should be denied everything." Blacks had a right to their freedom and to the fruits of their own labor, and Lincoln would do all in his constitutional powers to secure them these rights. Yet his efforts did not include support for meaningful black citizenship. Ever wary of being labeled by his political opponents as an advocate of black equality, he even refused in 1858 to sign a petition that called for the repeal of the section of the Illinois black code that prohibited blacks from testifying in court cases involving whites. It was no wonder that H. Ford Douglass, the black who circulated the petition through the state, would later "care nothing about that anti-slavery which wants to make the Territories free, while it is unwilling to extend to me, as a man, in the free States, all the rights of a man."

The unease that many black intellectuals felt over Lincoln's candidacy was registered by Frederick Douglass when he announced his support for Gerrit Smith, the presidential nominee of a splinter wing of the abolitionists. This was merely a symbolic gesture, for no one, including Smith, took his candidacy seriously. Most abolitionists, despite their misgivings, supported the Republicans as a party that at least was moving in the right direction. Furthermore, no politician was worried about the black vote. Blacks comprised barely over 1 per cent of the population in the free states, and, with the exception of New England, their vote was either restricted or not permitted at all.

Smith, running on a platform that demanded immediate and unconditional emancipation, polled fewer than three thousand votes. As a demonstration of independent abolitionist strength, his candidacy had failed; yet nearly all abolitionists and blacks could rejoice in Lincoln's election. For the first time a president had been elected who was utterly unacceptable to the South. One plank of the abolitionist program, the nonextension of slavery, had been ratified by a Northern majority. And, as Frederick Douglass ruefully noted, the Republican victory "demonstrated the possibility of electing, if not an Abolitionist, at least an *anti-slavery reputation* to the Presidency."

The secession winter of 1860–61 confronted the nation with its greatest constitutional crisis since 1787. The divergent interests and mutual jealousies of the North and South that had threatened to prevent the formation of any Union in 1787 had been resolved at the expense of the black man. The Constitution recognized the legality of holding human beings as property and placed the institution of slavery beyond the reach of national regulation. However, by simultaneously committing the nation to both liberty and slavery, the Founding Fathers had based the Constitution on a glaring inconsistency. Once their inconsistency was on the verge of tearing apart the Union after Lincoln's election, the sectional compromisers, Southerners in the Border states and conservative businessmen in the East, were willing once again to sacrifice blacks for the Union. Under the Crittenden Compromise, the only congressional plan that had any chance of forestalling secession, slavery was to be protected in all present and future territories below the Missouri Compromise line of 36° 30'; the permanence of slavery in those states where it already existed, as well as in the District of Columbia, was to be guaranteed against federal interference; and free blacks were to be disfranchised completely and sent abroad.

Blacks immediately saw that the Crittenden Compromise meant, in the apt phrase of Frederick Douglass, a "new drain on the negro's blood." Through public meetings and petitions addressed to white politicians, they denounced the plan as cruel and unjust. The Republican position was more cautious. For example, Lincoln's response to the Crittenden Compromise stretched his antislavery reputation almost to the breaking point. He accepted much of the plan and specifically disapproved only of the protection offered for the future expansion of slavery. Nonetheless, this protection was the very heart of the compromise, the *sine qua non* as far as the South was concerned, and Lincoln's opposition, and that of his party in Congress, made the plan worthless for the seceders.

The failure of the Crittenden Compromise ensured the breakup of the Union. Blacks praised the dissolution for, in truth, many of them saw little to respect in the old Union. In the spring of 1860, Robert Purvis, a wealthy black abolitionist from Philadelphia, revealed the depths of this disillusionment when he wrote, *"For such a government, I, as a man, can have no feelings but of contempt, loathing, and unutterable abhorrence."* The old Union, after all, was pledged to protect slavery. The coercive power of the federal government stood behind the enforcement of the Fugitive Slave Act, and both the federal armed forces and the state militias were constitutionally bound to help suppress any slave rebellions.

As the slave states were leaving the Union, few blacks permitted themselves the luxury of expecting that the federal government would take a strong stand against slavery. But the institution, now stripped of federal protection, appeared to be gravely weakened. Both the Garrisonian abolitionists and many Southern Unionists believed that slavery could not stand alone. "Without the aid and countenance of the whole United States, we could not have kept slavery," noted James Chestnut of South Carolina early in the war. "I always knew that the world was against us."

However, there was a danger in waiting for slavery to collapse of its own weight. A false optimism could easily be generated that would drain abolitionism of its commitment and drive. Relieved of the crushing sense of complicity in a national sin, abolitionists might well abandon the cause of the slave. What haunted blacks during the secession winter was the fear that the Union, unable to hold the South by sweeping concessions, would recognize the Confederacy and thereby postpone indefinitely the crusade for emancipation. Just before the firing on Fort Sumter, Frederick Douglass prophesied, "Our pulpit, now largely silent, will become absolutely dumb on the subject [of emancipation], and the moral sense of the North will in a few years probably die out; and thus will end the thirty years [of] moral warfare with the accursed slave system."

The belligerence of the South, not the moral outrage of the North, made Douglass a false prophet. Once war was launched, Americans were committed, knowingly or not, to a revolution that would destroy slavery. Although it would take two years of military stalemate before the majority of Northerners, Lincoln included, would accept the role of revolutionaries and strike at slavery, the cause of the rebellion, abolitionists and blacks realized at the outset that both slavery and liberty could not survive the war. "Let no more efforts be made to effect a union between light and darkness, liberty and slavery, heaven and hell. Reason testifies that it is impossible, and your own sad experience verifies her testimony," proclaimed the *New York Anglo-African* in May, 1861. The crippling ambiguity of the Constitution was about to be resolved.

Blacks welcomed the Civil War because it held the promise of the end of an oppressive Union and the creation of a new nation without slavery. In urging blacks to volunteer for armed service, A. M. Green, a Philadelphia schoolteacher, told his fellow blacks "not to cavil over past grievances." White racism must be resisted, "yet let us endeavor to hope for the future, and improve the present auspicious moment for creating anew our claims upon the justice and honor of the Republic." Throughout the North black leaders sounded the same theme: In the crisis of the Union lay the salvation of the black man.

Blacks had fought in America's past wars, notably the Revolution and the War of 1812, and they now offered their services. The resolution passed at a meeting of blacks in Boston in the spring of 1861 was typical: "We are ready to stand by and defend the Government as the equals of its white defenders." As soldiers, blacks felt that they could win a measure of dignity that had been denied them as civilians. By rallying to the support of the Union, blacks could prove their claim to citizenship while striking a blow against slavery. The self-respect that had been eroded by the oppression of whites could be regained on the battlefield. A black soldier, having learned how to defend his rights, would be less likely to resubmit after the war to the inferior caste position reserved for him by whites.

Precisely because black combat participation in the war was perceived by both races as a step toward racial equality, whites closed ranks and rejected all offers of blacks to serve as troops. Because the benefits of the antebellum Union were, by definition, for whites only, and because the preservation of the Union until 1863 had entailed the perpetuation of bondage for nine-tenths of the blacks in America, the military use of blacks was both unthinkable and repugnant to most Northerners.

In Providence, Rhode Island, the drilling of black troops was stopped on the insulting grounds that their exercises constituted "disorderly gatherings." Black volunteers in New York City disbanded on orders of the police chief, who told them that he was powerless to protect them against mob violence. A Cincinnati recruiting office for blacks was forcibly closed down by the city authorities. "We want you d—— niggers to keep out of this," explained a Cincinnati policeman; "this is a white man's war." Even where blacks succeeded in raising troops, their services were flatly refused. State governors referred to national legislation that forbade the enrollment of blacks in the militias. Meanwhile, the War Department made it clear that it had no use for black soldiers.

The Union, however, was not squeamish about employing blacks for noncombatant military labor. By the end of 1861 thousands of blacks were serving the military as cooks, teamsters, construction hands, and personal servants. Such duties, thought white Northerners, were consistent with a properly subservient role for the blacks. Having been forced by restrictions on their civilian employment into becoming, in the words of one contemporary black, "a race of cooks, waiters, barbers, whitewashers, bootblacks, and chimney sweeps," blacks were initially confined to the same subordinate role in the Union military.

The one quasi-exception early in the war was the recruitment of blacks for the Union navy. Service in the navy was unpopular with whites because of the rigid discipline and the harsh working conditions. In order to ensure an adequate supply of sailors, as well as to provide employment for the fugitive slaves picked up along the estuaries of the Virginia coast, Secretary of the Navy Gideon Welles authorized black enlistments in September, 1861. The color line was fixed, however, by a discriminatory pay scale and by the stipulation that blacks would be permitted no higher rank than "boys."

The reaction of Northern blacks was mixed once they realized that the war had brought no immediate change in the intractability of white racism. Some served in whatever capacity was acceptable to white opinion; others continued to drill surreptitiously in the hope that someday they would be permitted a combat role. But, increasingly, many blacks became embittered and alienated. The rejection of black troops had been particularly humiliating, and, as long as the North continued to define its cause as the restoration of a white supremacist Union with slavery intact, most blacks concluded that their race should remain neutral. "It being their fight I assure you they are welcome to it," wrote a Cincinnati schoolteacher. A black from Chillicothe,

Ohio, reasoned that military support of a racist government could be used against blacks in the future. "If the colored people, under all the social and legal disabilities by which they are environed, are ever ready to defend the government that despoils them of their rights, it may be concluded that it is quite safe to oppress them."

Disillusionment over the war increased black ambivalence toward the Union. For some this ambivalence could be resolved only by abandoning a nation that had made a mockery of its moral pretensions. In 1861 and 1862 about two thousand blacks migrated to Haiti, and in 1863 an additional five hundred settled on the Isle à Vache, an island off the coast of Haiti.

The 1861 movement was an expression of black separatism. In 1859 the black government of Haiti had offered to subsidize the immigration of Afro-Americans, and it extended liberal terms of citizenship, cheap land, religious freedom, and exemption from military service. The offer produced an intense debate in the American black community. Although the majority, under the leadership of Frederick Douglass, rejected emigration on the grounds that it was an open admission that the struggle against white racism was hopeless, a faction headed by Henry Highland Garnett, a prominent New York City minister, argued that American ideals could never be redeemed.

Blacks had no future in America, insisted Garnett, save that of being continually restricted and controlled in the interests of the white majority. The war would change nothing, wrote J. Willis Menard, another black emigrationist, "for the atmosphere of North America is interwoven and vocal with the blasting breath of negro prejudice. It is the first lesson taught by white parents to their children, that the negro is a low, debased animal, not fit for their association nor their equal." Blacks could not combat this prejudice, because white institutions coerced them into a life of poverty and ignorance that then served as a further justification for the belief in white supremacy. Emigrationist leaders felt that, if blacks were ever to secure their rights, they had no choice but to seize an opportunity to escape from degradation by leaving America and establishing a true nationality in a country not blinded by Negrophobia.

The high hopes of the Haitian-emigration movement were grounded more in desperation than in a realistic assessment of what would await black expatriates in Haiti. Mismanagement, broken promises by the Haitian government, disease, and the lack of job opportunities in an economy mired in grinding poverty quickly disenchanted the two thousand black expatriates. By 1864 fewer than 10 per cent of the original colonists were still on the island.

Even less successful were the efforts of the Lincoln administration to encourage black migration to the Caribbean. Provided with $600,000 in colonization funds appropriated by Congress in 1862, Lincoln tried to underwrite black colonies, first in northern Panama and then on the Isle à Vache. Black opinion was almost solidly against these schemes, for it was evident that they were motivated by a desire both to rid the nation of its blacks and to supply white entrepreneurs with cheap labor. The Panama project was connected with the development of American-controlled coal mines, and interest in the Isle à Vache was tied in with the exploitation of timber resources. Plans for the Panama colony were canceled once it was discovered that the coal deposits were worthless, but a settlement was founded on the Isle à Vache. Some four hundred fifty blacks migrated to the island in 1863; nearly one-quarter soon died from disease, and the remainder were swindled by Bernard Kock, the manager of American business interests on the island. In early 1864 Lincoln sent a ship to bring back the survivors.

Frederick Douglass, more than other black leaders, was responsible for checking the alienation that initially drove many of his race to remain neutral in the war or to consider leaving America. He set the tone for the guarded optimism that characterized the attitude of most Northern blacks toward the war. In spite of themselves, Douglass preached, Northern whites would have to free the slaves if they wanted to win the war. From the very beginning he declared that "the war now being waged in this land is a war for and against slavery; and . . . it can never be effectually put down till one or the other of these vital forces is completely destroyed." Certain that military logic would eventually force Northern opinion to recognize this conclusion, he saw that in protecting their nationality, white Americans were, however unwittingly, fighting for black liberation. And once emancipation was declared a war aim, once the black man had a cause for which to stake his life, the necessary corollary would be arming of the blacks.

Douglass, of course, was right. But his confidence was badly shaken by the conservative slavery policy of the Lincoln administration, and he devoted the first two years of the war to a campaign designed to educate Northern whites on the need for emancipation. He later recalled in his autobiography:

> . . . from the first I reproached the North that they fought the rebels with only one hand, when they might strike effectually with two—that they fought with their soft white hand, while they kept this black iron hand chained and helpless behind them—that they fought the effect, while they protected the cause, and that the Union cause would never prosper till the war assumed an antislavery attitude, and the Negro was enlisted on the loyal side.

After lecturing throughout the North in the summer and fall of 1861, Douglass met with other abolitionist leaders in Boston on December 16 to organize an Emancipation League. Disgusted by the enforced return to their masters of some of the fugitive slaves who had escaped behind Union lines, and alarmed over Lincoln's revocation of Frémont's emancipation order in Missouri, the abolitionists decided to mount a propaganda offensive. Within the next year the League churned out nearly one hundred thousand pamphlets, furnished newspapers with editorials, sponsored lecture tours, and organized petition campaigns directed at Congress.

In attempting to popularize the cause of emancipation, the Boston League, as well as similar associations in New York and Washington, was surprised that its efforts did not provoke violent retaliation from whites fearful over the social and economic consequences of emancipation. This had been the pattern in the past, and as late as the winter of 1861 abolitionist speakers were greeted by mobs throughout the North. To be sure, abolitionism had not suddenly become a mass crusade, and many Northerners shared the hatred of Senator Garrett Davis of Kentucky, a Unionist who fumed early in 1862, "If I had the power, I would take [the abolitionists] and the worst Seceshers [sic] and hang them in pairs." Nonetheless, abolitionists received a hearing in 1862, and there was an unmistakable buildup of pressure for emancipation.

Although the educational work of Douglass and other abolitionists cannot be ignored, Northern opinion was swayed more by the sacrifices and frustrations of the stalemated war. Abolitionism, popularly despised when it was a matter of principle and moral conviction, was becoming acceptable as it was transformed into a military weapon to defeat the Confederacy. The unexpected resistance of the Confederacy, coupled with the slackening of Union enlistments, documented what blacks had been preaching since the firing on Fort Sumter: that slavery was the backbone of the rebellion and that a Union victory required that the slaves be freed and armed.

The responsibility for changing the direction of the war rested with Lincoln. He moved inexorably toward emancipation and a combat role for blacks because of the relevance of these measures to victory. He had been driven, in his words, "to the alternative of either surrendering the Union, and with it, the Constitution, or of laying [a] strong hand upon the colored element." Lincoln had passed the test of leadership by revealing an incredible capacity to grow and learn while in office. But he never deluded himself or the public into believing that he had been motivated by anything but military necessity.

For the vast majority of white Americans, such a motive behind emancipation was sufficient because their paramount concern was the Union, not the condition of blacks. However, a minority foresaw that once black liberation had been separated from moral considerations, the resulting freedom would be illusory and as restricted as the prewar condition of free blacks. George Lawrence, an editor of the *Boston Pine and Palm,* a black pro-colonization newspaper, predicted in 1861 that the black man, even if freed and allowed to fight against the Confederacy, "will be rewarded with a mockery of thanks, and unceremoniously thrust aside." Lydia Maria Child, a white abolitionist, was nearly as pessimistic. She warned in 1862, "Even should [the slaves] be emancipated, merely as a 'war necessity,' everything *must* go wrong, if there is no heart or conscience on the subject." Federal policy toward the freedmen would do little to dispel the fears of either.

From Slave to Confederate

Unlike the Union, the Confederacy could not afford initially to ignore its blacks. Slaves and free blacks made up one-third of the population of the Confederacy, and their labor would have to be mobilized as a military resource if the Confederacy were to have any chance of equalizing the odds against itself in a total, industrial war. However, in both persuading and forcing blacks to contribute to the war effort, Southern whites unintentionally were blurring the distinction between blacks as property and as persons. Finally, by the last year of the war, many, including Jefferson Davis, were arguing that blacks should be viewed not as slaves but as Confederates. Thus, though the Confederacy approached the blacks from a perspective radically different from that of the Union, it was driven by the same military necessity toward a greater degree of racial tolerance.

The Confederacy was confident that slavery would enable it to win the war. In an editorial that was picked up and quoted by Northern abolitionists, the *Montgomery* (Alabama) *Advertiser* proclaimed in the fall of 1861 that the institution was a "tower of strength" and "really one of the most effective weapons employed against the Union by the South." Far from engaging in the self-deception that suffused much of the Southern thinking on slavery, the *Advertiser* was stating an obvious military fact. With slave labor to fall back on, the Confederacy could militarily mobilize a far higher percentage of its white manpower than could a free society. After the war, Grant admitted, "The 4,000,000 colored noncombatants were equal to more than three times their number in the North, age for age, sex for sex."

Whether in producing foodstuffs, extracting raw materials, manufacturing the implements of war, nursing the wounded, or building and repairing fortifications and railroads, black labor was indispensable to the Confederacy. Blacks performed not only the bulk of the physical labor but also a surprising amount of the skilled tasks. Railroad brakemen and firemen were typically slaves, and half of the workers at the Tredegar Iron Works were blacks, including thirty-two skilled slave technicians. As the war progressed, government shops and arsenals relied increasingly on slave labor. The Confederate naval arsenal in Selma, destroyed by Wilson's raiders in March, 1865, included 310 blacks among its 400 workers.

Although Southern whites correctly assumed that slavery was flexible enough to sustain a war economy, they could never be certain that war would not provide slaves with an opportunity to revolt. Fears over black behavior focused not so much on those who were employed in war occupations under direct supervision as on the free blacks and the slaves in rural areas that had been stripped of adult white males.

Southern free blacks were a group whose very presence contradicted the racial assumptions behind slavery. Barely tolerated in the antebellum South and legally consigned to a status closer to slavery than freedom, they faced much stricter controls over their lives once war had broken out. Only one out of twenty blacks in the Confederacy was free on the eve of the war. Nonetheless, as was so often the case in a time of crisis, free blacks became scapegoats for the anxieties of whites over internal security. Control legislation, with the dual purpose of intimidating the free blacks and ensuring their loyalty to the Confederacy, was passed.

A potential fifth column in the eyes of the whites, free blacks had to be isolated and their numbers restricted. Efforts were made to prevent any communication between free blacks and slaves or suspected Unionists. New restrictions were placed on movement, employment, the carrying of arms, and the ownership of slaves. To prevent any increase in the free black population, any loopholes in the manumission laws were closed. Freedom would now be granted by the state legislatures only in return for exceptional service to the Confederacy, such as exposing a plot against the government.

Beyond this, the tightness of controls varied. Six states legalized the impressment of free blacks into labor battalions, a practice that was nationalized by the Confederate Congress in February, 1864. It was extremely difficult to evade state service, because the impressment acts required that all adult free blacks register with the local courts. In addition, the national act of February, 1864, stipulated that free blacks should be impressed before slaves. Free blacks were now subject to periodic dragnets that forced all available labor into emergency service. When Rich-

mond was threatened by federal attack in the fall of 1864, free
black men were indiscriminately rounded up with slaves and put
to work on fortifications. "The Negroes," reported the *Richmond
Examiner*, "were taken unaware on the street, at the market,
from the shops, and at every point where they were found doing
errands for themselves or their masters." Impressment also pro-
cured for the Confederacy scarce economic skills that could be
exploited to maintain armaments production and the transportation system. Less than one-third of the free blacks impressed in
Virginia in the last two years of the war were common laborers;
the majority practiced diverse trades that could be diverted to
serve a war economy.

Much harsher than impressment was the legislation passed by
Georgia, Mississippi, and Arkansas to enforce submissiveness on
the part of free blacks. These states authorized slavery as the
punishment for any blacks whose behavior posed the slightest
threat to the Confederacy or to white supremacy. Mississippi free
blacks could remain in the state only if they were licensed by a
county board of police. Licenses were to be granted to those
who had demonstrated that they were "in no wise dangerous
to the community." Any black who remained without a license
was to be enslaved. In Georgia any black deemed idle or vicious
was liable to enslavement, with "viciousness" being defined as
"improper or mischievous influence upon slaves or mulattoes."
Bondage, or the threat of it, was also invoked to extract economic services from free blacks. In a perverse form of debt relief,
Arkansas decreed that the manumitted slaves of indebted masters
could be hired out as slaves whose wages would be used to pay
off the debts of their ex-masters. Temporary slavery was the
penalty in Georgia for nonpayment of an annual war tax of $25
required only of free blacks.

The South more than neutralized the potentially dangerous
presence of free blacks by coercing the bulk of them into supporting the Confederate cause. However, some blacks, particularly
the urban elite of the race, voluntarily contributed their money
and services. Desperately anxious to take some step toward
equality, these blacks hoped that their loyalty to the Confederacy
would result in a relaxation of the restrictions that confined their
every move. "No matter where I fight," explained a wealthy New

Orleans black in 1862, "I only wish to spend what I have, and
fight as long as I can, if only my boy may stand in the street
equal to a white boy when the war is over." Such expectations
were extinguished as the color line was drawn ever tighter in
the Confederacy and the status of free blacks deteriorated. Whites
were well aware that any improvement in the position of free
blacks would increase slave discontent.

The South gambled, on the whole successfully, that the control
mechanisms of slavery were sufficiently strong to prevent uprisings
in the absence of white men. Despite widespread fears in the
first year of the war that the slaves were preparing for a major
revolt, nothing of the kind occurred. "War . . . has now existed
for nearly four years," noted Thomas S. Gholson, a Confederate
congressman from Virginia, in early 1865, "and yet . . . there
has been no insurrection or attempt at insurrection. . . . Our
wives and children have been left on our plantations—frequently
with no other protection, than that afforded by our slaves."

Many Southerners, and Northerners as well, interpreted the
failure of slaves to revolt as confirmation of their belief in the
black man's inherent racial weakness. According to this racist
myth, blacks were, as Edmund Ruffin of Virginia wrote on the
eve of the war, "naturally timid, unenterprising, fearful of and
averse to change to any new and untried condition." As psychological reassurance that blacks did not represent a threat because they did not even aspire to freedom, the fiction of innate
black submissiveness was essential to both the moral and social
rationalization of slavery. Among themselves, however, when they
were not striking a pose for the outside world, Southern whites
confessed that they knew little of black motivations. "Are [the
slaves] stolidly stupid," mused Mary Chesnut in her diary, "or
wiser than we are, silent and strong, biding their time[?]"

Uncertain over the real black identity, whites were not willing
to entrust their lives entirely to the purported docility of the
slaves. Consequently, the outbreak of the war led to a strengthen-
ing of the enforcement machinery of slavery. Slave discipline was
grounded in fear, and no technique of control was more effective
than the slave patrols. The patrollers, generally intensely Negro-
phobic nonslaveholders, scoured the countryside for slaves off the
plantations without passes. Unrestrained by any property interest

in the blacks, the patrollers meted out terrible punishments. An ex-slave recalled that they kept "close watch on the poor niggers so they have no chance to do anything or go anywhere. . . . If you wasn't in your proper place when the patterrollers [*sic*] came they lash you till you was black and blue." Throughout the Confederacy patrol legislation was stiffened, and all white males not in the army were organized into home guards charged with maintaining internal security.

Increased surveillance was accompanied by immediate retaliation against suspected insurrectionary plots. "Within the last 12 months we have had to hang some 40 [slaves] for plotting an insurrection, and there has been about that number put in irons," reported a Confederate provost marshal from Mississippi in July, 1862. Self-appointed groups of whites known as vigilance committees interrogated alleged rebels and ordered their execution. What minor uprisings did occur were quickly put down wherever the Confederacy maintained a military presence. In the fall of 1864 thirty slaves in Amite County, Mississippi, armed themselves with their masters' weapons and headed for the Mississippi River. Before they could reach Union lines, most were killed by a party of Confederate scouts.

As effective as these security measures were in forestalling an insurrection, they were unable to prevent slaves from fleeing to Union armies in occupied or directly threatened regions. To close off this escape route, slaveholders, either voluntarily or under the orders of Confederate authorities, removed as many slaves as possible from the path of the federal advance. "Before de surrender de slaveowners begun to scatter de slaves about from place to place to keep de Yankees from getting them," remembered an ex-slave. "If de Yankees took a place, de slaves nearby was moved to a place further off." In the lower Mississippi Valley the pattern of migration was from the Gulf states to Texas, and in the East the major shift was from exposed coastal areas to the uplands.

Although slavery had been dislocated by the removal policy, much of its value had been salvaged. In a negative sense, the Union had been deprived of manpower. "Every sound male black left for the enemy," noted Kirby Smith, "becomes a soldier whom we have afterward to fight." The retention of that black man also preserved the economic stake of his owner in the Confederacy. As long as they still had some of their slaves, refugee masters had a source of income. Not only were nonslaveholders eager to hire servants, but the war economy in the unoccupied Confederacy offered a booming market for slave labor. In particular, saltworks and mines relied heavily on refugee slaves.

The number of fugitive slaves was also held down by the impressment of slave laborers. By placing slaves into Confederate service under direct military supervision, impressment combined policing functions with those of economic mobilization. After voluntary recruitments had fallen off by the end of 1861, slave impressments were authorized first by the states in 1862 and then, in legislation passed in 1863 and 1864, by the Confederate government.

Although bitterly criticized as an infringement on property rights, the practice did produce tangible results. Slave laborers, who might have escaped or otherwise been unavailable for the war effort, were extensively used in constructing fortifications and other defense projects. At the same time, potentially rebellious slaves were siphoned off the plantations and subjected to military control. In fulfilling their quota of able-bodied adult male slaves, planters selected the most troublesome ones. Some owners, like one Mississippi planter, even asked the impressment officers to "bring out a lot of the most unruly and place them at work." Despite their proximity to the front lines, few impressed slaves appear to have deserted. Discipline was extremely rigid, work was closely supervised, and at night the slaves were herded into camps under military guard.

Measured by its ability to retain most of its slaves and to extract labor from them, the Confederacy both protected slavery and benefited from it. Yet slave discontent and passive resistance, even in the absence of major revolts, eroded the internal discipline and economic efficiency of the institution. Slavery was not destroyed during the war, but much of its strength and stability had withered away. By the time Lee surrendered, about one-fifth of the slaves in the Confederacy had gained their freedom by moving behind Union lines. The tempo of escape was much faster in the second half of the war, not only because of the greater penetration of Union armies but also in response to the Emancipation Proclamation.

Short of violently rebelling or actively giving aid to the Union, flight from slavery was the best weapon that blacks could use against the Confederacy. By transferring their labor from the Confederacy to the Union, they committed in the eyes of Southern whites a treasonable act. Fugitives, stated the Reverend Charles Jones, "declare themselves enemies and at war with owners by going over to the enemy who is seeking both our lives and our property. They are traitors of the worst kind, and spies also, who may pilot the enemy into your bedchamber."

These "traitors" came from all ranks of slave society, but disloyalty was most rampant among two groups—house servants and the rebellious slaves whose spirit could not be broken. The behavior of house servants, especially those deemed most loyal by their masters and thereby treated most leniently, confirmed an observation of Frederick Douglass in his autobiography: "Give [a slave] a *bad* master, and he aspires to a good master; give him a good master, and he wishes to become his own master." By the same token a Maryland slaveholder noted that "those particular or individual slaves who have been most favored by their masters have been the first to leave."

Relative to the field hands, the slaves who waited upon the master and his family were a pampered elite that was generally treated more leniently and permitted more privileges. They were the least brutalized of the slave population, both physically and psychically. As a result, they had greater capacity and opportunity for individual initiative than most field hands. In daily and often intimate contact with the master's family and visitors, the house slaves had the additional advantage of being privy to the loose talk of whites. After relaying to the rest of the slaves military news and the information that the war was somehow related to emancipation, trusted servants often led escapes or took off on their own. Not as closely watched as the field workers, because their loyalty was assumed, house slaves also knew about the daily routine of the whites and could plan an escape accordingly.

Southern whites were shocked to discover that the average domestic slave would be far more likely to lead Union soldiers to the family silver rather than to hide and guard it. In the summer of 1863, an Alabamian observed that "the 'faithful slave' is about played out. They are the most treacherous, brutal, and ungrateful race on the globe." What especially distressed whites was the realization that no slave could be trusted. "The temptation of change, the promise of freedom and of pay for labor, is more than most can stand; and no reliance can be placed *certainly* upon any," conceded the Reverend Charles Jones, a disillusioned master who had always viewed himself as a Christian, paternalistic shepherd of black souls.

The submissiveness that whites equated with loyalty was often just a façade behind which the slave concealed his true motives. Personal servants were most adept at playing the role expected of them, because their training had taught them to anticipate every whim of the master and his family. Therefore, many house slaves, after escaping, had enough guile to return, persuade their masters that they were truly contrite, and then lead the remaining servants to freedom. One such slave in Georgia, as related by a friend of the deceived master's, insisted that "she had been convinced of her duty by reading the Bible and had returned to perform it, and during the months she remained was as humble and faithful as a servant could be."

The disloyalty of slaves who had stamped themselves as rebels was expected by whites and was sometimes met with a feeling of relief. When Jane, the slave cook of a Louisiana physician, fled to a Union camp with her two children in March, 1863, Kate Stone recorded in her journal, "I think we are all glad she had gone. We felt her a constant menace." Jane's master had not sold her or attempted to beat her, because she was too good a cook and too intimidating in her physical appearance. However, most recalcitrant slaves, particularly those without a valuable skill, were savagely and repeatedly punished. The fact that they could not be subdued made them a poor financial risk because they would run away at the first opportunity, and they were dangerous because of their possible influence on other slaves. Such slaves would be likely to escape and then return as Union soldiers.

The majority of the slaves who remained on the plantations were by no means the loyally docile of Southern legend. Although they did not completely deny the Confederacy their labor by escaping, these slaves commonly engaged in work slowdowns. One of the main factors behind the drop in Confederate agricultural yields was the refusal of slaves to work as hard or as efficiently as they had before the war. A complaint from a South Carolina planter in 1862 was typical: "We have had hard work to get along this season, the Negroes are unwilling to do any work, no matter what it is."

By necessity, supervision of the rural slaves was in the hands of women, the old, the disabled, and slave foremen. Concerned primarily with its own safety, the skeletal white managerial force lacked the coercive presence of able-bodied white men as overseers to maintain prewar production levels. Slaves stayed out of the fields by claiming sickness; those that did work abused and neglected livestock and farm implements. One Texas woman lamented in a letter to her husband that the greatest problem were the "black wretches," who tried "all they can . . . to agrivate [sic] me, taking no interest, having no care about the future, neglecting their duty." Complaints of insubordination rivaled those of idleness. Control usually broke down competely when federal troops were known or rumored to be in the vicinity. After the Yankees had passed by his plantation, Mark Valentine, a Louisiana planter, told his neighbors that his slaves "will not even pretend to work and are very impudent." Despite entrusting some plantations entirely to slave drivers, the whites could find no antidote for the semistrike of the slaves.

The slaves were not passive during the war. Some one hundred thirty thousand fought in the Union armies, another half-million fled from bondage and entered Union lines, where they performed support services for the military, and countless others aided the Union by serving as scouts or spies or by withholding much of their labor on Confederate farms and plantations. Still, the myth of passivity remains, chiefly because the slaves did not revolt. Indeed, so relieved were Southern whites over the failure of the slaves to rise up and kill them that they convinced themselves that most blacks must have been loyal and contented.

Southern slavery did not produce contented subjects, but it did stunt the development of widespread, violent rebellion. Within the limits of community standards and the endurance of the slaves, the master's control was absolute, and it was reinforced by the policing functions of the white majorities that surrounded the black belts. After the war, Robert Falls explained

just how controlled and dominated the life of a slave had
been:

> If I had my life to live over again, I would die fighting rather
> than be a slave. . . . But in them days, us niggers didn't know no
> better. All we knowed was work, and hard work. . . . Old Master
> and Old Mistress would say, "Do this!" and we done it. And they
> say, "Come here!" and if we didn't come to them, they come to
> us. And they brought the bunch of switches with them.

Falls had to step outside of slavery before he could realize that
he should have been a rebel. His life had to be freed from the
dependence on his masters that was the ultimate means of internally regulating slavery.

However, even for the potential slave rebels, their isolation
and enforced ignorance precluded any planning for a general
revolt. Slaves did have a grapevine that spread information more
quickly than whites imagined, but the effectiveness of this in-
formal means of communication had definite limits. Many slaves
in regions untouched by the fighting knew nothing about emancipation until their ex-owners informed them at the end of the war.

In keeping the nature of the war hidden from many of their
slaves, the owners also engaged in a none-too-subtle form of
psychological warfare. "All I done was for de Rebels," recalled
a North Carolina freedman. "I was afraid of de Yankee 'cause
de Rebels had told us dat de Yankees would kill us. Dey told us
dat de Yankees would bore holes in our shoulders and work us
to carts." Some slaves, of course, saw through these scare tactics,
but others were hardly certain that in freeing themselves from
the Confederates they would not be acquiring a harsher set of
masters. The enlistment of black Union soldiers on the South
Carolina Sea Islands was nearly scuttled because the ex-slaves
remembered that their former masters had told them that the
Yankees would sell them into Cuban slavery. The blacks, as an
abolitionist worker observed, saw recruitment as a "trap to get
the able-bodied and send them to Cuba to sell."

The cynicism and brutality of many Union soldiers toward
blacks lent substance to the psychological ploys of Southern
whites. Captain Silas Canfield of the 21st Wisconsin Volunteers,
while stationed in northern Alabama in the summer of 1862,
noted that "slaves came to us bringing information of the enemy

far south of our lines, and expecting protection and freedom, to be greatly disappointed." What especially infuriated Canfield was the illicit slave trade within his regiment, a racket that consisted of extracting bribes from masters for the return of their fugitive slaves who had come into Union camps.

The military slave trade was suppressed by 1863, but blacks' distrust again would be aroused by the continued arrogance of many of the Yankee soldiers with whom they came into contact. When these soldiers ransacked plantations, they often pillaged and carried away property that the slaves regarded as their own. The resulting resentment became open hostility when blacks were exposed to overzealous Union recruitment officers. Freedmen were rounded up either by details of white soldiers or by their prospective white officers, whose commissions depended on their success in filling up their proposed black regiments. Abuses were common under a system that was tantamount to ruthless impressment. Reports of the use of torture and the shooting down of resisting blacks prompted Lincoln on more than one occasion to caution his commanders against forcing blacks into military service.

Despite the association of the Union cause with emancipation, most slaves were wary of rebelling in support of the Union and their own freedom. They had no reason to believe that the risk of Confederate retaliation would be counterbalanced by a meaningful freedom in a Union that had always oppressed their race, whether they were free or slave. And, for the most part, the behavior of the Union army reinforced the slave's pessimism regarding his future. A minority of slaves were even indifferent as to who won the war, reasoning as did some ex-slaves at Port Royal, South Carolina, that "the white man [will] do what he pleases with us." One slave, upon hearing of the Emancipation Proclamation, is reported to have said that he doubted whether the North would ever consent to arming of the blacks and to have explained his reasoning thus: "Ain' yo' nebber seen two dogs fighten over bone 'fo now . . . well den, yo' ain' nebber seen de bone fight none is you?"

Even more important in precluding slave revolts than the ambivalence of blacks toward the Union was their ambivalence toward Southern whites. Very few slaves were the contented

Sambos of proslavery legend, but a considerable number, undoubtedly a majority, could not bring themselves to murder
whites. This rather negative demonstration of affection was
directly related to the ending in 1808 of the African slave
trade that had produced by the time of the Civil War a generation of slaves who had never known freedom. The consequences
in black-white relations were momentous. The planters had to
provide a sufficiently high level of physical well-being to ensure
a continuing supply of slave labor through natural increase.
In contrast to other slave systems in the Western Hemisphere,
where fresh imports maintained the servile populations, only
American slavery was able to perpetuate itself through slave
births. However, the greater physical comfort of the American
slave was gained within a more closed social system. The
rebelliousness of the African-born slave, a key factor in slave
uprisings elsewhere, was absent in the American South. Also
lacking was a direct experience with life-styles and expectations independent of slavery as regulated or tolerated by the
master class.

There was a degree of black autonomy that was expressed in
the culture of the slave quarters, the resiliency of the nuclear
slave family, and the presence on nearly every plantation of
black spiritual leaders described by whites as witch doctors
or conjurers. Moreover, blacks maintained their dignity by
resisting slavery through work slowdowns and sabotage, such
as arson or the destruction of farm implements. Nonetheless,
although the culture of the slaves preserved a sense of collective
identity, embodied a yearning for freedom, and sustained acts
of individual resistance, it did not produce a revolutionary
consciousness.

Frederick Douglass pointed out that slavery "must not depend
upon mere force—the slave must know no higher law than his
master's will." Thus, what crippled the development of revolutionary resistance was not so much the harshness of slavery
as the extent to which blacks, in their dependence on whites,
found their lives and values intertwined with those of the master
class. On some plantations the slave children eagerly awaited
a visit to the "Great House." "They knew no better, of course,"
remembered a slave woman, "and seemed to love Marster and
Missus as much as they did their own mother and father.

Marster and Missus always used gentle means to get the children out of their way when they bothered them and the way the children loved and trusted them was a beautiful sight to see." Adult slaves often quarreled among themselves over the relative kindness or other merits of their masters, related Frederick Douglass, because "they seemed to think that the greatness of their masters was transferable to themselves."

What further stabilized the inherently volatile nature of slavery and partially bridged the abyss between the races were the gray areas of shared experiences and personal contacts. The black mammy who nursed the master's children, the slave children who were raised in the master's house, and the mulatto offspring fathered by the planter or his sons were daily reminders of the physical intimacy between the races. To be sure, the accommodations and contacts necessary for a peaceful commingling of the races were grossly one-sided and monopolized by the authority and standards of whites. But in living together the two races came to accept, or at least tolerate, a measure of humanity in the other. For whites this often meant little more than that they viewed blacks as a childlike race of servants, to be cajoled and protected. But for blacks it meant that whites, although a hated master class, should not be murdered in a rebellion if freedom could be gained nonviolently.

Finally, there is no reason to doubt that many slaves consciously decided not to revolt, because they believed that freedom was at hand. The very absence of a white coercive presence also functioned as an unintentional safety valve for slave discontent. Slave codes were relaxed during the last half of the war, not only because whites increasingly lacked the means to enforce them but also because white fears of an uprising had subsided. Consequently, slavery lost much of its rigidity and blacks were emboldened to roam off the plantations, avoid work, and in general test the limits of what was becoming quasi-freedom. Meanwhile, talk of real freedom was spreading through the slave quarters. Although some slaves were sealed off from such rumors, the majority probably sensed that emancipation was imminent. As one Union soldier put it after talking with some freedmen, "They had long known that something was going to happen."

That something was usually the liberating presence of a Union army, but at least a few slaves were aware that Southern whites were considering freedom, and possibly land, for those slaves willing to fight for the Confederacy. The mere broaching of this subject, regardless of the small number of slaves who were actually armed, was dramatic evidence to both races that slavery was doomed. In forgoing a violent overturn of a system that was slowly crumbling from both internal and external pressures, the slaves were acting neither as passive subjects nor as loyal Confederates. Instead they were behaving as conscious political agents who had decided not to subject the South to a blood bath in order to gain a goal already within their grasp.

AND STILL A BLACK MAN

The recognition by the Union and the Confederacy that they could not win the war without the assistance of blacks led to greater racial tolerance by whites on both sides. Based as it was, however, not on a concern with blacks as human beings to be integrated into American society but overwhelmingly on military criteria, this tolerance fell far short of a commitment to political and civil equality for blacks. Moreover, some whites admitted that their support of emancipation signaled no modification of their racial attitudes. A Maryland Unionist and ex-slaveholder, Samuel Harrison, confided in his war journal in 1864 that he had "always since early boy hood [sic] looked upon the negro as a debased creature, hardly human, in the exalted sense of humanity." Now that he had worked for the inclusion of emancipation in the new Maryland constitution, he admitted that "I have done so from no humanitarian or benevolent feelings towards [blacks]." As the treatment of black soldiers and freedmen by the federal government was to document, the intransigent racism of a Harrison was hardly atypical.

Discrimination against black soldiers took many forms, the most obvious of which was an initially lower pay scale. Until June, 1864, when Congress retroactively equalized military salaries, white privates were paid $13.00 a month and provided a clothing allowance of $3.50, whereas blacks received $10.00 a month and had $3.00 deducted in advance for clothing. Despite the bitter opposition of blacks and abolitionists and near mutiny in the black 55th Massachusetts Volunteers, the inequality persisted for over a year. As Lincoln explained in an interview with Frederick Douglass in the summer of 1863, lower pay for blacks was a "necessary concession" to popular prejudice until whites were shown proof that blacks were effective combat soldiers. For the same reason blacks also received no enlistment bounties until after June, 1864.

By 1865 blacks comprised about 10 per cent of the Union armies and nearly one-quarter of naval enlistments. But the number of their commissioned officers was never commensurate with the proportion of blacks in the military. Aside from chaplains, barely one hundred blacks were granted military commissions. Exclusion of blacks from leadership positions was a calculated policy designed to maintain the morale of the white soldiers. Career advancement for whites was linked to the combat use of blacks by reserving for whites the commissioned ranks in the new black regiments. The result was, as Horace Greeley observed, "There are few, if any, instances of a White sergeant or corporal whose dignity or whose nose revolted at the proximity of Blacks as private soldiers, if he might secure a lieutenancy by deeming them not unsavory, or not quite intolerably so."

White-supremacist attitudes were not necessarily softened with the enlistment of blacks but, rather, were channeled into militarily useful directions. Therefore, blacks could expect discriminatory treatment at the hands of their Union allies as well as their Confederate enemies. They were assigned to excessive fatigue details and garrisoned, whenever possible, in districts where the ranks of the white soldiers had been decimated by yellow fever and malaria. This unhealthy garrison duty, in combination with inadequate medical care that was inferior to that provided for whites, was a major contributor to a black mortality rate that was 40 per cent higher than that of white Union soldiers. Another factor was the refusal of many Confederates to treat captured black soldiers as prisoners of war. On more than one occasion blacks were wantonly murdered, the most notorious incident occurring in April, 1864, when the Confederates overran Fort Pillow, a Union outpost on the Mississippi River.

While 37 per cent of the black soldiers were dying during the war, the noncombatant freedmen in the Union camps were confronted with hardships and discrimination that resulted in an appalling amount of suffering. The camps into which freedmen were herded after they had crossed behind Union lines were condemned as charnel houses by most observers. In late 1863 James E. Yeatman, president of the Western Sanitary Commission, reported squalor and misery in all the camps in the Mississippi Valley, "At Natchez is a camp of twenty-one hundred freedmen, all in cabins which are without proper light and ventilation, overcrowded and most prolific sources of disease. Seventy-five had died in one day. I was informed that some had returned to their masters on account of the suffering."

Survival was frequently the most pressing problem for the freedmen. As noted by John Eaton, a military chaplain under Grant, the refugees from slavery encompassed "every stage of disease or decrepitude [and were] often nearly naked, with flesh torn by the terrible experiences of their escapes." The emergency medical care, food, and shelter that were provided were totally inadequate. "Thousands must die for want of medicines and medical attendance this winter," concluded Yeatman in his investigative report of 1863. The contributions of Northern benevolent societies notwithstanding, the mortality rate in the black refugee centers averaged no lower than 25 per cent during the war.

The failure of the Lincoln government to ease for blacks the transition from slavery to freedom resulted in part from the lack of a federal tradition of responsibility for individual social and economic welfare. The very concept of a federal relief agency empowered to intervene directly in social problems was foreign to a generation that accepted the Jacksonian equation of good government with the negation of power at the national level. The unprecedented and overwhelming magnitude of the South's social dislocation finally induced Congress in March, 1865, to pass a bill for a Bureau of Refugees, Freedmen, and Abandoned Lands. Created far too late to have been of any service to blacks freed during the war, and never supplied with adequate appropriations or strong leadership after the war, the Bureau was important more in setting a precedent than in actually relieving misery.

Quite apart from the conceptual and constitutional limits on federal authority, the plight of the freedmen was directly related to the priorities assigned by Lincoln and his commanders. Their primary concern in responding to the problem of the freedmen was how best to use ex-slaves in the Union war effort while calming white fears that hordes of blacks were on the brink of migrating northward.

On the surface, federal policy toward Southern blacks was simple enough by the spring of 1863. "That policy," explained General Halleck, Lincoln's chief military adviser, in a letter to Grant, "is to withdraw from the use of the enemy all the slaves you can, and to employ those so withdrawn to the best possible advantage against the enemy." An obvious corollary of this military approach to the dismantling of slavery was the recruitment of black soldiers, a move that demonstrated to many skeptical Northerners that emancipation would be a military and political asset to the Unionist cause.

But most freedmen, as a result of age, sex, or physical infirmities, were ineligible for combat duty. As they milled around the Union camps in a state of limbo, confused and impoverished, the black refugees were denounced as a threat to military efficiency. Their apparent helplessness confirmed for white supremacists the notion of an inferior race incapable of caring for itself. After citing the sickness "among the poor lazy blacks," a Union soldier wrote home from his army camp in Kentucky that the former slaves "are filling all the vacant houses and even sleeping under the trees, so anxious are they to get near 'de Lincoln soldiers.' They live on scraps and whatever they can pick up in camp and they will shine our shoes or do any camp work for an old shirt or cast-off coat." Lincoln, reacting to complaints from his commanders and to the sneers of the Democratic press that emancipation was a burden to the Union armies and to the blacks themselves, labeled the refugee problem in April, 1863, the "most difficult with which we have to deal."

The solution of the problem entailed a massive employment of the refugees within the South in whatever capacity promised useful service to the government. In practice, this meant imposition of forced-labor controls that differed little from open exploitation. Intended to relieve the government of the financial burden of supporting the refugees, as well as to demonstrate to critics of emancipation that blacks would work once freed, the controls also systematically and cheaply marshaled black labor into national service. In the infighting that erupted between the War and Treasury departments, the former claiming control over all civilian affairs within the occupied South as a matter of military necessity and the latter arguing that its own jurisdiction over abandoned plantations made it responsible for the freedmen, the military won out. The controls were usually administered through the War Department, and commanders were given wide latitude in using the refugees as military and agricultural laborers.

The stabilization of the contraband situation in the interest of greater military efficiency was the keystone of the Union army's program regarding the freedmen. Labor battalions of ex-slaves were formed to supplement, or in many cases replace, the employment of white soldiers in the commissary and quartermaster's departments. "There exists the greatest demand for their labor, and they are anxious to supply the demand," reported a correspondent of the *Philadelphia Christian Recorder,* after visiting a contraband camp at Fort Monroe, Virginia. "They are kept at Government quarters till employed—they do not have to wait long for this." As cooks, teamsters, stevedores, hospital attendants, woodchoppers, and laborers on fortifications, blacks were an indispensable adjunct to the Union military in the latter half of the war. They chopped the wood needed to fuel the gunboat flotillas on the Western rivers, built the breastworks that secured the Union enclaves, and raised the combat level of the armies by performing much of the heavy work and camp drudgery.

Not only was this labor physically exhausting and often dangerous because of exposure to Confederate raids, it was also underpaid and markedly exploited. The white soldiers, both the officer corps and the privates, could never quite divest themselves of the belief that they were doing the freedmen a favor by giving them an opportunity to work for wages. Indeed, most whites had to be convinced that blacks would be willing to work without compulsion. Representative of Northern opinion in this regard was a statement by John Murray Forbes, a wealthy Boston businessman. Before he visited the occupied

South Carolina Sea Islands in 1862, Forbes "used to think emancipation only another name for murder, fire and rape." A white private from Massachusetts was amazed when he saw former slaves working as stevedores at a Union naval base in Virginia; "they were at work as quietly and industriously as though they were men, and not 'miserable niggers!'" Owing to their negative preconceptions of the black character and because they interpreted black *free* labor as a threat to white supremacy, whites supervised the black military laborers with an arrogance that often shaded into brutality.

Although some whites in the military, especially the officers, were humane and just in their dealings with the freedmen, the typical attitude was contempt. In a pamphlet issued by the Emancipation League, a chaplain in the Western theater accused the privates of treating the ex-slaves "as savages and brutes." A reporter for the *New York Evening Post* described white behavior on the South Carolina Sea Islands as "some of the vilest and meanest exhibitions of human depravity that it has ever been my lot to witness. Many, very many of the soldiers, and not a few of the officers, have habitually treated the negroes with the coarsest and most brutal insolence and inhumanity."

One of the most galling forms of discrimination concerned the paying of the black laborers. Blacks frequently worked months without any compensation, and when the wages finally arrived, some commanders withheld them pending a decision on whether part of the funds should go to former masters. The wages that were issued were well below both what whites were paid for comparable work and what blacks could receive in the open market had their labor not been conscripted into the army. James Yeatman, in a study released in 1864, noted that in the Memphis, Tennessee, area the wages of blacks in government service were one-third to one-fifth of the prevailing market rate that blacks could command. Black firemen on steamboats refused to disembark at Memphis for fear that they would be seized and forced to labor on government installations at a reduction in wages of 75 per cent.

The bulk of the freedmen, however, did not work directly for the federal government as military laborers. Rather they were encouraged and, if that failed, forced to return to the planta-

tions as a cheap labor force for the production of cotton. Part
of the rationale for this policy, which was firmly decided upon
by the summer of 1863, was expressed by Lincoln in August
of that year: "The able bodied male contrabands are already
employed by the Army. But the rest are in confusion and
destitution. They better be set to digging their subsistence
out of the ground."

Aside from Lincoln's paternalistic assumption that whites
would have to be responsible for seeing that ex-slaves resumed
useful employment, pressing war-related needs prompted the
re-establishment of blacks as a rural work force. Returning the
blacks to the plantations freed the armies from the encumbrance
of a displaced class with no military value. At the same time,
Unionism within the South was strengthened by providing labor
to loyal planters. Where Unionism was negligible, Northern
entrepreneurs were more than willing to move in and lease
abandoned or confiscated plantations from the Treasury Department in the expectation of high profits from the war-inflated
prices of raw cotton. By redeploying blacks so as to maximize
the amount of Union-produced cotton coming out of the South,
Lincoln also ensured the continued support of the New England
textile manufacturers who were worried about the cotton
shortage.

With considerable justification, blacks viewed this labor program as a reimposition of the controls and restraints from which
they had just fled. Blacks found within Union lines who were
unfit for military duties were defined as "vagrants" and sent
back under military guard to work on the plantations. The
terms of their employment were regulated by annual contracts
that were drawn up in conferences between the federal commanders and the local planters. The contracts stipulated hours
and wages on a sliding scale according to age and sex and
permitted fines for any missed work and deductions for supplies,
clothing, and medical services advanced by the employer.

Designed to stabilize a tractable supply of cheap agricultural
labor, the contracts left few safeguards for the former slaves.
Exploitation was flagrant, and conditions on many of the leased
plantations approximated slavery at its worst. For the South-
ern-born lessees, slavery, however illegal, was still a psychological

and social reality; Northern speculators were characteristically denounced as camp followers and "army sharks," motivated only by the desire for quick profits. Blacks, even before the end of the war, were already all but trapped as a rural proletariat. Ironically, the responsibility for their plight rested more with the Union army than with their former masters.

Underlying the federal program regarding the freedmen was the assumption that the political needs of the Republican party and the racial stability of Northern society required containment of the blacks within the former slave states. On the eve of the Civil War, 95 per cent of American blacks lived in the slave states, and Northern whites were determined to keep them there. Northern attitudes toward blacks in 1862, as acidly summarized by Edward Dicey, consisted of "an equal desire to make an end of slavery, and to get rid of the Negro." Because emancipation had resulted from military necessity rather than from any radical transformation of racist public opinion, it ultimately could be reconciled with white supremacy only by a settled policy of keeping the freedmen out of the original free states. Lincoln had hoped to gain this objective through his colonization and emigration plans for blacks. Faced with the failure of this program by 1863, he turned to the alternative of preventing any sizable northward migration of Southern blacks. Political expediency and the intransigence of Northern racism had left him no other choice.

For a brief period in the fall of 1862, Union commanders at Cairo, Illinois, under authorization from the War Department, attempted to find private employment in Illinois for the surplus contraband population that had been funneled into Cairo, a river town at the southern tip of the state. But Illinois authorities immediately invoked the state's black exclusionary law and local communities resorted to physical intimidation to drive off the black refugees and to coerce prospective employers into shunning black labor. The War Department soon reversed its policy, but the Republican party had already been damaged. By exploiting the alleged dangers of "Africanization" and popular dissatisfaction with the military stalemate and Lincoln's suspension of the writ of habeas corpus, the Democrats regained control of Illinois politics in the state and congressional elections of 1862.

The white fears that had been so quickly galvanized in Illinois were widespread. In 1862 and 1863 sporadic racial violence directed against the employment of blacks broke out in Northern cities and throughout the Ohio Valley. The Ohio River was patrolled at several points to seal off an escape route for fugitive slaves. A regiment of Indiana soldiers, proclaiming that its "object in going to war was not to make Indiana an asylum for negroes," blocked a group of blacks from crossing the river in November, 1862.

The worst eruption of white violence occurred in New York City in July, 1863. A predominantly Irish, working-class mob, egged on by the Democratic press and panic-stricken at the thought of losing its unskilled jobs to an influx of blacks, savagely lashed out at the city's black population. Triggered by the recent federal conscription law, which permitted a wealthy American to buy his way out of the draft, the riot focused first on the draft-enrollment office and then became an antiblack pogrom. The city's Colored Orphan Asylum was looted and burned, and for four days blacks were the victims of murderous mob violence. An account of the riot, published in 1867 by the black author William Wells Brown, related that "every place known to employ negroes was searched: steamboats leaving the city, and railroad depots were watched, lest some should escape [the mob's] vengeance. . . . Blacks were chased to the docks, thrown into the river and drowned; while some, after being murdered, were hung to lamp-posts." Many blacks fled New York in terror, as reflected by the 20 per cent drop in the city's black population between 1860 and 1865. Estimates of the casualties in the riot, which was finally quelled by calling in combat-hardened army units, ran as high as one thousand.

Avoidance of such explosions of white hatred was an explicit objective of the program worked out by the Lincoln government after emancipation. In deciding upon a massive mobilization of the ex-slaves behind the war effort, Lincoln and his commanders rejected the option of encouraging blacks to move northward and thereby ease the labor shortages in the Northern economy. Lorenzo Thomas, the adjutant general responsible for raising black troops and organizing black labor in the lower Mississippi Valley beginning in the spring of 1863, made it clear that his mission was one of containment. Before leaving for the South, he told Secretary of War Edwin Stanton that "it will not do to send [black refugees] in numbers into the free states, for the prejudices of the people of those States are against such a measure, and some of the states have enacted laws against the reception of free negroes."

The guidelines set down by Thomas reinforced and regularized the tendencies of most Union commanders to employ the contraband blacks within the South. Occasional deviations, such as Grant's authorization in January, 1863, for the transporting of some blacks to Ohio under the care of an Ohio philanthropist, were countermanded. Only a trickle of ex-slaves entered the North. Most came as laborers consigned to military installations and as the servants of loyal Southerners or Northern military personnel. The majority of blacks probably had no desire to leave the South and most certainly lacked the means of financing any migration to the North. Nonetheless, black immobilization was guaranteed through the systematic denial of transportation passes by the Union military and the herding back onto the plantations of the militarily surplus freedmen.

In their relief over the lack of any sizable black migration to the North, most Northerners overlooked the deliberate federal policy of containment. Instead, they saw in the fixed position of Southern blacks confirmation of the prevalent racial notion that blacks were inherently fit to live and prosper only in a tropical or semitropical climate. "In the Northern Hemisphere, the Negro is an exotic, and does not flourish except under an artificial system," explained Edward Diccy, as he repeated a popular racial axiom that had been intellectualized by nineteenth century anthropologists. This belief in a climatically ordained restriction of black mobility was immensely comforting to Northerners because it enabled them to reconcile emancipation with the continuation of white supremacy. As the moderately antislavery *New York Tribune* assured its readers in 1862, white nationalism apparently could be maintained even without expatriation of freed slaves.

> . . . the negro race, wherever free, will gradually migrate southward, colonizing the less populous West Indies, Central America, and the adjacent portions of South America. . . . Climate, soil,

natural products, ease of obtaining a rude yet ample subsistence, and the ready fraternisation of blacks with the Indian and mongrel races who now exist in those regions, and who are nowise above our Southern negroes in the social scale, not even in their own opinion, will all attract them that way.

Carried to its logical conclusion, the specious thermal law of nature also promised the elimination from America of a race whose presence was an embarrassment to whites and whose treatment was a standing contradiction of the nation's ideals. Most white Americans, regardless of their stand on slavery or the Union, interpreted emancipation as a death knell for the black race. Samuel Gridley Howe, a noted philanthropist and abolitionist from Massachusetts, was certain that emancipation would "allow fair play to natural laws, by the operation of which . . . the colored population will disappear from the Northern and Middle States, if not from the continent, before the more vigorous and prolific race." Mary Jones of Georgia, a diehard Confederate and the wife of a planter, put the matter more bluntly: "with their emancipation must come their extermination."

Survival in a free society was equated with ambition, enterprise, and the desire to work, attributes that white Americans dogmatically insisted were deficient in the black character. Therefore, by viewing the end of slavery as the removal of a paternalistic institution that, for all its brutality, had artificially encouraged and fostered a growth of black population, whites could convince themselves that the end of the black race itself in America was not far off. It was confidently predicted that blacks, now bereft of the protection and services of their masters, would gradually die off, the helpless victims of their own inability to compete as free agents with the more energetic whites in a temperate climate. Blacks would be no more able to compete with whites in North America than Indians were. "To leave the negro to himself, and put him in competition with the white man," declared Senator Edgar Cowan of Pennsylvania, "is to destroy him as effectually as our civilization has destroyed the red man of the forest."

The war had destroyed slavery, but white racial attitudes

remained all but frozen. Whether as Unionists or Confederates, soldiers or laborers, blacks were continually reminded that the war had not affected the stigma attached to the color of their skins. Freedom was about to become a reality for all blacks, but not acceptance in white America. Prophetically for race relations in America, even the limited nature of this freedom owed much to the white belief that, in freeing the slave, the nation was ridding itself of the black man.

5

Lincoln's Republic

The restructured Union had to balance the hatred and bitterness of the South against the exultation and power of the North. These tensions were never resolved, only sublimated at the expense of the blacks. The conversion of the nation into an urban, industrial society was advanced by both the war legislation of the Republicans and the removal of the divisive slavery issue. Above all, the sources of credit, organization, and mobilization spawned by the war effort were to expand opportunities for the middle-class aspirations that had fueled so much of the original Republican crusade. Although Northerners quickly began to delude themselves with the myth that the Civil War was a glorious struggle to end slavery, the treatment of the freedmen during and after the war revealed that, if the war had wrought any revolution, the chief beneficiaries were the Northern bourgeoisie, not the ex-slaves.

THE VICTORIOUS NORTH

The North emerged from the war in an expansive, self-confident mood. Plantation slavery had been removed as an obstacle to national unity, and an integrated home market, far larger than any counterpart in Europe, had been ensured. The economy appeared to be strengthened during the war, and Lincoln could proclaim to Congress in December, 1864, "Material resources are now more complete and abundant than ever." Stimulated by wartime demands for its products, both at home and abroad, and aided by national legislation that expanded the economic functions of the federal government, the economy had begun a marked shift from a predominantly agrarian and entrepreneurial base to a maturing condition of industrial capitalism.

Most Northerners either prospered or held their own during the war. The total nature of the conflict mobilized all the productive energies of Northern society until, as even staunch Confederates such as the Reverend Charles C. Jones of Georgia were forced to admit, "The whole old United States is one workshop of war. The war gives the masses their daily bread and rolls up fortunes for thousands. It is to them now the great pursuit for support and fame, and their furor runs in this channel." The resulting prosperity was sufficiently widespread to sustain both the fortunes of the Republican party and the initial Union consensus behind the war effort.

It was by no means a foregone conclusion that the Northern economy would be able to meet the demands of a total war. Agriculture was one sector that was threatened with severe dislocations. The outbreak of war shut down the Mississippi River trade, which had siphoned off much of the agricultural surpluses of the Midwest. Although the establishment of rail communications with the East had reduced the relative importance of this trade for the Midwest, immense quantities of foodstuffs continued to be shipped downriver in the 1850's. The upper Mississippi Valley annually marketed 10 million bushels of grain, including flour, and one-third to one-half of its pork through New Orleans. The blocking of this natural trade outlet produced a sharp recession in the Midwestern agricultural economy that persisted until the summer of 1862.

The potential agricultural depression that had existed in 1861 gave way to prosperity in the latter half of the war. The annual wholesale price index of farm products, which had stood at 77 in 1860 and climbed to 86 by the end of 1862, peaked at 162 in 1864. Military demand and war-induced shortages contributed to part of the turnabout. Purchases by the army quartermasters had driven up the price of hay after 1861, and sales ran between $25 and $35 a ton, almost triple the prewar price. The scarcity of cotton and military orders of wool for army uniforms created a boom in the sheep industry. As the price of coarse wool more than doubled, farmers responded by enlarging their sheep herds and tripling their output of wool.

Overshadowing the domestic market as a stimulant to agricultural prosperity was a huge increase in foreign demand. Triggered by crop failures in England between 1860 and 1862, and generally poor harvests throughout Europe in the same two years, this demand absorbed most of the North's agricultural surpluses. Whereas American wheat exports had averaged about 20 million bushels annually in the 1850's, 60 million bushels were shipped abroad in the second year of the war. Higher prices, coupled with greater demands, raised the total value of exports of pork, beef, corn, and wheat products from $28 million in 1860 to $128 million by 1863. The demand had slackened after 1863, but U.S. agricultural exports still totaled $82 million in 1865.

Not only had the loss of the Southern market been more than compensated, but, also, England was more firmly riveted to the Union cause than at the outbreak of the war. Although it would be an oversimplification to argue that King Wheat had replaced King Cotton in the policy considerations of the British, the wheat that flowed into England in return for munitions was solid proof that the Union had more to offer England than the Confederacy had. English cotton-textile interests had a large backlog of raw cotton, which they tapped while new sources of supply were being developed in India. While England was discovering that its economy could survive without Confederate cotton, Union wheat served as the chief means of exchange for British exports of munitions to the Union. This trade declined sharply after 1863, but by then the British already had made an irrevocable decision not to intervene. Confederate ships and privateers were destroying enough of the Union merchant marine to re-establish British supremacy in the Atlantic trade, and the Northern navy was striving to enforce the maritime demands that Britain traditionally had asserted.

The ability of Northern agriculture to produce huge surpluses during the war that could influence foreign policy was remarkable in light of the drain on rural manpower by the Union armies. At least half of the farm families contributed men to the armed services, and in some states as many as one-third of the farm laborers went off to war. A home missionary in the Midwest reported in 1862 that "the drain of young and able-bodied men to meet the demands of the army has left farmers very much in need of help, and great difficulty has been felt in securing the crops properly."

To relieve this labor shortage, women assumed much of the work load. Along with the men who were left on the farms, they were able to maintain agricultural output because of the widespread introduction of farm machinery. By creating a need for labor-saving devices, the war accelerated the rate of agricultural mechanization. The advantages of using a horse-drawn mower that could cut a field of hay ten times faster than a man with a scythe were manifest when labor was scarce and hay was fetching war-inflated prices. The conversion from hand power to animal power is evidenced by the tripling of the amount of agricultural machinery on Northern farms between 1860 and 1865, and by the 13 per cent rise in productivity per farm worker in the 1860's, an increase surpassed in only one other decade in the nineteenth century.

At the start of the war, Northern businessmen had had no more reason to be optimistic than the commercial farmers. The bid for Southern independence had meant at least a temporary loss of a home market that the *Philadelphia Press* estimated was "of as great value annually to the free States as that of the Union is to all Europe, Asia, and South America." Commercial towns in the Ohio Valley feared depression and social unrest if their Southern trade were cut off. So grave was the economic threat that most major businessmen opposed policies that pointed toward war. In particular, those businessmen who were directly dependent on the slave economy, either through providing the Southern market with goods or services or through marketing or manufacturing cotton products, were understandably in favor of a compromise in 1860–61. Any compromise favored by the leaders of Northern capitalism was ruled out because the majority of Republicans, America's rising bourgeoisie of farmers, smaller entrepreneurs, and mechanics with a vision of themselves as employers, wanted to protect themselves against slave competition by denying slavery room to expand.

Initially, the fears of the business leaders were realized. Secession resulted in the repudiation by the South of some $300 million in debts owed to Northerners and in the sequestration by the Confederate government of all property belonging to alien enemies. Retrenchment and uncertainty gripped the Northern economy as businessmen waited to determine what impact the war would have. Retail sales and manufacturing production fell off, and economic activity, reported the *New York Tribune* in March, 1861, seemed "checked and chilled by vague apprehensions, which find no relief as yet." In the first year of the war nearly 6,000 Northern commercial firms failed, some 2,000 more than had gone under in the panic year of 1857. Only an influx of European gold in payment for grain exports prevented a general suspension of banking.

Business recovery, while uneven and of less than boom proportions, was nonetheless dramatic. In March, 1865, the New York *Sun* editorialized, "There never was a time in the history of New York when business prosperity was more general, when the demand for goods was greater, and payments were prompt, than within the last two or three years." The prosperity of New York, the mercantile and financial center of the Union, was shared by the manufacturing and commercial regions in the interior. Northern cities and larger towns grew rapidly, as labor was drawn off the countryside to work in the war industries. A sharp rise in both the number of individual bank depositors and the value of their deposits reflected an increase in disposable income.

Military demand was the immediate stimulant to the economic resurgence that set in by 1863. Arming, clothing, feeding, and transporting the 2.3 million men that were eventually mobilized into the Union armies required the procurement and distribution of supplies on an unprecedented scale. Besides the constant need for food and munitions, the soldiers had to be resupplied continuously with shoes, which wore out in two months, and uniforms, which lasted about four months. The civilian staff of the Quartermaster's Department ballooned from 890 men to 130,000 as an army of civil servants had to be created to coordinate the flood of provisions and to settle military accounts.

Production increases were greatest in those industries directly concerned with the logistical support of the armies. The military market accelerated the growth and consolidation of the meat-packing industry. Chicago, in more than tripling its output of packed hogs, far outstripped its previous rivals in the Mississippi and Ohio valleys, whose livestock sources and distribution outlets were disrupted by the war. That city's postwar hegemony in meat packing was ensured by the establishment of the Union Stock Yards, the largest cattle yards in the world. To the east, in the mining and manufacturing valleys of Pennsylvania, the North's prewar nucleus of heavy industry was expanded. Production of the pig iron essential for the booming armaments industry reached new highs in 1864, and its price had more than doubled since 1860. Similar gains in output and profits were registered in mining. Anthracite from Pennsylvania and iron ore from upper Michigan fueled the growing complex of rolling mills around Pittsburgh and in the Schuylkill and Lehigh valleys of eastern Pennsylvania.

The woolens, ready-made–clothing, and shoe industries enjoyed spectacular profits. The scarcity of cotton, coupled with military demand for uniforms and blankets, tripled the dividend rates of woolen textile firms. At the height of the war the mills were consuming twice as much raw wool as in 1860. Much of their output went into ready-made clothing, especially for the military. Clothing as well as shoe manufacturers were able to cope with a labor shortage, cut costs, and standardize production by relying more heavily on labor-saving machinery. The adoption of the Howe and the McKay sewing machines, the latter a mechanical device for sewing uppers to soles in shoe production, accelerated the shift in both industries from household manufacturing to the factory system.

Although new track construction during the war was but 40 per cent of the yearly averages in the 1850's, the Union railroads prospered. They had been built in anticipation of future demand and now, for the first time, their full carrying capacity was utilized. As the major trunk lines doubled their freight tonnage, passenger miles, and rolling stock, profits and stock values rose accordingly. A leading journal of the industry, the *Railroad Record,* observed that "the year 1862 will ever be remembered as one of the most prosperous that has ever been known. The railroads never earned so much in the whole course of their existence as they have during this much-dreaded year." Competition was keen, and freight rates generally declined, but the volume of traffic was so great that the first substantial earnings and stock dividends of many lines came as products of the war years. Lines that controlled key links in the flow of east-west traffic, such as the Erie and the Pennsylvania, and those that dominated the north-south supply routes of Union armies, such as the Illinois Central and the Louisville and Nashville, generated enough income to begin modernizing their equipment and preparing for postwar expansion. A major step toward consolidation during the war was taken by the Pennsylvania Railroad when it acquired the Pittsburgh, Fort Wayne and Chicago Railroad, thereby completing the first through trunk line between Chicago and the Atlantic Coast.

However dramatic was the recovery from the near-panic conditions of 1861, the extent of wartime prosperity and economic growth can be exaggerated. The index of manufacturing production showed only slight gains, rising from 16 in 1860 to 18 1864 and then dropping back to 17 in 1865. A major industry, the merchant marine, received a crippling blow from which it never recovered: The number of American ships decreased by five thousand during the war and the volume of American shipping by 60 per cent, as a result of Confederate depredations and the transfer of ships to foreign registry in an effort to escape Confederate raiders. In other industries, war-inflated prices increased profits while actual production was declining. For example, the output of Northern cotton mills was down sharply from prewar levels, yet Amos Lawrence, a cotton-textile magnate, wrote a friend in the spring of 1864 that business was "better than ever." Pepperell, a large, established mill, multiplied its prewar profits sixfold.

Moreover, business prosperity did not extend to labor. There was nearly full employment, and skilled labor probably held its own, but the average worker experienced a drop in real income. Wages rose but not as fast as prices. From an 1860 base figure of

100, real wages in the North steadily fell to 83 in 1864 before rebounding to 87 in 1865. Economic discontent was partially defused by the success of skilled labor in resorting to trade unionism and strikes in order to protect its position. However, most workers, unskilled and divided by sex, nationality, and religion were insufficiently organized to mount any effective protest actions. One-quarter of the nonagricultural work force was women in desperate need of wages to supplement family income while their husbands were away fighting.

Nonetheless, despite the burdens placed on them, laborers remained loyal to the war effort. As a group, only professionals contributed a higher proportion of their numbers to the Union armies. The source of this loyalty lay in the identification by labor of the Unionist cause as an effort to achieve the victory of free-labor principles over the hereditary caste system of compulsory, bonded labor for which the Confederacy was struggling. Even in 1864, when the Lincoln government began using federal troops to smash strikes in the war industries, labor leaders held back from provoking a major confrontation. In citing these antilabor actions, William Sylvis, president of the Molders' Union, explained in January, 1865, "In ordinary times a collision would have been inevitable. Nothing but the patient patriotism of the people, and their desire in no way to embarrass the government, prevent it."

The uneven economic development and the failure of labor to keep pace with the cost of living were two factors limiting Northern prosperity. Also, the fact that so much of the North's manpower was employed in a nonproductive, military capacity was bound to have a dampening effect on the economy. Thus, it is not surprising that the economic growth rate, as measured by commodity output, was only 23 per cent in the Civil War decade as opposed to rates of 60 per cent or higher in the 1850's and 1870's. However, given the disruption and devastation of the war, the ability of the economy to sustain substantial growth in the 1860's was remarkable, and the postwar decade from 1865 to 1875 registered significant gains over the 1850's, in both absolute and relative terms, in such important indicators as railroad-track construction and pig iron and bituminous-coal production.

Production statistics alone cannot measure the economic impact of the war. The political nationalism that the Union was fighting to establish had as its counterpart institutional changes in the nation's political economy. In effect, the federal government underwrote a shift of ideological, economic, and political power from the laissez-faire agrarians of antebellum America to the industrial capitalists who would dominate the postwar United States. These changes presaged and largely explained the direction, scope, and control of economic development both during and after the war.

The Republican war Congresses, aware of the need to restructure the economy to meet the demands of total war, enacted one of the most sweeping economic reform programs in American history. In order to finance the first of the modern mass wars, the Republicans learned that they would have to create additional purchasing power through the issuance of greenbacks, non-interest-bearing Treasury notes acceptable as legal tender for all debts, private and public. The need for greenbacks became imperative by the winter of 1861–62. The leading Eastern bankers, worried over their dwindling gold reserves and the projected deficits in the federal budget, suspended specie payments in December, 1861. Confronted with insufficient revenue from customs duties and internal taxation, unable to market its securities successfully because the banking market for them was surfeited, and unwilling to let private bankers reap the profits of issuing irredeemable bank notes, the federal government responded to the financial crisis by passing the First Legal Tender Act in February, 1862. Subsequently, one-sixth of the cost of the war was met by issuing some $431 million in greenbacks.

Of more significance than their immediate value as a source of war finance was the effect of greenbacks on the bond market. By simultaneously raising purchasing power and contributing to inflation, the greenbacks created the conditions under which government bonds could be sold at par. During the latter half of the war, bond purchases were no longer a prerogative of the banking elite but, as the success of Jay Cooke's marketing organization revealed, a means by which the average Northerner could identify emotionally and financially with the Unionist cause. More than 60 per cent of Union war revenue came from the sale of bonds, and these bonds were the chief item in the huge increase in the per capita debt of the federal government from $2.06 in 1860 to $75.01 in 1865. In gross figures the public debt had risen to $2.6 billion, an immense capital fund that provided a credit base for industrial expansion. Thus, both as a form of cheap credit to entrepreneurs and as a stimulant to the successful financing of the war, the greenbacks had accelerated industrial development.

In addition to creating more currency, the Republicans stabilized the nation's money through the reorganization and rationalization of the banking system. Before the passage of the National Banking Act in 1863, banks were chartered and regulated under a hodgepodge of state laws. The existence by 1863 of 1,600 state banks of issue with about 12,000 different kinds of bank notes in circulation was ample evidence of the lack of uniformity. Much of this paper currency was unsound because it was not backed by adequate reserves and none of it was acceptable as legal payment to the national government. The strains of coping with, first, the outbreak of war and, then, the upsurge in economic activity accentuated the weaknesses of the state banks. The collapse of many banks in the Midwest and the Border states early in the war was followed by a flood of new, and often unsecured, bank notes in 1862 and 1863.

Intent on widening the market for government loans and providing for "circulation of notes bearing a common impression and authenticated by a common authority," Secretary of the Treasury Salmon Chase pushed for a national bank system that was approved by Congress in 1863. The system astutely balanced private interests with the needs of the federal government, a mutually profitable arrangement that was the hallmark of the Republicans' economic nationalism. The National Bank Act created a system of federally chartered banks that were divided into three categories, depending upon the population of the area they served. Member banks—whether in the country, in the designated reserve cities, or in the central reserve city of New York—had to accept exclusive federal supervision, meet specie and capital requirements, and agree to issue notes only against federal bonds. In return, bankers were promised stability and the dual profits from the interest on their government bonds, which had to be deposited with the Treasury, and from the lending of their bank notes.

Eastern bankers, who already controlled credit resources through their sound and profitable network of banks in the Northeast, had to be won over to the new system. They were placated by the redeposit provisions of the national system, which permitted reserves to be pyramided from the smaller country banks up through the central reserve banks in New York. In this manner 40 per cent of the reserves of the entire system were concentrated in New York, ensuring its financiers continual dominance of the national money market. In effect, New York bankers had the advantages of a central bank with none of the responsibilities. All national bankers were rewarded with the elimination of the wildcat banks that had proliferated under the various state laws. The number of state banks dropped rapidly even before Congress slapped a 10 per cent tax on state bank notes in 1865, which virtually destroyed any banking outside of the national system.

Beyond enlarging and stabilizing the capital fund available for industrial development, the Republicans provided specific economic services in the form of tariff protection and subsidies for railroads. First exploiting the need for increased government revenues and then resorting to the argument that industry was entitled to compensation for wartime taxes on manufactured goods, the protectionists pushed up the average tariff rates from 19 per cent to about 47 per cent at the end of the war. In reversing the drift of the 1840's and 1850's toward lower tariffs, the Republicans gave Northern factory owners a virtual monopoly in the domestic market. The tariff wall, in combination with the issuance of greenbacks, was of particular value to newer, undercapitalized industries such as iron manufacturing. Ironmasters, hampered by a lack of investment capital and unable to compete with British manufacturers of high-grade iron products before the war, turned to the federal government for the currency inflation and protection that enabled them to expand their output and gradually come to dominate the American market.

After steady growth during the war, pig iron production more

than doubled between 1865 and 1873, a boom that was geared
to the expansion of a railroad industry subsidized by the Republicans. Although the precedent of land grants to railroads
from the public domain had been set in 1850 in the charter of
the Illinois Central Railroad, sectional bickerings and Southern opposition to federally assisted internal improvements had
stalled any large-scale commitments. The break-through came in
July, 1862, with the chartering by Congress of two corporations,
the Union Pacific and Central Pacific railroads. These federal
charters underwrote railroad development militarily and economically. Protection from Indian attacks was provided, alternate
plots of public land on either side of the right-of-way were
granted, and national credit was pledged through the loan of
bonds. European investors, lured by the prospect of land
ownership, added their capital to that lent by the federal
government to the railroads.

The four land-grant railroads that were eventually chartered
by Congress were allotted, until outright subsidies were stopped
in 1873, 155 million acres of land (94 million of which were
actually patented) and $64 million in government-backed credit.
There was certainly much waste in the Republicans' lavish use
of public resources, but federal largess did speed up the development of a transcontinental common market by at least a decade.
Built between the Mississippi and the Pacific through unsettled
territory, the land grant railroads preceded the formation of the
markets they were designed to serve. However, as consumers
of heavy industrial products and as market outlets for commercial agriculture in the Great Plains, the railroads proved to
be a sound venture in government-supported capitalism. Not only
did the entire economy benefit, but the federal government also
profited from the railroad charters. The alternate strips of land
retained by the government rose in value as the railroads opened
up areas, and until 1940 government freight received a 50 per
cent discount from the land-grant railroads.

The positive liberalism of the Republicans was justified as a
program that furthered the interests of all classes. The public
domain was used to subsidize agriculture and public education
as well as the railroads. The Homestead Act of 1862 granted
160 acres of unoccupied public land to citizens who would live

on the land for five consecutive years. Despite the agrarian idealism of its backers, the act was often subsequently administered in such a way as to rationalize the interests of speculators and land monopolists. Nonetheless, the act did accelerate the spread of family farms throughout the trans-Mississippi West. During the war some twenty-seven thousand homestead entries were registered, and more than half of the homesteaders took title after five years. The Morrill Act of 1862 allotted those states that established public agricultural colleges thirty thousand acres for each of their congressmen. Representing an endowment equivalent to $10 million in the free states alone, the act signaled the first major effort by the federal government to underwrite higher education. In the long run this legislation probably yielded a larger social return than the Homestead Act. The diffusion of public education was stimulated, and specialized agricultural research was developed that would result in greater farm productivity in the twentieth century.

Labor benefited the least from the new political economy. Rather than receiving subsidies from the federal government, labor was confronted with a drop in real wages attributable to both the inflationary impact of greenbacks and the imposition of heavy taxes and import duties that diverted resources to the war effort and thereby raised the cost of goods and services for consumers. Responding to the wartime labor shortages and to the widespread, but erroneous, assumption that the Homestead Act would function as a safety valve for Eastern labor, the Republican Congress catered to business demands in 1864 by establishing an Immigration Bureau and legalizing the importation of cheap contract labor from Europe and China. Government intervention on behalf of capital was most evident when martial law and federal troops were used to break strikes at the R. P. Parrott Works in Cold Spring, New York, a production center for heavy military ordnance, and in Saint Louis and Louisville, two hubs of the gunboat traffic on the Western rivers.

The political economy of the Republicans, despite its one-sidedness, was based on free labor, and for this reason labor would continue to support the Republicans. Believing that the Union represented the world's greatest political democracy, and understanding that its preservation meant the destruction of slavery (a labor system described by trade unionists as inherently antagonistic to free labor), Northern workers usually submerged their immediate class interests in their loyalty to the war effort. Although oppressed by starvation wages, the Cincinnati seamstresses who petitioned Lincoln to be paid directly for their work rather than through subcontracting clothing merchants stressed, "We are in no way actuated by a spirit of faction, but desirous of aiding the best government on earth, and at the same time securing justice to the humble laborer." By the end of the war the mood of labor was less deferential. Speaking for trade unionists, Ira Steward, a leader of the Machinists' and Blacksmiths' International Union, proclaimed in November, 1865, that labor would "bear with patient endurance the burden of the public debt," but "we . . . want it to be known that the workingmen of America will in future claim a more [nearly] equal share in the wealth their industry creates in peace and a more [nearly] equal participation in the privileges and blessings of those free institutions, defended by their manhood."

Labor was prepared to be militant after the war, and a spate of labor reform parties would be formed. But, aside from token acceptance by Republicans of the movement for an eight-hour day, labor's demands would continue to be frustrated; the imbalance of the political economy in favor of capital was too great to be overcome. When the Republicans had redefined the relationship of the federal government to the economy, they assumed they were acting in the best interests of all the people. They justified the new institutional arrangements with the egalitarian rhetoric of democratic capitalism. Yet, often being entrepreneurs themselves, they approached political economy and the needs of the people from the perspective of the emerging elite of promoters and manufacturers who had benefited directly from wartime legislation. Thus, however unwittingly, the Republicans, in striking down the slave oligarchy, had laid the foundations for a new industrial oligarchy.

THE BURDEN OF DEFEAT

In blinding contrast to the North, the South emerged from the war defeated and impoverished. Both races were crushed by the burden of defeat. Even before the war ended, the problems of rebuilding the economy and restructuring race relations had been pressing. Yet the generation of Southerners who had fought the war, or had been freed by it, would not live to see full economic recovery or the beginnings of a racial ethos not grounded in the forced subjugation of blacks. The postwar Southern economy in the remainder of the nineteenth century was as severely crippled by the lack of productive capital as race relations were by the debilitating legacy of slavery.

The condition of the South in 1865 was a grim witness to the resolve of the Confederacy. The sheer physical damage to the economy was staggering. In the single blow of emancipation, the South had suffered the greatest act of confiscation in American history. The value of slaves at the start of the war had exceeded $1.5 billion, easily the largest capital investment in the nation. Still, exclusive of slaves, Southern wealth had shrunk by 43 per cent as a result of the war. The hardest-hit sector was agriculture, which had been neglected by Confederate authorities, subjected to heavy direct taxes and impressment, and exposed to Union raids. The desolation in an area fought over by the armies was described by W. L. Nugent of Mississippi in early 1864, when he noted of the region north of Jackson, "The largest plantations are thinning out, grown up in weeds & pastured upon by a few scattering cattle; fences are pulled down & destroyed; houses burned; Negroes run off. A general gloom pervades everything." This was the war damage encapsulated in the statistics that show that the assessed value of Southern real estate was cut in half and the number of livestock dropped by one-third between 1860 and 1870. Comparable losses were registered in the value of agricultural implements; the Southern share of the national total fell from one-third on the eve of the war to just over 13 per cent in 1870.

The full cost of the losses to Southern agriculture can be measured by the slowness of its recovery. Although the output of cotton and corn, the South's two major crops, surpassed its prewar level by 1880, the total values of farms, farm products, and livestock in the eight older states of the Confederacy did not recover to their 1860 levels until 1900. Only the newer states, Arkansas, Florida, and Texas, were able to increase their prewar agricultural capital and values in the generation after the war. In the meantime, the 1860 value of Northern farms had more than doubled by 1900.

Southern industry, although nearly as badly crippled as agriculture by 1865, was in a better position to recover. Industrial development had been force-fed during the war as a result of the heavy military demand for manufactured products and the blockade, which sharply restricted the importation of finished goods. Confederate businessmen were hampered by a number of problems, such as competition with government bureaus for raw materials, the unsettling effects of conscription regulations, and the rapid drop in the real value of money, but they enjoyed high profits because of the lag between the increases in wages and prices. The cost of living rose approximately thirtyfold between 1861 and 1865, whereas wages rose only tenfold. Although the Confederacy always suffered a shortage of skilled labor, especially machinists and metalworkers, an ample supply of unskilled labor was available. Attracted by cash wages that were quite high by prewar standards, and forced to add to their income in a time of inflation, many rural families entered the industrial work force for the first time. The lure of high returns, coupled with the shrinkage of the cotton export market, also induced more planters to sell or rent out slaves to mills, factories, and railroads.

Despite an absolute increase in industrial resources and output and the prosperity of businessmen as a class, Confederate industrialization could not serve as a springboard for the postwar economic development of the South. Much of the prosperity was based on inflationary paper profits and the hothouse effect of special wartime conditions. Directed and controlled by the military, the industrialization effort had demanded sacrifices bearable only in the context of the intense patriotism of most Confederates. Labor had complained that it was being driven to the point of destitution, and bread riots had broken out, but massive unrest had been avoided because the work force had been willing to accept a lower standard of living before it would destroy from within the Southern bid for independence. With the defeat of the Confederacy and the removal of wartime patriotism as a control mechanism, Southern labor would no longer be so willing to subsidize high business profits. Exploitation would continue, but not as flagrantly as during the war years.

In addition, most of the expanded industrial base of the Confederacy was gutted by the end of the war. Railroads and factories had been singled out as military targets by Union raiders. In two of the most extensive raids, the march of Sherman through Georgia and the Carolinas in the fall and winter of 1864–65 and the cavalry incursion of General James Wilson through Alabama and Georgia in the spring of 1865, the previously untouched munitions and rail complex of the interior Confederacy had been smashed. As Sherman's army had moved south from Atlanta, Oliver O. Howard, commander of the Army of the Tennessee, recalled, "wrecked engines, bent and twisted iron rails, blackened ruins and lonesome chimneys saddened the hearts of the few peaceful citizens who remained there." The destruction of rails had been refined to an art by Sherman's soldiers. Special work details had been assigned to uproot and heat the rails and then twist them into the shape of a doughnut. It was estimated that one thousand men could destroy 5 miles of track per day, and Sherman reported that about 300 miles of track had been obliterated during his campaign.

Nonetheless, the greatest success of Sherman's march lay in its devastating impact on Confederate morale. For all the notoriety of the march as an exercise in the terror tactics of psychological warfare, the heaviest blow to Confederate industry had been struck by the cavalry columns of General Wilson. Advancing down the valleys of the Black Warrior and Cahaba rivers and then swinging eastward across central Alabama into Georgia, Wilson's raiders had wrecked the last significant centers of Confederate industry and their rail network. The equipment of three railroads, the Montgomery and West Point, the Alabama and Florida, and the Mobile and Girard, had been almost totally destroyed. Selma, Alabama, and Columbus, Georgia, had been eliminated as factors in the war-making potential of the Confederacy. The destruction in Columbus, as summarized by Wilson in his report, had consisted of "15 locomotives, 250 cars, the railroad bridge and foot bridges, 115,000 bales of cotton, four cotton factories, the navy yard, foundry, armory, sword and pistol factory, accouterment shops, three paper mills, over 100,000 rounds of artillery ammunition, besides immense stores of which no account could be taken."

The very thoroughness of the Union armies created favorable conditions for the rehabilitation of Southern industry after the war. Cities had to be rebuilt, production centers for consumer goods and agricultural implements had to be established, and a new rail network had to be laid down while what was left of the old one was refurbished. Atlanta, Charleston, and Richmond experienced building booms, and as early as the end of 1865 the track mileage of Southern railroads was but 32 miles short of the 1860 figure. In one of the few instances of federal economic assistance to the postwar South, the government returned to its previous owners the approximately 2,000 miles of track that had come under the control of the Union military during the war. Most of this mileage had already been repaired. Government-held rolling stock was also returned at less than its market value on favorable terms of short-term credit. In the 1870's federal generosity extended to writing off $3 million in delinquent debts on this rolling stock.

By 1870 the South had nearly 80 per cent more business firms than in 1860, and 30 per cent more workers were engaged in nonagricultural pursuits. However, the extent of this recovery, though more complete and faster than that of agriculture, was still limited. The reintegration of the South into a national market after 1865 placed its economy under the same competitive disadvantages that had existed before the war. Having but limited access to capital and skilled labor, and lacking the demand of a purchasing power within the South sufficient to sustain an industrialization effort, Southern businessmen could do little more than produce for small, local markets. Manufacturing remained confined largely to the initial processing of crops and resources by cheap, unskilled labor. The Southern share of the nation's manufacturing output, which had stood at 7.2 per cent in 1860, fell to 4.7 per cent in 1870, and did not regain its prewar level until 1900.

Most important as a brake on the postwar economic development of the South was the lack of capital. In gold dollars the Confederacy had spent approximately $570 million on the war, a debt that had to be repudiated as part of the terms for readmission to the Union. Therefore, none of this debt could serve after the war as the basis of a Hamiltonian-type funding program for capital accumulation. Indeed, the very opposite occurred. The defeated South was eventually drained of at least a billion dollars in tax revenue that was used as a war indemnity to help pay for the Northern war debt and pensions for Union soldiers. This aggravated what was already a desperate credit problem. The situation the *New York Times* described in South Carolina in the summer of 1865 was typical: "The funds of churches, colleges, charitable institutions, $15,000,000 in bank stock, and nearly all the funds of private individuals which were available have been almost entirely sunk [into the war]." Throughout the South between 1860 and 1870 the banking capital had been reduced from $61 million to $17 million, and the proportionate loss in circulating currency had been as great. The gap was not filled by an influx of capital from the North, because investors there had more profitable and secure outlets than the politically and socially unstable South.

The shortage of agricultural capital was particularly critical, for over 90 per cent of the South's labor force worked on the land, and the sale of agricultural surpluses was fundamental to any economic recovery. Because the North provided no assistance, the capital necessary for commercial agriculture would have to be generated internally. Given the steady decline in cotton prices that persisted after the late 1860's and the dominance of cotton in the Southern economy, capital accumulation would be an expensive and slow process with exploitative social consequences.

In the absence of capital, plantation agriculture was reorganized through sharecropping, a labor system in which the landlord supplied the use of his land and passed along credit in return for one-half of the tenant's crop. What little credit was available commanded interest charges of from 25 to 70 per cent. Even at these prices, credit was extended only in anticipation of a quick cash return on a staple crop, usually cotton. At the very time its price was dropping because of a world-wide glut, attributable in part to the development of new sources of production by Britain during the Civil War, cotton became ever more important to the Southern economy. In turn, the low economic return of cotton per worker doomed the South to poverty. An individual working full-time could produce annually 2,000 pounds of cotton, which, at the prices prevailing in the 1870's and 1880's, would gross about $220. After the crop had been divided with the landlord and interest charges had been deducted, the sharecropper would be left with a net monthly income of about $10.

Although defeat for most whites and freedom for blacks resulted in the impoverishment of both races, the burden was not shared equally. For example, by 1900 white farmers were almost three times as likely to be the full owners of their farms as were blacks; 57 per cent of the former owned their own farms as compared to 21 per cent of the latter. Any chance for economic democracy for blacks had been ruled out during the Civil War or immediately thereafter. The failure of blacks to secure land ownership removed most of their bargaining power relative to their ex-masters and left them economically helpless. It ensured that black labor would be divorced from control over the means of production, and it thwarted efforts to initiate communal use of the land by blacks.

Few Southern whites were prepared to encourage or even permit ownership of the land by their former slaves. In the debate over arming the slaves and how best to motivate them to fight for the Confederacy, a few Southern newspapers had suggested that, in addition to freedom, a homestead would have to be granted to black soldiers. As heretical as was the idea of emancipation, many Southern whites were able to countenance it during the last half of the war because of the gathering momentum of military emancipation by the Union and the unsolved wartime problems of imposing discipline and extracting efficient labor from the slaves. But the distribution of land to the freedmen, which implied an economic basis for black equality after the war, was too obviously a threat to white supremacy to be seriously considered. The few whites who favored land for black Confederate veterans were denounced as race traitors. In January, 1865, the Raleigh *North Carolina Standard* warned that "the *negro* is to be the pet, and the gallant white veteran . . . is to be turned off to work as a tenant, if he have [sic] no land, and must be jostled and insulted in his neighborhood as long as he lives, by his black comrade,

who is to have a homestead provided for him by the state!"
The paper added that even the Yankee enemies "have appeared
disposed thus far to spare us this humiliation."

The proposition for black homesteads was stillborn, but in
contemplating for the first time the role of most blacks as
free men in Southern society, many Confederates formulated a
rationale for keeping the ex-slaves subservient. As explained
in December, 1864, by Judah P. Benjamin, a member of the
Confederate cabinet, this rationale was a succinct statement
of what in fact would be the status of blacks after the war.
Stressing the need to create some "intermediate stage of serfage
or peonage" before the eventual emancipation of the families
of black soldiers, Benjamin wrote:

> We might then be able, while vindicating our faith in the doctrine
> that the negro is an inferior race . . . , yet so modify and ameliorate
> the existing condition of that inferior race by providing for it
> certain rights of property, a certain degree of personal liberty, and
> legal protection for the marital and parental relations, so as to
> relieve our institutions from much that is not only unjust and
> impolitic in itself, but calculated to draw down on us the odium
> and reprobation of civilized man.

Ratified into law by the Southern Black Codes of 1865, and
then enforced by white majority opinion after the repeal of
these codes during Radical Reconstruction, this twilight zone
between freedom and slavery was nearly as confining to blacks
as their antebellum legal bondage had been.

The intransingence of whites meant that any land reform in
the South had to rest either on the external agency of the
federal government, working through confiscation of rebel
estates and subsequent redistribution, or on the forcible seizure
of land by blacks. The Confiscation Act of July, 1862, and the
failure of Southern landowners to pay the direct war tax levied
by Congress in August, 1861, had established a legal basis for
federal expropriation of rebel property. At Lincoln's insistence,
however, Congress passed a joint resolution that limited the
forfeiture of property to the lifetime of the offender. Because
this resolution gave the heirs of rebels the legal right to reclaim

their property, the act was emasculated as far as land redistribution was concerned.

The sale of rebel land for the nonpayment of the direct tax could benefit the ex-slaves only if special safeguards were provided. In open competition with Northern investors and speculators for these tax lands, blacks would be at a clear disadvantage because they lacked capital. Thus, when the first major tax sale occurred in March, 1863, on the South Carolina Sea Islands, Northern interests purchased 90 per cent of the auctioned plantation lands. The government still held some 60,000 acres on the islands, part of which had been set aside for "charitable purposes," to benefit the freedmen. At the urging of Secretary of the Treasury Salmon P. Chase and abolitionist-oriented missionaries and teachers who were working among the blacks, the government announced that the heads of black families could pre-empt 40-acre plots of this reserved land at the fixed price of $1.25 per acre. This liberal policy was reversed before the next land auction in February, 1864. Opposition from the tax commissioners and Edward Philbrick, the manager of the Boston group that had speculated in abandoned plantations on the Sea Islands, convinced Chase to rescind the pre-emption order. The land was sold in large blocks at an average price of $11 per acre, and the freedmen acquired less than 2,500 acres at the pre-emption price.

The amount of land expropriated for blacks during the war was quite limited. While Republican congressional efforts to extend the provisions of the Homestead Act to include abandoned and confiscated lands in the South were bogged down in legal technicalities, the racial containment and plantation-leasing policies of the Lincoln government were ensuring that blacks would be a landless proletariat within the South. The results were painfully obvious to black spokesmen. "The slaves were made serfs and chained to the soil," charged the *New Orleans Tribune* in the fall of 1864. "Such was the boasted freedom acquired by the colored man at the hands of the 'Yankees.' " Yet, just before the end of the war, the land question was revived and the hopes of blacks suddenly raised by General Sherman's "Special Field Order No. 15." In conjunction with a previous program in black separatism initiated by Grant in the lower Mississippi Valley, Sherman's order implied that the federal government was about to pledge itself to reserving land within the South for the field slaves.

Burdened with a train of several thousand refugee blacks as his army entered Savannah in December, 1865, Sherman, joined by Secretary of War Edwin Stanton, held a conference with the black leaders of Savannah in a effort to learn how to free his army from caring for the refugees. The black response was unanimous: "The way we can best take care of ourselves is to have land. . . . We want to be placed on land until we are able to buy it, and make it our own." Consequently, in January, 1865, Sherman designated for the exclusive settlement of blacks the South Carolina–Georgia Sea Islands and the coastal area from Charleston to Jacksonville, extending 30 miles inland. Black families were permitted to settle 40 acres under "possessory titles" that subsequently were to be regulated by Congress. By June, 1865, forty thousand blacks, under the supervision of General Rufus Saxton, had colonized the region set aside by Sherman.

At Davis Bend, Mississippi, a peninsula extending into the Mississippi River 25 miles south of Vicksburg, nearly two thousand freedmen had been resettled on more than 5,000 acres of prime plantation land in 1864 and 1865. This agricultural community had been protected from guerrilla raids by the Union military and allowed to govern itself. The blacks had administered their own judicial system, managed their economic affairs, and provided welfare services for the elderly, sick, and orphaned. In 1865 the community had a net profit of $159,200 from its agricultural production. More importantly, the colonists had revealed that a communal approach to agriculture, based on voluntary partnerships and sharing of the land, was a workable and even desirable alternative to small and scattered individual holdings.

These experiments in black land ownership were soon aborted by President Andrew Johnson. Four of the six antebellum plantations that comprised the bulk of Davis Bend were restored to their original owners in 1865. Within the next two years the other plantations, which belonged to the family of Jefferson Davis, were also returned. Through another lavish use of his pardoning powers, Johnson dispossessed from the land those blacks who had taken the government at its word and settled in the coastal strip south of Charleston. The freedmen protested to no avail that "to turn us off from the land that the Government has allowed us to occupy, is nothing less than returning us to involuntary servitude." Abolitionists bitterly denounced Johnson's policy, and General Saxton, then commissioner of the Freedmen's Bureau in South Carolina, had to be removed from office before Johnson's orders could be carried out. But in the end the blacks lost most of the land to its former owners.

As compensation for their expulsion from land they had controlled at the end of the war, the freedmen received the unfulfilled promise of land reform written into the bill establishing the Freedmen's Bureau in March, 1865. The Bureau was given supervision over the abandoned and confiscated Southern land held by the federal government and was authorized to divide this land among the freedmen and "loyal refugees," with the provision that the land might be purchased under "such title thereto as the United States can convey." However, as noted previously, the government did not have complete title to these lands, which were claimed by the legal heirs of former rebels. The rebels themselves were pardoned in wholesale numbers by Johnson under terms that included the full restitution of property rights. Moreover, the Bureau never controlled enough land to take more than a token step toward its redistribution. At most, the Bureau could have provided about one-quarter of the ex-slave population with family garden plots of 5 acres each.

Additional confiscations after the war were out of the question. The egalitarian arguments of Thaddeus Stevens in favor of dividing the landed estates of the wealthiest seventy thousand Confederates into 40-acre farms for freedmen were futile. Insisting that the economic substructure of the South had to be reshaped radically if a biracial democracy were ever to emerge, he rhetorically asked, "How can republican institutions, free schools, free churches, free social intercourse exist in a mingled community of nabobs and serfs?" In 1867 the confiscation proposal of Stevens received only thirty-seven affirmative votes in the House. Congress settled for two far more moderate measures.

It gave the dispossessed freedmen in the region encompassed by Sherman's Order No. 15 the option of leasing government-owned land on the Sea Islands. The lessees had a six-year option to purchase up to 20 acres at $1.50 per acre. Second, the Homestead Act was extended to cover the public domain in Alabama, Arkansas, Florida, Louisiana, and Mississippi, and the settlement of these lands was to be closed until January 1, 1867, to anyone who had supported the rebellion. Very little fertile acreage was made available by this legislation, and few freedmen benefited from it.

Blacks yearned for land and argued eloquently that they had a morally legitimate claim to a fair share in the estates of their former masters. Writing in the *Philadelphia Christian Recorder* in June, 1863, a North Carolina black reasoned that "if the strict law of right and justice is to be observed, the country around me, or the Sunny South, is the entailed inheritance of the Americans of African descent, purchased by the invaluable labor of our ancestors, through a life of tears and groans, under the lash and the yoke of tyranny." Nevertheless, this moral claim was denied.

Reliance on the federal government clearly had been a weak and ineffectual prop for black aspirations to land ownership. Yet the freedmen had no other alternatives open to them. Any forcible seizure of the land had to rest on an independent base of political, and especially, military power. Such a base had never developed, because the slaves had been able to achieve their freedom without resorting to revolutionary violence. Without their own armed forces independent of white control, and without a cadre of leaders responsive to the needs of a revolutionary organization, the freedmen could not compel whites, whether Unionists or Confederates, to consider seriously their demands for land. Quite to the contrary, most whites saw little reason to respect any black program, because they perceived the freedmen as passive agents even in their own emancipation. "What have the negroes done to secure freedom at this time, when the course of their masters seems especially to invite them to strike for liberty?" Senator Cowan of Pennsylvania asked early in the war. "Nothing; they simply rely on their masters with a sort of blind instinct." Edward Dicey, the English observer, agreed. "I should think more highly of the Negro race than I do, if I believed there was any probability that, unarmed and unassisted by white men, they would rise against their owners." Thus, while tending to congratulate themselves on their benevolence in bestowing freedom upon a race that they believed was too weak and docile to fight for its own freedom, Northern whites were unresponsive to what they saw as ungrateful and unreasonable black demands for land during and after the war.

To be sure, sparks of revolutionary agitation over the land question did flare up in 1865 and 1866. The implicit belief of freedmen that they had a right to the land had been reinforced not only by Sherman's order but also by warnings in the Confederate press that Southern defeat meant confiscation of the plantations and their division among the ex-slaves. When black expectations were thwarted in 1865, many freedmen refused to surrender the farms they had gained during the war. When the pardoned planters returned to reclaim their estates on the Sea Islands, the blacks armed themselves with whatever weapons they could find. The planters were forced to leave and were admonished: "You had better go back to Charleston, and go to work there, and if you can do nothing else, you can pick oysters and earn your living as the loyal people have done—by the sweat of their brows." This militancy, as well as the extremely heavy concentration of freedmen on the Sea Islands and the nucleus of black ownership that dated back to the tax sales of 1863 and 1864, influenced the conciliatory response of Congress. Black ownership of tax lands was confirmed, leases on confiscated lands were converted to full ownership, and the remaining government lands on the islands were offered to the freedmen at $1.50 per acre. Consequently, the proportion of black ownership of farms in this region was the highest in the postwar South.

Elsewhere in the South, black militancy was in vain. Scattered incidents of armed attempts to seize or protect landholdings were reported, but they were quickly put down by either Southern whites or the federal military. Moreover, blacks were driven off the land if they balked at accepting white control. The freedmen were relatively defenseless because of the rapid demobilization of the Union army. By June 1, 1866, the combined strength of the regular army and the volunteers was fewer than seventy thousand men. In particular, the removal of the black troops deprived the freedmen of their sole potential military allies. Whites in both sections accused these soldiers of fomenting discontent among the ex-slaves over the land issue. Advised by Grant to withdraw black regiments because they "demoralize [black] labor," and urged to do so by Southern whites who feared that the ex-slaves would turn to the black military for the leadership of a mass uprising, Johnson reduced the army of occupation to a skeletal force within a year. In the meantime, as former Confederates gained control of the state governments under the Johnson guidelines, the freedmen were disarmed, first forcibly and then under the legal cover of the Black Codes, which prohibited black ownership of weapons.

The potential (and it was never more than that) for a revolution to gain land was gone by 1866. Although the freedmen would try to withhold their labor in an effort to gain higher wages or a better sharecropping arrangement, their position was barely above that of serfdom. An abolitionist who traveled in the South in 1866, the Reverend John Savary, was struck by the resignation of those who had once dared to hope that the rewards of freedom might be commensurate with the sacrifices of slavery. The freedmen "appear to have neither mind nor hope above their present condition, and will continue to work on from day to day, and from year to year, without more than enough to keep soul and body together." In the future, black spokesmen and their white allies could but repeat the obvious —the legal bonds of slavery had been dissolved, only to be replaced by the economic bonds of poverty and exploitation.

THE AMBIVALENCE OF REUNIFICATION

The Civil War was the terrible price that Americans paid for the inadequacies of the Constitution. Fundamentally flawed by the ambiguity of dual sovereignty and by the absurdity of excluding the black tenth of the population from the protection of the Bill of Rights, the antebellum Union collapsed during the secession crisis from the weight of its own contradictions. As its minimal objective, the ensuing war of reunification had to establish whether sovereignty ultimately rested with a national government or with the states. To the extent that the slaves had to be freed in order to achieve a Union victory, emancipation became a war aim after 1863. Victory, attained at the cost of more than six hundred thousand war dead, was possible only through a radical restructuring of the definition and application of national power. Yet, and this was the enduring tragedy of the Civil War, the political revolution was arrested. Once the military confrontation had been resolved in favor of the Union, the political implementation of power again became imprisoned in a traditional constitutional framework that precluded the effective use of centralized power. Reconstruction would be aborted, not so much by the lack of idealism or commitment as by the failure to conceive a philosophy of national power capable of administering the vast social and economic changes wrought by the war.

As Lincoln put it so well in 1862, "The dogmas of the quiet past, are inadequate to the stormy present. . . . As our case is new, so we must think anew, and act anew." It was this recognition of the need for far-reaching changes, as well as his skill in exercising the war making powers of the executive, that made Lincoln a great wartime president. Under his leadership, although not always at his initiative, the United States became a nation in the full meaning of the word. Emancipation, by destroying the legal power of the master class over slaves, made all Americans direct subjects of the government; the draft embodied the principle of compulsory military service; the Legal Tender Acts created government-controlled currency and credit; and the heavy wartime taxes on producers and consumers extracted financial support for the bureaucratic and military machinery of the government. By exercising for the first time federal controls over the lives of individual citizens, these four war measures amounted to a revolution in the application of national power. But this revolution was justified and supported only in the context of a military emergency. Having established by 1865 the permanence of the Union, most Northerners balked at any extension of the nationalistic concepts and controls that had been indispensable for victory. In particular, few Northerners could conceive of the need for a peacetime nationalism under which the federal government would assume responsibility for rebuilding the South and integrating the freedmen into American society.

This failure of imagination ensured a bitter legacy of hatred in the postwar years. Reunification brought together in a common experience the victors, the defeated, and the former slaves. For the nation to be successfully reconstructed, the distinctions between these groups had to be eliminated. Reconciliation between Unionists and Confederates would be all the more difficult because these groups lacked a common external enemy against whom they could unite. Whereas the perceived threat of aggressive Communism allied the United States after World War II with the same Axis powers it had been instrumental in defeating, no such foreign menace was present to drive together the American belligerents after the Civil War. Spain would eventually perform this function, but not until the late 1890's.

Another deterrent to reconciliation was the lack of a formal peace treaty. Without this ritualistic release of war hatreds the antagonisms between Unionists and Confederates continued to fester. The South did not know exactly what terms of submission would be demanded by the North, which in turn never had the gratification of receiving concrete assurances that the South recognized its defeat. All that had been established in 1865 was that the South had been militarily defeated and had lost slavery. Left unsettled were the future status of the freedmen, the extent of the Southern defeat, and the meaning of the Northern victory—in short, the overriding issue of what the war in fact had settled.

In time an accommodation was worked out in which the North specified its minimum guarantees of victory. Immediately after the war Southern whites insisted on turning to ex-Confederates for their leadership. They harassed wartime Unionists and attempted to reduce the freedmen to a submissive rural peasantry with few political or civil rights. These actions, openly encouraged and supported by Northern Democrats and by President Johnson, convinced the majority of Northerners that their sacrifices might have been in vain, that they had won the war only to face the immediate danger of losing the peace.

Consequently, Congress formulated and then compelled ratification of what amounted to a peace treaty—the Fourteenth and Fifteenth amendments. These measures, when added to the Thirteenth Amendment, which was in the process of ratification at the war's end, freed the blacks, invested them with national citizenship, and granted them suffrage. As the price of readmission to the Union, the rebel states had to acquiesce in this new legal definition of black status, repudiate their war debts, and accept as a penalty the temporary loss of officeholding and voting rights by former Confederate officials.

Measured by its leniency and speed in restoring the seceded states to the Union, this peace package was an undoubted success. Not a single Confederate was executed for political crimes. By 1868 most of the Southern states had been accepted back into the Union, and by 1870 the Union was again intact. Northerners felt they had received confirmation of their original belief that secession had been a great aberration, an inexplicable form of mass delusion on the part of Southerners who would eventually come to their senses and seek to rejoin the best and most democratic government on earth. It seemed as if Lincoln had been correct when he had told the Maryland Union Committee in November, 1864, that "those who had differed from us and opposed us would see that it was better for their own good that they had been defeated, rather than to have been successful."

Nevertheless, these amendments failed both as a catharsis for the hostilities of the war years and as an institutional framework that would aid blacks in the transition from slavery to freedom. In the spring of 1865 Southern whites had been prostrate, expecting the worst from their conquerors. "A joyless future of probable ignominy, poverty, and want is all that spreads before us," lamented Eva B. Jones of Augusta, Georgia. "We are scattered, stunned, the remnant of heart left alive in us filled with brotherly hate," noted Mrs. Chesnut. "We sit and wait until the drunken tailor who rules the United States of America issues a proclamation and defines our anomalous position." But the Southern position was not immediately defined. Although no Southerners were shot as soldiers or hung as political traitors, the uncertainty in existence at the war's end persisted through the rest of the decade. Because Northern peace terms were not presented quickly and dramatically in 1865, but instead were issued piecemeal over a period of four years, the agony of agreeing on these terms was continually re-enacted. Repeatedly Southerners felt aggrieved because additional demands were being forced on them, whereas Northerners were frustrated over what they saw as the absence of true repentance.

However, quite aside from the question of the timing of the peace terms was the problem of implementation. The North undoubtedly could have forced more strenuous terms on the South if it had moved immediately in 1865, but this would not necessarily have resulted in Southern acceptance of these conditions. Southerners, both black and white, had to be re-educated if the dehumanizing attitudes and racist assumptions of slavery were ever to be removed and if blacks were to be provided with the skills necessary for a successful adjustment to freedom. This re-education had to be imposed from without by the federal government, and it had to be a long-range commitment. It could be accomplished not in a year but only after a generation of sustained effort backed by military force. Tragically, not only was the North ill prepared and unequipped for such an unprecedented use of federal police power, but most Northerners were incapable of conceiving of the need for such power.

With the exception of the use of the army to coerce compliance with the Military Reconstruction Act of 1867, military reconstruction was more fiction than fact, a failure because of its brevity more than its brutality. Federal troop strength in the postwar South hovered just above ten thousand men, enough of a force to be an irritant to Southern whites and a reminder of their defeat, but far too small to constitute an effective army of occupation. Real police power was exercised by white sheriffs in rural areas who were supported by paramilitary organizations along the lines of the Ku Klux Klan. These organizations, instruments of community violence and intimidation, were an almost spontaneous Southern reinstatement of police control over the blacks.

The Freedmen's Bureau was as far as Congress would go in assuming national responsibility for a welfare role in the postwar South. The Bureau issued some 21 million rations to refugees of both races, treated nearly half a million cases of illness, established more than forty hospitals, and spent more on educational facilities than $5 million. In the context of the limited government assumptions of antebellum Americans, the Bureau was indeed revolutionary. Moreover, as an emergency relief agency, a temporary shield for the legal rights of the freedmen, and a regulatory mechanism for stabilizing the plantation labor market, the Bureau was a success. But when set against the widespread poverty and devastation of the South, the achievements of the Bureau appear distinctly limited. Most of its programs had been phased out in the late 1860's, and the agency was formally disbanded in 1872. In the interval, the Bureau had barely touched the most pressing of all Southern problems, that of the overwhelming need for capital with which to finance economic recovery and redevelopment.

Lincoln saw this need and proposed the only major plan that would have pumped capital into the South for rehabilitation. At a cabinet meeting in early February, 1865, he submitted to Congress a draft of a joint resolution calling for the executive issuance of $400 million in 6 per cent government bonds to all 16 slave states (including West Virginia) in proportion to the number of slaves resident in those states in 1860. Half of the bonds would be issued on the condition that the Confederacy submitted to federal authority by April 1, 1865; the second installment would be paid once all resistance ceased, provided that the Thirteenth Amendment freeing the slaves was ratified by the requisite number of states by July 1, 1865. For once Lincoln misread the temper of his party. However appealing his proposal was as a means of ending the war through negotiations rather than unconditional surrender, and however shrewd an attempt it was to give the South an economic stake in a reunited government and thereby create a centrist Whiggish party led by a bisectional coalition of the propertied classes, his plan met with little support. Union armies were on the verge of victory regardless of any negotiations, and Republicans were shocked at what appeared to be an unnecessary and perhaps immoral recognition that slave interests should receive special considerations by the very government that the planters were pledged to destroy. Gideon

Welles, the Secretary of the Navy, summed up the reaction of the cabinet when he wrote, "The earnest desire of the President to conciliate and effect peace was manifest, but there may be such a thing as so overdoing as to cause a distrust or adverse feeling."

Congressional Republicans were as concerned as Lincoln with ensuring the majority status of their party under peacetime conditions. Lincoln had been a minority president in 1860, elected with but 39 per cent of the popular vote, and his re-election over the Democratic candidate, George McClellan, clearly had occurred under abnormal circumstances. Indeed, without the soldier vote in such pivotal states as Indiana and Pennsylvania, Lincoln might well have been defeated in 1864. Because it was implicitly understood that after the war the seceded states eventually would be restored to their former position in the Union, the Republicans faced the dilemma of balancing a military victory with the retention of political power in a restored Union in which they might well be a minority party. Lincoln's solution was a revival of Whiggery through an alliance of planters and Northern businessmen who would supervise a national commitment to rehabilitate the Southern economy. Most congressional Republicans, while Lincoln was alive but especially after President Andrew Johnson had estranged himself from his nominal party through his refusal to cooperate in any readjustment policy, sought to protect their party and the fruits of victory by enfranchising the freedmen and disfranchising some of the Southern whites. This effort to create a new balance of power, commonly called Radical Reconstruction, was supported initially by a Northern public anxious to create in some form a "more perfect" Union than the one that had collapsed in 1860. However, without the economic pragmatism that was at the heart of Lincoln's plan in 1865, this effort would be an exercise in futility.

The minimum condition for Radical Reconstruction to have succeeded in the postwar South was economic stability. The very term "reconstruction" would be a misnomer unless the agents of Republican control could in fact rebuild what the war had destroyed. The "carpetbaggers," the pejorative label pinned on Northerners resident in the South after the war who entered politics as Republicans, were small-risk capitalists who did bring in some entrepreneurial capital. Nonetheless, without access to large-scale capital funds from the North, either public or private, the carpetbaggers themselves became an unsettling element, hated by Southern whites as protectors of the black man's newly won status and as symbols of exploitative Yankee domination. The "scalawags," former Southern Whigs and Unionists who looked to the Republican party for stability and Northern capital, were likewise miscast as reconstructionists. Denounced by their fellow Southerners as traitors to their race and to the South, discredited for their failure to restore the economy, and blamed for the heavy postwar taxes that had to be levied to begin rebuilding the South, the scalawags shed their Republicanism in the early 1870's. The freedmen, the major prop of the Republican governments in the South had nothing but their vote to bring to reconstruction. Although blacks made immense strides in literacy and in structuring a community life centered around church organizations, they remained an economically vulnerable, impoverished class whose very freedom reminded whites of what the South had lost in the war.

Radical Reconstruction was formally ended in 1877, when, as part of the price for his presidency, Rutherford B. Hayes removed the last federal troops from the South. Despite laying a foundation for social democracy in the South, Radical Reconstruction had failed, and its failure called into question the whole meaning of the war. Had it been fought, as Lincoln and the North had originally insisted and as Johnson and Northern Democrats persisted in arguing, to restore the Union as it was in 1860? If so, then the experiment in reconstruction from 1865 to 1877 was the more tragic for having been conceived in the first place. Or had the war, once emancipation became a condition of victory, taken on revolutionary characteristics that would remold Southern society and integrate the former slaves into American society? If this were the case, the tragedy of Radical Reconstruction lay in the refusal of Northerners to grant the federal government the power to make it a success.

Americans could never decide on the meaning of their civil war, and their indecision was reflected in the ambivalence of reunification. On the one hand, Northerners wanted assurance that the Union they had fought to preserve was indeed mankind's last, best hope, and Southern efforts to re-enter the Union as quickly as possible after their defeat offered just such assurance. On the other hand, Northerners did not want readmission to involve sacrificing the interests of either Southerners who had stood by the Union during the war or those blacks whose freedom both removed the root cause of sectional discord and promised that the restored Union would be a "more perfect" one. Reconciling these conflicting attitudes toward the settlement of the war was the in-but-out interpretation of the status of the seceded states. As geographical entities, these states were viewed as having never left the Union, but as political bodies they theoretically had forfeited their rights and were to be reconstructed under a republican form of government. Although the in-but-out approach was a necessary compromise tailored to the mood of Northerners at the end of the war, in practical terms it stymied any revolutionary application of national power. No state boundaries were obliterated and no uniform, positive system of national law was proclaimed. Indeed traditional state-federal relations were re-established before the end of the 1860's, and Southern whites were already using their control of federal courts in the reconstructed states as a constitutional means of undermining black civil rights.

A revolution was spawned in the Civil War, but it was not a political one. Democrats in both the North and the South were never reconciled to the social and economic transformations of the war. Their rearguard efforts to immobilize political nationalism and to entrust power to white majorities on the local level resulted in major victories even before the Republicans acknowledged the defeat of Reconstruction in the aftermath of the presidential election of 1876. The Republicans did embrace the changes of the war years, but they failed to translate their commitment to change into a program of action. Although the Thirteenth, Fourteenth, and Fifteenth amendments declared both the end of dual sovereignty and the subordination of the states to national authority, the incipient political nationalism was negated by the failure to entrust the federal government with institutions of centralized power. No enforcement machinery was established to implement the civil rights promised blacks in the Fourteenth and Fifteenth amendments. No federal agencies were created to rebuild the South, and the radical governments lacked the capital means to do so. Not until 1950 would the South's relative share of per capita national income climb back to its 1860 level. This overriding fact of poverty in the postwar South would exacerbate race relations as whites continued to equate their economic plight with the black man's freedom.

The revolutionary legacy of the war was not the ideals of Radical Reconstruction, however important a precedent they set for the future, but the impetus given to industrial capitalism. The partnership of the federal government with Northern businessmen that was necessary to win the war was not dissolved in 1865. The retention of protective tariffs and federal subsidies for internal improvements was coupled with a quick removal of wartime business taxes. The national banking system remained under the control of New York City bankers who would exercise an imperial domination over the economies of the South and the West. Above all, the expanded credit base created by the federal government would continue to fuel industrial development. Industrialization and urbanization would be as much consequences of the war as the freeing of the slaves. Southerners, recalling the Northern confiscation of the capital they had invested in their slaves and the Confederate war effort, would understandably attribute much of the North's postwar prosperity to their own defeat.

Lincoln's America would remain a bitterly divided nation. Unionists, Confederates, and freedmen were not reconciled so much as they learned to coexist. The revolution in political attitudes that was necessary if economic resources were ever to be harnessed to national reunification never occurred, or at best was aborted when the war was over. Fearful that the federal government might limit their freedom to compete in an expanding economy, Americans had insisted during the Jacksonian period that power devolve into the hands of first the states and then individual entrepreneurs. Despite a temporary reversal of this process during the Civil War, social planning, or even the exercise of power through national agencies, remained unthinkable. With no culturally sanctioned sources of public power to act as a counterweight to the immense private sources of economic power created by industrial capitalism, and with no administrative framework with which to cope with the social dislocations of the war, postwar America was as incapable of democratizing economic growth as it was of integrating the ex-slaves into American life with any measure of equality. The same gap between the decentralized political philosophy of Jacksonian America and the concentration of economic power in Lincoln's America that resulted in a generation of rapid industrialization and urbanization unrestained by government controls or any notion of the public welfare would also make a mockery of Reconstruction—an experiment that failed because Americans could not summon the imagination to embrace any fundamental changes in the Constitution. The very lack of centralized power that made secession conceivable was also to ensure that the postwar settlement would eventually lead to the abandonment of the blacks. The power vacuum that existed in the South during the era of Reconstruction enabled the defeated Confederates to maneuver until they secured peace on their own terms. By the 1880's Northern and Southern whites were in near agreement that Reconstruction, with its uncertain commitment to racial democracy, had been a tragic mistake. Southern whites gained through peace what they had felt they could obtain only through war—full control over their region's black minority without any federal interference. In perhaps the greatest irony of the war, the North won the battles but the South dictated the peace terms.

Bibliographic Essay

Although the flood of literature dealing with the Civil War reduces any effort at a selective bibliography to an act of faith, the following brief guide is offered to alert the reader to the major works drawn upon in this study and to suggest sources for further areas of inquiry.

Allan Nevins, James I. Robertson, Jr., and Bell I. Wiley, eds., *Civil War Books: A Critical Bibliography*, 2 vols. (Baton Rouge, 1967–69), and the survey in James G. Randall and David Donald, *The Civil War and Reconstruction* (Boston, 1969), provide an excellent vantage point from which to begin sorting out the hundred thousand or so volumes on the Civil War. The continuous efforts to explain the coming of the war and its meaning are well canvassed in Thomas J. Pressly, *Americans Interpret Their Civil War* (New York, 1965).

For its well-rounded perspective on the Civil War years and its detailed yet lucid narrative, the Randall and Donald textbook *The Civil War and Reconstruction* has yet to be surpassed. Recent volumes that concisely summarize much of the latest research include: Elbert B. Smith, *The Death of Slavery: The United States, 1837–65* (Chicago, 1967); Thomas H. O'Connor, *The Disunited States: The Era of Civil War and Reconstruction* (New York, 1972); Robert H. Jones, *Disrupted Decades: The Civil War and Reconstruction Years* (New York, 1973); and David M. Potter, *Division and the Stresses of Reunion, 1845–1876* (Glenview, Ill., 1973), an interpretative work particularly adept at showing how the Civil War generation avoided any direct approach to the central issues of slavery and the integration of blacks into American society.

The most readable account of the war itself will be found in Bruce Catton, *Centennial History of the Civil War*, 3 vols. (New York, 1961–65). E. B. Long, *The Civil War Day by Day: An Almanac, 1861–1865* (New York, 1971), is an exhaustive but coherent summary that can be read both as a statistical compendium and as a factual account of the war years. Irwin Unger, ed., *Essays on the Civil War and Reconstruction* (New York, 1970), brings together recent interpretative articles. Five different approaches to the question of the Union victory are offered in David Donald, ed., *Why the North Won the Civil War* (Baton Rouge, 1960). The social and economic impact of the war provides the theme for William E. Parrish, ed., *The Civil War: A Second American Revolution?* (New York, 1970), and Ralph Andreano, ed., *The Economic Impact of the American Civil War* (Cambridge, Mass., 1967).

Of the many collections of contemporary reactions to the war, Henry Steele Commager, ed., *The Blue and the Gray* (New York, 1950), is unexcelled for its breadth of coverage of both the home fronts and the military theaters. Otto Eisenschiml and Ralph Newman, eds., *Eyewitness: The Civil War as We Lived It* (New York, 1956), and William B. Hesseltine, ed., *The Tragic Conflict* (New York, 1962), are useful shorter compilations.

BATTLES AND GENERALS

No aspect of the Civil War has been subject to more intricate study than the actual fighting. Book after book on battle after battle, to say nothing of the contentious memoirs, has resulted in such a stultifying mountain of details, claims, and counterclaims that many mistakenly dismiss the military history of the war as an exercise in trivia, of interest only to armchair generals. In truth, much of this military literature does bear but a peripheral relationship to the larger issues raised by the war. However, superb studies do exist that either treat the war as a social process or provide the raw material for doing so.

Despite its formidable length and chaotic organization, *The*

War of the Rebellion: A Compilation of the Official Records of the Union and Confederate Armies, 4 series, 128 vols. (Washington, D.C., 1880–1901), is an essential starting point for grasping the war through the perspective of the combatants. Available in most university libraries, the *Official Records,* even when consulted randomly, are invaluable for appreciating the totality of the war. Also indispensable in this regard are the recollections gathered in Robert U. Johnson and Clarence C. Buel, eds., *Battles and Leaders of the Civil War,* 4 vols. (New York, 1956: reprint of the 1884–88 edition). U. S. Grant, *Personal Memoirs of U. S. Grant,* 2 vols. (New York, 1885), is the best known of the military memoirs. From the profusion of accounts by lesser figures, two are particularly successful in describing conditions in the armies: Major Abner R. Small, *The Road to Richmond,* ed. by Harold A. Small (Berkeley, Calif., 1959), and George Cary Eggleston, *A Rebel's Recollections* (Bloomington, Ind., 1959). Mark M. Boatner, III, *The Civil War Dictionary* (New York, 1961), provides a useful guide to battle, military terms, and the officer corps.

Russell F. Weigley, *The American Way of War* (New York, 1973), pp. 92–152; B. II. Liddell IIart, *Sherman: Soldier, Realist, American* (New York, 1958); and J. F. C. Fuller, "The Place of the American Civil War in the Evolution of War," *Army Quarterly,* XXVI (1933), 316–25, are superb on explaining how the war produced a revolution in strategy and tactics. The best study on generalship remains J. F. C. Fuller's *Grant and Lee* (Bloomington, Ind., 1957). Most suggestive for insights into strategic problems and the question of civil-military relations are: T. Harry Williams, *Lincoln and his Generals* (New York, 1952), and *McClellan, Sherman and Grant* (New Brunswick, N.J., 1962); Kenneth P. Williams, *Lincoln Finds a General,* 5 vols. (New York, 1949–59); Grady McWhiney, ed., *Grant, Lee, Lincoln and the Radicals* (New York, 1966); Stephen E. Ambrose, *Halleck: Lincoln's Chief of Staff* (Baton Rouge, La., 1962); Thomas Lawrence Connelly and Archer Jones, *The Politics of Command: Factions and Ideas in Confederate Strategy* (Baton Rouge, La., 1973); and Ludwell H. Johnson, "Civil War Military History: A Few Revisions in Need of Revising," *Civil War History,* XVII (June, 1971), 115–30. Outstanding on the Eastern theater are Bruce Catton, *Mr. Lincoln's Army* (New York, 1951), *Glory Road* (New York, 1952), *A Stillness at Appomattox* (New York, 1953); and Douglas Freeman, *Lee's Lieutenants*, 3 vols. (New York, 1942–44). For the West, see Bruce Catton, *Grant Moves South* (Boston, 1960); Ludwell H. Johnson, *Red River Campaign: Politics and Cotton in the Civil War* (Baltimore, 1958); Grady McWhiney, *Braxton Bragg and Confederate Defeat: Field Command* (New York, 1969); and Thomas Lawrence Connelly, *Army of the Heartland: The Army of Tennessee, 1861–1862* (Baton Rouge, La., 1967), and *Autumn of Glory: The Army of Tennessee* (Baton Rouge, La., 1971).

Biographical sketches of the generals will be found in Ezra J. Warner, *Generals in Gray* (Baton Rouge, La., 1959), and *Generals in Blue* (Baton Rouge, La., 1964). The organization and command structure of their armies are detailed in Fred A. Shannon, *The Organization and Administration of the Union Army, 1861–1865*, 2 vols. (Cleveland, 1928), and Frank E. Vandiver, *Rebel Brass: The Confederate Command System* (Baton Rouge, La., 1956). The experiences and attitudes of the common soldiers are analyzed by Bell Irwin Wiley in *The Life of Johnny Reb* (Indianapolis, 1943), and *The Life of Billy Yank* (Indianapolis, 1951). Military casualties in the Civil War still exceed the total of American lives lost in all our foreign wars; Thomas L. Livermore, *Numbers and Losses in the Civil War in America: 1861–65* (Boston, 1900), and Paul E. Steiner, *Disease in the Civil War* (Springfield, Ill., 1968), tabulate the deaths resulting from battles and disease.

THE UNION

To an extraordinary degree, Lincoln both mirrored and shaped the Union consensus on the war effort. Lincoln's leadership, as well as his growing capacity to learn while in office, can be traced in Roy P. Basler, *The Collected Works of Abraham Lincoln,* 9 vols. (New Brunswick, N.J., 1953–55). Quite helpful for revealing the complexity and shrewdness of Lincoln, and superb in showing his flexibility on the emancipation issue, is Richard N. Current, *The Lincoln Nobody Knows* (New York, 1958). Benjamin P. Thomas's *Abraham Lincoln* (New York, 1952) is the best single-volume biography, but for the war years it should be supplemented by James G. Randall, *Lincoln the President*, 4 vols., the last volume completed by Richard N. Current (New York, 1945–55).

The surprisingly neglected question of why Northerners enlisted and fought for the Union is partially answered by Phillip S. Paludan in "The American Civil War Considered as a Crisis in Law and Order," *American Historical Review*, LXXVII (Oct., 1972), 1013–34. Allan Nevins, *The War for the Union*, 4 vols. (New York, 1959–71), provides the fullest treatment of the North at war. For an excellent collection of source material on the home front, see George W. Smith and Charles Judah, *Life in the North During the Civil War* (Albuquerque, N.M., 1966). Three outstanding contemporary accounts of Northern society are Edward Dicey, *Spectator of America*, ed. by Herbert Mitgang (Chicago, 1971), a work by an English observer into the Jacksonian period whose insights rival those of Alexis de Tocqueville; Auguste Laugel, *The United States During the Civil War*, ed. by Allan Nevins (Bloomington, Ind., 1961, which is particularly strong on the Midwest during the last two years of the war; and Allan Nevins, ed., *The Diary of George Templeton Strong* (New York, 1962), a journal of a member of the New York City elite who had frequent occasion to visit Washington as treasurer of the U.S. Sanitary Commission.

Historians, attracted to Lincoln's role and the details of military campaigns, have yet to produce a major synthesis on the impact of the war on Northern society and politics. Emerson D. Fite, *Social and Industrial Conditions in the North During the Civil War* (New York, 1910), remains the best general account of social and economic changes. The crucial issue of labor's support for the war is covered in David Montgomery, *Beyond Equality: Labor and the Radical Republicans, 1862–1872* (New York, 1967). Paul W. Gates, *Agriculture and the Civil War* (New York, 1965), and Wayne D. Rasmussen, "The Civil War: A Catalyst of Agricultural Revolution," *Agricultural History*, XXIX (Oct., 1965), 187–96, are both excellent on the relationship between the war and the accelerated use of farm machinery. The debate over the industrial consequences of the war touched off by Thomas C. Cochran's "Did the Civil War Retard Industrialization?" *Mis-*

sissippi Valley Historical Review, XLVIII (Sept., 1961), 197–210, can be followed in David T. Gilchrist and W. David Lewis, eds., *Economic Change in the Civil War Era* (Greenville, Del., 1965). Harry N. Scheiber, "Economic Change in the Civil War Era: An Analysis of Recent Studies," *Civil War History,* XI (Dec., 1965), summarizes the debate.

Leonard P. Curry, *Blueprint for Modern America: Nonmilitary Legislation of the First Civil War Congress* (Nashville, Tenn., 1968), is hopefully but the first of the much needed studies on the Civil War Congresses. The interplay between congressional and presidential efforts to shape reconstruction is superbly handled by Herman Belz, *Reconstructing the Union: Theory and Practice During the Civil War* (Ithaca, N.Y., 1969), a work that provides a corrective to the overbearing Lincoln presented in William B. Hesseltine, *Lincoln's Plan of Reconstruction* (Tuscaloosa, Ala., 1960). Robert P. Sharkey, *Money, Class, and Party: An Economic Study of Civil War and Reconstruction* (Baltimore, 1969), and Irwin Unger, *The Greenback Era: A Social and Political History of American Finance, 1865–1879,* subtly examine the origins and repercussions of the Union's fiscal legislation.

In the absence of a full-length study of either major party during the war, political biographies, memoirs, and specialized studies must fill the void. Two provocative essays on the differing impact of the Union and Confederate political systems on the respective war efforts are Eric McKitrick, "Party Politics and the Union and Confederate War Efforts," in F. Gatell, P. Goodman, and A. Weinstein, eds., *The Growth of American Politics: Volume I Through Reconstruction* (New York, 1972), 426–46, and Roy F. Nichols, "The Operation of American Democracy, 1861–1865: Some Questions," *Journal of Southern History,* XXV (Feb., 1959), 31–52. Benjamin P. Thomas and Harold M. Hyman, *Stanton: The Life and Times of Lincoln's Secretary of War* (New York, 1962), and David Donald, *Charles Sumner and the Rights of Man* (New York, 1970), stand out among the biographies. Tyler Dennett, ed., *Lincoln and the Civil War in the Diaries and Letters of John Hay* (New York, 1939); Howard K. Beale, ed., *The Diary of Edward Bates, 1859–1866* (Washington, D.C., 1933); David Donald, ed., *Inside Lincoln's Cabinet: The*

Civil War Diaries of Salmon P. Chase (New York, 1954); and Howard K. Beale, ed., *Diary of Gideon Welles, Secretary of the Navy under Lincoln and Johnson,* 3 vols. (New York, 1960), are well edited and informative. Federal-state relations within the Union and the organization of the Republican party are treated in William B. Hesseltine, *Lincoln and the War Governors* (New York, 1948), and Harry Carman and Reinhard Luthin, *Lincoln and the Patronage* (New York, 1943), respectively. For the thesis that the war fundamentally changed the Republican party, see William A. Dunning, "The Second Birth of the Republican Party," *American Historical Review,* XVI (Oct., 1910), 56–63.

Hans W. Trefousse, *The Radical Republicans: Lincoln's Vanguard for Social Justice* (New York, 1968), is a solid work on the left-wing Republicans. However, Lincoln's relations with the radicals, and indeed the question of what constitutes a consistent radical posture in Republican politics, remain controversial. T. Harry Williams, *Lincoln and the Radicals* (Madison, Wis., 1941), presents the case for deep ideological differences, whereas David Donald in Chapter 6 of his *Lincoln Reconsidered* (New York, 1961), pp. 103–27, sees considerably more flexibility and agreement.

At the opposite end of the political spectrum, the Copperheads have received more attention than the Northern War Democrats. Wood Gray, *The Hidden Civil War: The Story of the Copperheads* (New York, 1942), and Frank Klement, *The Copperheads in the Middle West* (Chicago, 1960), are the two standard accounts. Klement is prone to view the Copperheads more as disgruntled agrarians than as conspiratorial traitors. Leonard P. Curry, "Congressional Democrats, 1861–1863," *Civil War History,* XII (Sept., 1966), 213–29, reminds us that the Democrats in Congress behaved as a loyal opposition that voted for most war measures.

Unsurpassed on intellectual, literary, and constitutional developments are George M. Frederickson, *The Inner Civil War: Northern Intellectuals and the Crisis of the Union* (New York, 1965); Edmund Wilson, *Patriotic Gore: Studies in the Literature of the American Civil War* (New York, 1962); Daniel Aaron, *The Unwritten War: American Writers and the Civil War* (New York, 1973); James G. Randall, *Constitutional Problems Under*

Lincoln (Urbana, Ill., 1951); and Harold M. Hyman, *A More Perfect Union: The Impact of the Civil War and Reconstruction on the Constitution* (New York, 1973). Among the more specialized works on the North, Paul P. Van Riper and Keith A. Sutherland, "The Northern Civil Service, 1861–1865," *Civil War History,* XI (Dec., 1965), 351–69, and Robert W. Bremner, "The Impact of the Civil War on Philanthropy and Social Welfare," *Civil War History,* XII (Dec., 1966), 293–303, are excellent.

THE CONFEDERACY

Two fine essays in Arthur S. Link and Rembert W. Patrick, eds., *Writing Southern History: Essays in Historiography in Honor of Fletcher M. Green* (Baton Rouge, La., 1965), discuss the literature on the Confederacy: John G. Barrett, "The Confederate States of America at War on Land and Sea," and Mary Elizabeth Massey, "The Confederate States of America: The Homefront." Also helpful, though more impressionistic, is Robert C. Black, III, "Thoughts on the Confederacy," in Donald Sheehan and Harold C. Syrett, eds., *Essays in American Historiography in Honor of Allan Nevins* (New York, 1960), pp. 20–36.

E. Merton Coulter, *The Confederate States of America, 1861–1865* (Baton Rouge, La., 1950), is the most complete history of the Confederacy. Charles P. Roland, *The Confederacy* (Chicago, 1960), is a good short history, and Clement Eaton, *A History of the Southern Confederacy* (New York, 1954), is the best-balanced general treatment. Robert L. Kerby, *Kirby Smith's Confederacy: The Trans-Mississippi South, 1863–1865* (New York, 1972), gives details of the disintegration of the Confederate West after the fall of Vicksburg. An interesting, but often overstated, interpretation of the Confederacy is provided by Emory M. Thomas, *The Confederacy as a Revolutionary Experience* (Englewood Cliffs, N.J., 1971). The war's unforeseen consequences for Southern women are revealed in Anne Firor Scott, *The Southern Lady: From Pedestal to Politics, 1830–1930* (Chicago, 1970), pp. 81–102.

Of two popular collections of documents, Albert D. Kirwan, ed., *The Confederacy* (New York, 1959), and Richard B. Harwell, *The Confederate Reader* (New York, 1957), Kirwan's edition is more tightly organized and more helpful on internal problems. W. H. Russell, *My Diary North and South* (Boston, 1863), and A. J. L. Fremantle, *Three Months in the Confederate States, April–June, 1863* (Edinburgh, 1863), are two of the more perceptive accounts by foreign observers.

Many published letters, journals, and diaries are richly evocative of the Confederate experience. John B. Jones, *A Rebel War Clerk's Diary,* ed. by Earl Schenck Miers (New York, 1958), and Edward Younger, ed., *Inside the Confederate Government: The Diary of Robert Garlick Hill Kean* (New York, 1957), are informative on debates within the Confederate government and on social conditions in Richmond. Legislative maneuvering and the personnel of Congress are among the subjects discussed in Bell Irwin Wiley, ed., *Letters of Warren Akin, Confederate Congressman* (Athens, Ga., 1959). For insights into conditions on the home front, see Kenneth Coleman, ed., *Athens, 1861–1865* (Athens, Ga., 1969); Spencer Bidwell King, Jr., ed., *Ebb Tide, as Seen Through the Diary of Josephine Clay Habersham, 1863* (Athens, Ga., 1958); John Q. Anderson, ed., *Brokenburn, The Journal of Kate Stone, 1861–1868* (Baton Rouge, La., 1972); Mary Boykin Chesnut, *A Diary from Dixie,* ed. by Ben Ames Williams (Boston, 1949); and the Civil War letters in Robert Manson Myers, ed., *The Children of Pride: A True Story of Georgia and the Civil War* (New Haven, Conn., 1972). Especially useful for perceiving the Southern reaction to defeat is Spencer Bidwell King, Jr., ed., *The War-Time Journal of a Georgia Girl, 1864–1865* (Macon, Ga., 1960).

Allan Nevins and James D. Richardson, eds., 2 vols., *The Messages and Papers of Jefferson Davis and the Confederacy, Including Diplomatic Correspondence, 1861–1865* (New York, 1966), is a solid beginning for study of the political history of the Confederacy. Two contrasting opinions on Jefferson Davis's relations with his cabinet and his effectiveness as a national leader are presented by Burton Hendrick in *Statesmen of the Lost Cause* (Boston, 1939) and by the more sympathetic Rembert Patrick in *Jefferson Davis and His Cabinet* (Baton Rouge, La., 1944). Wilfred Buck Yearns, *The Confederate Congress* (Athens, Ga., 1960), now supplemented by the statistical profile of voting in Thomas B. Alexander and Richard E. Beringer, *The*

Anatomy of the Confederate Congress (Nashville, Tenn., 1972), combines political analysis with biographical information on Confederate congressmen. The establishment and growth of the bureaucracy are covered in Paul P. Van Riper and Harry N. Scheiber, "The Confederate Civil Service," *Journal of Southern History,* XXV (Nov., 1959), 448–70. Frank L. Owsley, *King Cotton Diplomacy,* second ed. (New York, 1959), is an exceptionally sound history of Confederate foreign relations, and James M. Callahan, *Diplomatic History of the Confederacy* (New York, 1968), is also useful.

Confederate efforts to procure manpower and build up supplies of ordnance are set forth in Albert Moore, *Conscription and Conflict in the Confederacy* (New York, 1924), and Frank Vandiver, *Ploughshares into Swords* (Austin, Texas, 1952). The labyrinth of fiscal manipulations is explored in Richard C. Todd, *Confederate Finance* (Athens, Ga., 1954). For an understanding of the over-all economic legislation of the Confederacy, an old study by John C. Schwab, *The Confederate States of America, 1861–1865* (New York, 1901), is still indispensable. The importance and pervasiveness of the nationalistic controls over the economy can be studied in Charles W. Ramsdell, "The Control of Manufacturing by the Confederate Government," *Mississippi Valley Historical Review,* VIII (1921–22), 231–49; L. B. Hill, *State Socialism in the Confederate States of America* (Charlottesville, Va., 1936); and Raimondo Luraghi, "The Civil War and the Modernization of American Society," *Civil War History,* XVIII (Sept., 1972), 230–50.

The forced resourcefulness of Southerners is meticulously documented in Mary Elizabeth Massey, *Ersatz in the Confederacy* (Columbia, S.C., 1952). The ability of the Confederacy to trade cotton for specie and vitally needed supplies and the willingness of the federal government to countenance such trade are explained in A. Sellew Roberts, "The Federal Government and Confederate Cotton," *American Historical Review,* XXXII (Jan., 1927), 262–75; Thomas H. O'Connor, "Lincoln and the Cotton Trade," *Civil War History,* VII (March, 1961), 20–35; and Ludwell H. Johnson, "Contraband Trade During the Last Year of the Civil War," *Mississippi Valley Historical Review,* XLIX (March, 1963), 635–52.

Eugene M. Lerner, "Money, Prices, and Wages in the Confederacy, 1861–1865," in the previously cited Andreano, ed., *The Economic Impact of the American Civil War,* 31–60, clearly presents the factors behind the devastating inflation of Confederate currency. Weaknesses in transportation are stressed in Robert C. Black, III, *The Railroads of the Confederacy* (Chapel Hill, N.C., 1952), whereas Frank L. Owsley, *State Rights in the Confederacy* (Chicago, 1925), argues that Southern defeat was attributable to inherent political weaknesses. The range of internal problems is analyzed in Charles W. Ramsdell, *Behind the Lines in the Southern Confederacy* (Baton Rouge, La., 1944), and Bell Irwin Wiley, *The Plain People of the Confederacy* (Baton Rouge, La., 1944). Despite the role of Southern churches in promoting the war, documented in James W. Silver, *Confederate Morale and Church Propaganda* (Tuscaloosa, Ala., 1957), resistance to the Confederacy was a persistent problem that grew worse, as shown in Georgia L. Tatum, *Disloyalty in the Confederacy* (Chapel Hill, N.C., 1934), and Ella Lonn, *Desertion During the Civil War* (New York, 1928).

The magnitude of the social dislocation is ably presented in Mary Elizabeth Massey, *Refugee Life in the Confederacy* (Baton Rouge, La., 1964). The scope of the economic crisis facing the postwar South can be understood from the data collected in James L. Sellers, "The Economic Incidence of the Civil War in the South," *Mississippi Valley Historical Review* XIV (Sept., 1927), 179–91, and Eugene M. Lerner, "Southern Output and Agricultural Income, 1860–1880," *Agricultural History,* XXXIII (July, 1959), 117–25.

Blacks

No major work has yet captured the blend of pathos, ambivalence, and unrealized expectations that characterized the experience of black Americans during the Civil War. However, Philip S. Foner, ed., *The Life and Writings of Frederick Douglass,* Vol. III (New York, 1952), and the autobiographical *Life and Times of Frederick Douglass* (Hartford, Conn., 1882; new paperback edition, New York, 1962), provide a superb introduction to this experience from the perspective of the most important black leader in the North. Invaluable for its wide-ranging and judicious selection of source material, drawn largely from black newspapers, is James M. McPherson's *The Negro's Civil War* (New York, 1965). Benjamin Quarles, *The Negro in the Civil War* (New York, 1953), a standard treatment, is a bit thin in its coverage, while Herbert Aptheker, *The Negro in the Civil War* (New York, 1938), is incisive but excessively polemical.

Helpful for background are the Civil War chapters in general black histories such as John Hope Franklin, *From Slavery to Freedom* (New York, 1969); August Meier and Elliott M. Rudwick, *From Plantation to Ghetto* (New York, 1966); and Leslie H. Fishel, Jr., and Benjamin Quarles, *The Black American: A Documentary History* (Glenview, Ill., 1970). Three useful accounts of uneven quality by black contemporaries are William Wells Brown, *The Negro in the American Rebellion* (Boston, 1867); Joseph T. Wilson, *The Black Phalanx* (Hartford, Conn., 1882); and George W. Williams, *History of the Negro Troops in the War of the Rebellion, 1861–1865* (New York, 1888).

Dudley T. Cornish, *The Sable Arm: Negro Troops in the Union Army, 1861–1865* (New York, 1956), and John Hope Franklin, *The Emancipation Proclamation* (New York, 1963), are excellent on the arming and freeing of the blacks. See also Jack D. Foner, *Blacks in the Military in American History* (New York, 1973). For the development of these themes in a politically volatile Border state, see Charles L. Wagandt, *The Mighty Revolution: Negro Emancipation in Maryland, 1862–1864* (Baltimore, 1964). Although James M. McPherson's *The Struggle for Equality: Abolitionists and the Negro in the Civil War and Reconstruction* (Princeton, 1964) documents the continuing idealism and reform efforts of abolitionists, the persistence of a white-supremacist ideology in the North is glaringly apparent in V. Jacque Voegeli's *Free but Not Equal: The Midwest and the Negro During the Civil War* (Chicago, 1967) and Forrest G. Wood's *Black Scare: The Racist Response to Emancipation and Reconstruction* (Berkeley, Calif., 1970). George M. Frederickson, *The Black Image in the White Mind* (New York, 1971), pp. 130–97, perceptively analyzes the racial dilemma of mid-nineteenth century Americans; the Negrophobia of Northern workers and the racial violence sparked by fears of economic competition are covered in Williston Lofton, "Northern Labor and the Negro

During the Civil War," *Journal of Negro History*, XXXIV (July, 1949), 251–73, and Albon P. Man, Jr., "Labor Competition and the New York Draft Riots of 1863," *Journal of Negro History*, XXXVI (1951), 375–405.

Bell Irwin Wiley, *Southern Negroes, 1861–1865* (New Haven, Conn., 1936), is still the only comprehensive study of blacks in the Confederacy. Bernard H. Nelson, "Legislative Control of the Southern Free Negro, 1861–1865," *Catholic Historical Review*, XXXII (April 1946), 28–46, remained the best introduction to the role of free blacks until the appearance of James H. Brewer, *The Confederate Negro: Virginia's Craftsmen and Military Laborers, 1861–1865* (Durham, N.C., 1969), a provocative and ground-breaking study that, with its very notion of a black Confederate, took sharp issue with the portrayal of blacks outlined in the early chapters of W. E. B. DuBois's *Black Reconstruction in America, 1860–1880* (New York, 1935). The revolutionary expedient of resorting to slaves as soldiers is covered in the source material appraised in Robert F. Durden, *The Gray and the Black: The Confederate Debate on Emancipation* (Baton Rouge, La., 1972), and in three early articles: Nathaniel W. Stephenson, "The Question of Arming the Slaves," *American Historical Review*, XVIII (Jan, 1913), 295–308; Thomas R. Hay, "The South and the Arming of the Slaves," *Mississippi Valley Historical Review*, VI (June, 1919), 34–73; and Charles H. Wesley, "The Employment of Negroes as Soldiers in the Confederate Army," *Journal of Negro History*, IV (July, 1919), 239–53.

Louis S. Gerteis, *From Contraband to Freedman: Federal Policy Toward Southern Blacks, 1861–1865* (Westport, Conn., 1973), draws together and amplifies the themes of military utilization of freedmen and racial control developed by J. Thomas May in "Continuity and Changes in the Labor Program of the Union Army and the Freedmen's Bureau," *Civil War History*, XVII (Sept., 1971), 245–54, and by Vernon Lane Wharton in *The Negro in Mississippi, 1865–1890* (Chapel Hill, N.C., 1947), pp. 9–57. The tension between the humanitarian and economic motives of Northerners involved in wartime reconstruction is set forth by Willie Lee Rose in *Rehearsal for Reconstruction: The Port Royal Experiment* (Indianapolis, 1964). The harsh reality of life in the contraband camps is best described in James E. Yeatman, *A Report on the Condition of the Freedmen of the Mississippi*

(Saint Louis, 1864), and John Eaton, *Grant, Lincoln, and the Freedmen* (New York, 1907). Black demands for land are presented most forcibly in James S. Allen, *Reconstruction: The Battle for Democracy, 1865–1876* (New York, 1937), and the halting federal response is covered in Martin Abbott, "Free Land, Free Labor, and the Freedmen's Bureau," *Agricultural History,* XXX (1956), 150–56; Patrick W. Riddleberger, "George W. Julian: Abolitionist Land Reformer," *Agricultural History,* V (July, 1955), 108–15; and LaWanda Cox, "The Promise of Land for the Freedmen," *Mississippi Valley Historical Review,* XLV (Dec., 1958), 413–40.

The most neglected aspect of black history during the war has been the attitudes and reactions of the slaves, the majority of whom never made it behind Union lines during the war. Joel Williamson's *After Slavery: The Negro in South Carolina During Reconstruction, 1861–1877* (Chapel Hill, N.C., 1965), pp. 3–63, is helpful, as are sections in Wiley's *Southern Negroes* (cited above), but unsurpassed are the relatively untapped recollections of ex-slaves in such sources as Federal Writers' Project, *Slave Narratives* (Washington, D.C., 1941), and the shorter and more accessible Norman R. Yeatman, ed., *Life Under the "Peculiar Institution"* (New York, 1970).

Convenient sources for understanding of conditions in the South under which both races had to restructure relations are Whitelaw Reid, *After the War: A Tour of the Southern States, 1865–1866,* ed. by C. Vann Woodward (New York, 1965), and John Richard Dennett, *The South as It Is, 1865–1866,* ed. by Henry M. Christman (New York, 1965). The unmet preconditions for peace are examined in Eric McKitrick, "A Democratic Society Emerges from Total War," in *New Perspectives on the American Past,* ed. by Stanley N. Kutz and Stanley I. Kutler, Vol. I (Boston, 1969), pp. 309–36. The larger and enduring problem for postwar America of how to achieve racial and social justice in the face of constitutional barriers erected by those who would resist change is analyzed in Harold M. Hyman, ed., *New Frontiers of the American Revolution* (Urbana, Ill., 1966), pp. 1–58, and is the central theme of W. R. Brock's masterful study *An American Crisis: Congress and Reconstruction, 1865–1867* (New York, 1963).

Index